GLIDING

A Handbook on Soaring Flight

GLIDING

A Handbook on Soaring Flight

DEREK PIGGOTT

Fifth edition

BARNES & NOBLE BOOKS
TOTOWA, NEW JERSEY

First published in the USA 1987 by
BARNES & NOBLE BOOKS
81 ADAMS DRIVE
TOTOWA, NEW JERSEY, 07512

Library of Congress catalog card number: 59-22654

ISBN: 0-389-20748-9

Published by A & C Black (Publishers) Limited
35 Bedford Row, London WC1R 4JH

Fifth edition 1986
Reprinted 1978 & 1983 (with corrections)
First published 1958
Second edition 1967
Third edition 1971
Fourth edition 1976

© 1986, 1976, 1971, 1967, 1958 Derek Piggott

Typeset from data by Datatrend (Hull) Ltd
Printed in Great Britain by The Garden City Press Limited
Letchworth, Hertfordshire SG6 1JS

CONTENTS

Introduction, 6

Section I Learning to Glide, 7
1 Facts and formalities, 8
2 Launching, 19
3 Before your first flight, 26
4 Early flights, 31
5 Launching by aerotow, 41
6 Wire launches, 56
7 Stalling and spinning, 64
8 Control of the approach, 73
9 Circuit planning, 81

Section II Further training and soaring, 97
10 More about turning, 98
11 Better car and winch launches, 111
12 Landing out of wind, 115
13 More about stalling and spinning, 120
14 Safe flying in high winds, 131
15 Sideslipping, 141
16 Local soaring and efficient cruising, 144

Section III Exploring the skies, 151
17 The instruments and their limitations, 152
18 Thermals, 171
19 Thermal soaring, 185
20 Hill soaring, 203
21 Wave soaring, 214
22 Landing in strange fields, 221
23 Cross-country soaring, 235
24 Cloud flying, 261
25 Flying high, 274
26 Going faster and farther, 279
27 Motor gliders and self-launching sailplanes, 297

Appendices, 305
1 Gliding awards and records, 305
2 The gliding movement in Great Britain, 308
3 Owning your own glider, 310

Index, 314

INTRODUCTION

The excitement and fascination of soaring flight must be experienced to be appreciated. On a summer's day huge warm buoyant bubbles of air are continually leaving the ground to form thermals, rising currents of air which a glider pilot can use to gain height. These invisible air currents often rise hundreds of feet a minute, carrying the glider with them up to the little white cumulus clouds at 4,000 or 5,000 feet. By circling inside the thermal, adjusting the position of the glider until it is in the strongest part of the up-current, the glider pilot gains his height before setting off in search of the next area of lift.

Thermals occur almost everywhere on a fine sunny day, but the airflow over hills and mountain ranges also provides a source of rising air. In this case, unlike thermal activity, the strength and direction of the wind are the most important factors. Hill lift was the first form of lift used by gliders and many of the older gliding sites are on hills. Wave lift occurs in some circumstances when the airflow over hills or mountains takes up a wave motion, producing strong up-currents capable of taking gliders up to 20,000 or 30,000 feet. Since hill and wave soaring do not depend on the sun's heat they are possible in the winter, which makes it an all-the-year-round sport.

The modern glider pilot tries to master all ways of soaring. Each has its particular fascination, but the majority of flights are made in thermals and on a good day a skilled pilot can cover two or three hundred miles.

This kind of flying may seem remote to you if you are only just starting to learn. It is difficult to comprehend that if you fly regularly you will be solo in a few weeks or months. Once you are solo it is only a matter of practice before you will be making flights of hours instead of minutes.

SECTION I

Learning to glide

This section gives you the information you will need before you make your first few solo flights. However, if you have not had the necessary flying experience, do not expect this, or any other book, to teach you to fly. A book can only be a useful supplement to your gliding instructor and cannot replace him.

Although the handling of a glider is rather different from that of a modern light aircraft, any piloting experience will help to reduce the time spent learning to glide. Some clubs encourage their members to start their training by having a few lessons on any powered aircraft available and this is particularly worthwhile for beginners who have only a limited amount of spare time. However, these people will do even better to start their training with some concentrated flying on a motor glider. These machines have the handling and flying characteristics of a normal glider but are independent of launching cables, etc. After about three or four hours on a motor glider, most students require only a few flights in a glider before being ready for solo.

Solo flight is the first step towards becoming a soaring pilot.

1 Facts and formalities

Training—Motor gliders—Cockpit size and weight limitations—Clothing—
Log books—Gliding and soaring periodicals—Licences—Facts and
theory—The controls—How an aeroplane flies—Flying speed—Turning—
Launching—Performance

Every glider pilot will tell you that soaring is the greatest sport. The flying,
of course, is wonderful but we cannot all be in the air together. There
must be wingtip holders, tug pilots, signallers, tow car or winch drivers
and others willing and able to help push your glider out to the launch
point or back for another flight. Alternatively, someone must be paid to
do the work, making your gliding much more expensive. Rich or poor,
you alone can decide whether this is worth your while. If you want to
be able to book your flying and have the aircraft waiting for you to step
into, then you should go to your nearest power flying club or a commercial
gliding school.

  If you decide that you want to learn to glide, this book will give you
most of the information you will need to supplement your flying
instruction.

Training

There are various ways in which you can learn to glide. It will not take
very long if you are already a power pilot. But in any case it is a good
plan to visit your nearest gliding clubs, talk to the members and have at
least one flight *before* you commit yourself to joining as a full flying
member. If you are discouraged by finding that you must wait your turn
to fly and that even as a prospective member you will not receive any special
priority, then perhaps club gliding is not the sport for you. Give up the
idea now, rather than begin over-enthusiastically, only to lose interest after
a few flights.

  Training can either be on a casual day-to-day basis as a member of a
gliding club, or on a residential course of a week or longer. Two or three
weeks of training may get you solo but it is only by flying regularly that
you will become really proficient. Eventually, that means becoming an
active member of a club.

  If you are learning to glide at your own expense you will want to obtain
the best value out of the flights you have. It is seldom possible to arrange
for a perfect training programme: this would take the form of a fortnight's
continuous instruction, making a minimum of three or four flights a day.

If the training is carried out over a long period of occasional days, the final sessions before solo should be as close together as possible.

It is tempting to try to save money by making occasional single flights instead of three or more at a time. In the long run this is wasteful and results in a much greater number of launches to first solo, besides a lower standard of flying in many cases. It is, therefore, wiser to be prepared for the expense of six or eight flights in a day towards the end of training.

Because there are usually other students learning to fly and always launches for advanced flights going on, it is not possible to guarantee continuous training except on a special training course. Most gliding clubs run such courses during the summer months and details can be obtained by writing to the club concerned or to the British Gliding Association (see page 308 for the address).

Bad weather will also hold up your training but you should take every opportunity to fly, even in windy conditions or when the cloud base is low. You will also learn by helping in the workshops or hangar and by talking about flying when the weather is too bad to fly.

A small minority of people benefit from training over a long period since they take longer to acclimatise themselves to flying and to learn to relax.

Motor gliders

The two-seater motor glider has proved an unqualified success for all stages of training. If anything, it is less expensive than normal gliding because of the better utilisation of the aircraft and the instructor.

Besides speeding up the training, it relieves the launching facilities of most of the training flights and so allows more solo flying.

Although many of the modern motor gliders are just a sailplane fitted with a 'tuck away' engine, other types are high performance light aircraft with glider handling and performance. The Scheibe Falkes were the first really successful machines for training purposes and these are being superseded by glass fibre machines. These have a conventional layout, with the engine in the nose but with a glider wing. Like any other light aircraft they have electric starters and are able to taxi out and take off unaided. After climbing under power the engine can be stopped and the propellor blades feathered (turned on edge) to reduce the drag. Once in the glide these machines have a performance and soaring capability very similar to a two-seater trainer. But, of course, they are capable of touch-and-go landings, which speeds up the training enormously.

Each training session lasts twenty to thirty minutes and can include up to ten landings. Once the engine has been throttled back or stopped, it is not used again until after landing. This ensures that the student learns to treat the aircraft as a glider and not to rely on the use of the engine.

After three to four hours the beginner is ready to convert to the glider and go solo. This does not take long and is mainly a matter of getting used to the type of glider and the method of launching.

Cockpit size and weight limitations

The majority of two-seater gliders can cater for pilots of up to 6 feet tall and 220 lb (100 kg) weight. However, a person with a very long back or particularly long legs would be well advised to try sitting in one before joining a club and starting to learn seriously.

The problem may be worse in the single-seaters, for although some will take almost anyone, others are fiendishly uncomfortable for the majority of well-built men.

Being slightly overweight is usually relatively unimportant. In most cases it is sufficient to limit the maximum diving speed and to prohibit violent manoeuvres and aerobatics. The overweight pilot must fly with an extra few knots for every approach and landing or he may find it difficult or impossible to hold off properly for a landing. He also has an increased risk of damaging the glider if he makes a heavy landing.

Very tall or heavy people should consult an experienced instructor and make quite sure that they can sit comfortably in both the single- and two-seater gliders they will be flying, bearing in mind that at some later date they will need to sit in those cockpits for five hours or more on long flights.

Very small and light people can easily carry extra weight and use more packing behind them, together with packing blocks on the rudder pedals or fixed to a pair of shoes.

If you weigh under about 145 lb (60 kg), it is almost certain that you will require some ballast for solo flying to bring the cockpit load well above the minimum permissible. It is dangerous to fly with less than the minimum weight shown on the placard and inadvisable to fly early solo flights or in a new type unless you are well over that limit. This is because moving the centre of gravity forward improves the stability and so makes the aircraft easier to fly. With a cockpit load below the minimum the stalling and spinning characteristics are always worse and may be dangerous.

Any ballast weights put on the seat must be securely tied down to ensure that, in a crash or heavy landing, they cannot break loose and move forward.

Most gliding clubs have ballast available for solos in two-seaters but if you are a lightweight you will probably need your own for single-seaters.

Clothing

It is not necessary to buy expensive clothes specially for gliding. Any old clothes that you do not mind getting dirty would be suitable. However, most gliding sites are situated in exposed places and, except in the summer, warm clothing is needed on the airfield.

Some inexpensive sort of boiler suit or overall will help to keep the wind out and save your clothes from getting too dirty. The ideal flying suit for gliding is an ex-R.A.F. lightweight flying suit. This is shower-proof and wind-proof but is not too hot for strenuous work.

In winter, warm pullovers and gloves and waterproof boots or Wellingtons are necessary to keep warm and dry.

Of course there is no cockpit heating in a glider but all modern machines have an enclosed cockpit and are reasonably warm.

Since you are bound to get dirty sooner or later when you are gliding, do not make a habit of arriving in your best suit. This will imply that you are not willing to help with the work involved in keeping the aircraft flying.

Log books

As soon as you start your glider flying you will need a log book in which to record your flights. An inexpensive glider pilot's log book can be obtained from your club or gliding school.

An accurate record of all your gliding is essential so that, if you visit another club, you have documentary proof of your gliding experience and ability. Your log book should be signed by your chief flying instructor periodically, particularly if you are visiting a gliding club in another country and you hope to fly there.

As you gain experience your log book begins to have a considerable personal value when you look over the pages. Most pilots like to keep barograph charts, photographs and notes on flights of interest in their log books. It is well worth while spending an extra few minutes writing the entries in neatly rather than finishing up with a log book of which you are ashamed.

Gliding and soaring periodicals

Most countries have their own periodicals devoted to the sport and published by the National Association or Aero club. Although much of the contents are often the results of competitions and accounts of epic soaring flights, they also contain hints and tips for instructors and student pilots, news of the various clubs and schools, and information on new design and developments. They all make useful and interesting reading if you are learning to glide.

Licences

In Great Britain there are very few restrictions placed on the glider pilot. No glider pilots' licence is required but there are internationally recognised certificates and badges to mark the pilot's progress. Many other countries have glider pilots' licences involving a medical, and flying and ground examinations similar to those for a Private Power Pilot Licence. In addition each pilot keeps a personal log book and the entries and comments by instructors give a good indication of the pupil's competence. However, even an experienced pilot would expect to make at least one dual check flight at a new site or club before flying solo there.

Provided that you are reasonably healthy and do not suffer from epilepsy, blackouts or fainting fits and have average eyesight (if necessary with glasses) you are almost certainly fit to glide. At some clubs you may be asked to get your doctor to sign a statement to this effect.

As you gain experience you will have to learn about the special rules of the air regarding airways etc., but this need not worry you until you are solo and are beginning to think about flying across country.

The first step is to learn to fly the glider.

Facts and theory

Readers who are interested in glider design and the reasons why a glider behaves as it does should read my other book, *Understanding Gliding*. The explanations are all non-technical and illustrated. However, if you are learning to glide it is not necessary for you to understand more than the fundamentals which are in this book. Learning to glide is mainly a practical affair.

Most of the necessary information you will pick up during your training. If you know how the controls work and a little about how an aeroplane flies, you know more than enough for your first few flights.

Fig. 1 shows the main parts of a glider. The long span and short chord of the wings give the glider the high lift and very low drag necessary for a flat glide and low rate of descent. Very careful attention is paid to streamlining in order to keep the drag to a minimum to obtain a good gliding performance. Gliders are designed to very stringent airworthiness requirements and are structurally very strong. They are usually built to withstand loads over five times greater than normal flying loads at speeds of over 120 m.p.h., and they can perform simple aerobatics such as loops, chandelles and spins. Landing shocks are taken by the main wheel and tail wheel or skid under the tail. On high-performance machines the main wheel is invariably retracted in flight to reduce the drag. Training aircraft and many other medium-performance gliders have a fixed main wheel

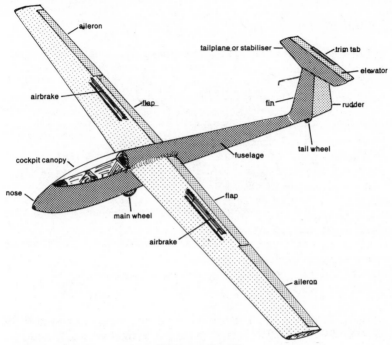

1. The parts of a glider.

and an additional wheel or nose skid to absorb the shocks of a bad nose-down landing on rough ground.

The wings and tailplane of gliders can be quickly removed to allow the glider to be retrieved by road in a long trailer. Although a few training machines are still constructed in metal or a combination of wood and metal, the vast majority are now made of glass fibre using some carbon fibre and Kevlar for highly stressed parts. These newer materials enable much smoother and more accurate contours to be made, which result in a considerable increase in performance. The modern two-seater trainer has a better all-round performance than the high-performance single-seat competition gliders of the 1950s-1960s and are all capable of long cross-country flights in the hands of a competent pilot.

The controls

The cockpit and main controls of a glider are identical to those of any other aircraft and consist of the stick (or control column) and the rudder pedals (Fig. 2). The stick is always held in the *right* hand and both feet are rested against the rudder pedals. Forward and backward movements

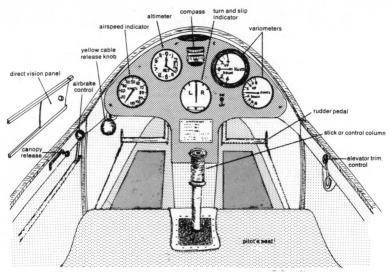

2. A typical cockpit layout for a two-seater training glider.

of the stick operate the *elevator* and result in nose-down and nose-up *pitching* movements. Movements to the left or right operate the *ailerons* out on the wingtips, and these control surfaces move in opposite directions. A movement to the left on the stick moves the aileron on the left wingtip up, and the one on the right wingtip down. The left wingtip loses a little lift and the right wingtip gains a little additional lift, resulting in a *rolling* or *banking* to the left (Fig. 3). The movements of the stick soon become instinctive. You lean or press the stick in the direction you want the glider to go, so you press the stick forward to put the nose down. Move the stick to the left to bank over to the left.

The rudder movements are not instinctive. Left foot forward moves the rudder surface to the left and swings or *yaws* the nose to the left. Right foot on right rudder pedal swings the nose to the right. If the rudder is applied and held on while the wings are kept level, the nose swings a little to the side and then stops swinging. The glider skids sideways through the air as if skating on ice and scarcely changes direction. When the rudder is centralised again the nose swings back and the aircraft returns to accurate straight flight. Sideways movements like this result in the fuselage creating much more drag and there is very little tendency to turn. For efficient flight the rudder is used to *prevent* any sideways slipping or skidding, particularly as the glider is changing its angle of bank.

The glider is always banked over to make it turn and once it is turning very little rudder is required. Flat unbanked turns are practically impossible.

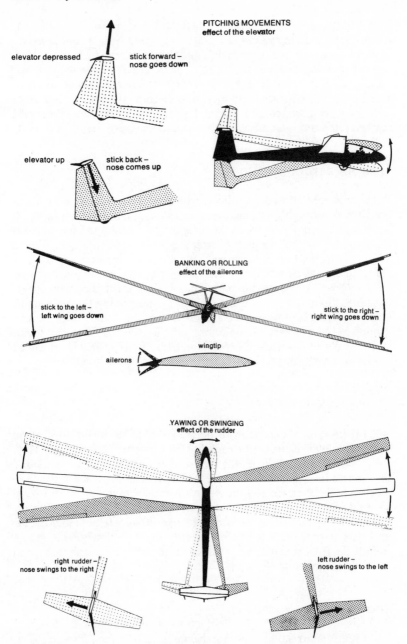

3. The controls and their effects. The elevator controls pitching movements, the ailerons rolling or banking, and the rudder yawing.

In smooth air the glider can be made to fly 'hands and feet off' and it will continue flying steadily by itself. In more turbulent conditions the glider is disturbed from time to time and the pilot has to make corrections to bring the wings level and occasionally to reposition the nose in the correct attitude. But it is stable and tends to correct itself if allowed to do so. During early flights students invariably become too tense, make jerky movements and over-control. The glider will often fly far better if the pilot relaxes on the controls and allows the natural stability of the glider to work.

How an aeroplane flies

With a powered aircraft, the thrust from the engine or propeller drives the aircraft through the air to overcome the resistance we call 'drag'. If there is sufficient flying speed the wing generates enough lift to support the weight. The tail keeps the wing steady and the fuselage pointing accurately in the line of flight so that there is no unnecessary drag.

Flying is, in some respects, rather like cycling. In level flight or on level ground, power is required to overcome the drag and to maintain speed. In gliding flight the speed is maintained by descending the glide slope, much like freewheeling down a hill. As the weight of the glider must be supported by lift a certain minimum speed is essential for steady flight. In steady flight the airspeed depends on the attitude, which is controlled by the elevator (the stick movements forwards or backwards).

Flying speed

The lift from the wings depends on the speed of the airflow over them and on the angle of attack (the angle at which the wing meets the airflow). If the speed is high, enough lift is created at a small angle of attack and the aircraft flies rather nose down. At low speeds the wing is pulled to a larger angle of attack and the aircraft is rather nose high. (See Fig. 4) In reality the speed and angle of attack are controlled by the elevator.

Beyond a certain angle the wing becomes very inefficient and the lift decreases so that there is a definite limit as to how slowly each type of aircraft can fly. For this reason a glider has to maintain a minimum speed of about 40 knots or 45 m.p.h.

Turning

The aircraft is turned by banking the wings so that the lift force acts at an angle, thus pulling the aircraft round in the turn. In a turn the wing still has to support the weight, but in addition it provides the turning force, so that more lift is required for a turn. This is obtained by making a small backward movement of the stick to pull the wing to a larger angle relative to the airflow. (See Figs. 42 and 43 on pages 101 and 102.)

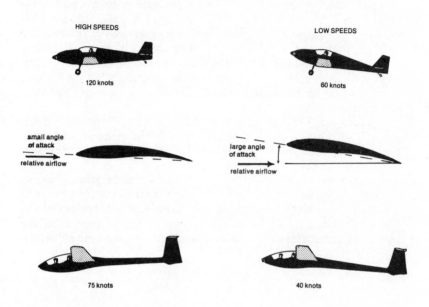

4. Flying at high and low speeds. Notice the nose-high attitude and the larger angle of attack of the wing at low speed.

Launching

Briefly, gliders are usually launched by towing them up to height with a light aircraft. They can also be launched by catapult (bungee), or with a winch, or towing by motor car. Once the tow has been released, the gliders drift down, losing height gradually, unless they are flown into an area of rising air. From a 2,000 feet launch height a training glider will take about 10 to 15 minutes to glide down for a landing. In soaring conditions, with skill, the flight can be extended for as long as the weather remains favourable.

Performance

Most training gliders have a normal flying speed of about 45 knots (50 m.p.h.) and a maximum permissible speed in a dive of about 120 knots. In many countries knots or nautical miles per hour are used in preference to miles an hour or kilometres per hour. 1 knot is almost exactly equal to 100 feet per minute and by using these units it is possible to make quick estimates of the gliding performance. For example, if the rate of descent is 3 knots or 300 feet per minute and the airspeed is 60 knots, the gliding angle is $60 \div 3 = 20 : 1$. This means that the glider will fly a distance of 20 times its height or, in no wind, just under 4 miles per thousand feet of height lost.

The normal rate of descent of most gliders is 150 to 200 feet per minute (1½ to 2 knots) at a speed of about 45 knots. At higher speeds, of course, the glider is gliding much more steeply and the rate of sink is far greater.

Whenever the glider is flown at normal speeds into air which is rising more rapidly than about 200 feet per minute it will be gaining height. The art of soaring is to fly the glider into the strongest up-currents to gain height quickly. The height is then turned into distance during the flight to the next area of lift enabling long distances to be covered. Staying up is just a matter of finding suitable areas of lift and using them efficiently.

2   Launching

Ground handling—Running the wingtip—The flying log—Driving
vehicles—Attaching the cable—Launching procedure and signals

If you become a member of a gliding club you will be expected to help
at the launch point, and at first it may all seem very bewildering. Every
launch involves several helpers and it is much more fun if you know
something about the various jobs so that you can give a hand. Probably
you will be asked to help while you wait your turn to fly.

Ground handling

Figs. 5 and 6 show the parts of a glider which should not normally be
handled. You can push anywhere on the front, leading edge of the wing
but never on the sharp trailing edge which can easily be damaged. Do
not hold or push on any control surface or on the tailplane. There are
usually special handles or hand holds on the fuselage just ahead of the
tail and only these can be used at the tail end.

Running the wingtip

One person is always required to steady the wing and keep it level for the
start of the take-off run. This should be the downwind tip so that any
slight dragging helps to prevent the glider swinging into wind. One hand
is all that is required and it is important to walk with it and let go as it
accelerates. Do not drag the wingtip; hold it lightly and let it go.
Occasionally the pilot will allow one wing to drop and he may have to
release and abandon the launch. This, if it happens, is not your fault.
Note that only one wingtip is held, never both.

The flying log

Another important duty that you may be asked to do is to keep the log
of all the take-offs and landings. A clear and accurate log is important
for every flying organisation and even one or two flights not logged and
not paid for will be a serious financial loss to most gliding clubs. They
all run on a very tight budget and only just break even each year. Make
quite sure that someone explains the log sheet to you before you take on
this job. Other members may easily assume that you know all about it.

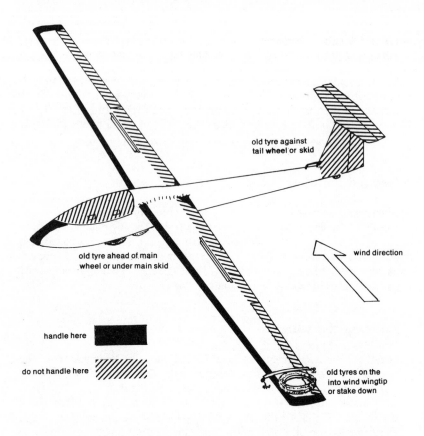

old tyre against
tail wheel or skid

wind direction

old tyre ahead of main
wheel or under main skid

handle here

do not handle here

old tyres on the
into wind wingtip
or stake down

5. Parking the glider. Gliders are parked at right angles to the wind and are never left
   unattended unless they are properly parked.

Driving vehicles

If you are invited to drive a tractor or car to retrieve the cables or gliders,
do not assume that you understand what is needed. Insist that someone
comes with you for at least one run and make sure you know what to do
if things go wrong. A willing volunteer who is not properly briefed can
bring the whole launching operation to a halt by doing the wrong thing.
Nearly everything has its 'dos and don'ts'.

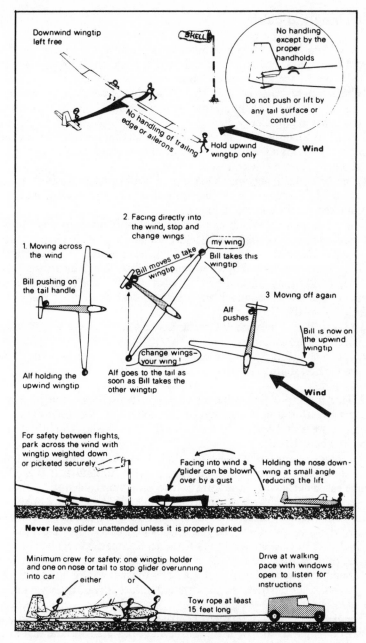

6. Ground handling. Gliders must be handled correctly on the ground or they can easily be damaged.

Attaching the cable

Some gliders are fitted with two launching hooks, one in the nose for aerotowing and a second one, much further back and known as a 'c.g. or belly hook', for winch or car launches.

Where a nose hook is fitted, it should always be used for aerotow launching as it makes keeping straight on take-off and staying in position on the tow much easier.

Launching on a belly hook the glider will tend to nose up into a steep climb and if this is allowed to happen on an aerotow launch, it could pull up the tail of the tug with disastrous results.

Other types have only one hook in a position suitable for both kinds of launch. In this case special care is needed to ensure that the glider is not allowed to pitch up on aerotow.

The hook used for winch or car launching will automatically release the cable at the top of the launch if the pilot fails to pull the release knob. As soon as the load in the cable is pulling backwards, it releases itself.

This system was devised by a well-known British gliding instructor, John Furlong, and first produced by Ottley Motors. It is the basis of almost every release hook today and the automatic over-ride part is still often referred to as the Ottfur.

The nose hooks have no automatic device and therefore should *never* be used for wire launches.

It is normal good practice to test both methods of releasing the cable before the first flight of the day to make quite sure that the release is fully serviceable.

A Terylene or polypropylene rope is generally used for aerotowing and the last 10 – 20 feet of this should be checked over before each flight for excessive wear and knots. (A knot usually reduces the strength of any rope by about half.)

For winch or car launching some kind of drogue or simple parachute is used on the cable to keep it tight and prevent kinking as it falls after it is released at the top of the launch. The launching cable itself is either 11 or 12 gauge steel wire or stranded flexible cable and has a breaking strain of 3,000 lb or more. This necessitates using a weak link to prevent inadvertently overstressing the glider. This may be a simple shear pin or a small plate link designed to fail if the tension gets too high.

The rope or the cable should not be attached to the glider until the occupants are strapped in and are ready for the launch. Should the flight be postponed or delayed, the pilot should release immediately so that at no time is it attached to the glider unless it is actually about to be launched.

The person attaching the rope or cable is expected to carry out a quick check of the parachute, weak link, rope and rings to make sure that they are serviceable.

The release rings should be inspected before every flight to see that they are not elongated. The small rings should pass into the release easily and, after attaching the cable, the rings should be rattled to make sure that they are free to move. If the rings will not rattle, it is possible that they are either bent or oversized, and that they may prove difficult to release at the top of the launch.

An elongated or oversized ring is the *only* possible cause of the cable failing to release with this type of release. On *no* account may home-made or non-standard rings such as links of chain be used for launching gliders.

After attaching the cable, it should be given a strong tug to make sure that it is secure.

Launching procedure and signals

In the early days of gliding there were many dangerous incidents directly attributable to poor procedure leading up to the launch. Slack procedure may result in the glider being launched before the pilot is fully prepared or while onlookers are standing too near or even in front of the aircraft.

At one gliding site a pupil was actually launched off while waiting for the instructor to climb into the back seat of a two-seater. Fortunately he was almost ready for his first solo and had no difficulty in making a circuit and landing. This incident shows the need for the pilot to give clear orders for launching and for the signaller to insist on an order and to take no notice of vague hand signals from the pilot. Otherwise the pilot may find himself launched before he is ready if he happens to so much as scratch his face.

Whereas only the pilot should be able to initiate the launch, anyone can give the order to stop it. On hearing a shout of 'Stop', the pilot must release the cable immediately. It is the duty of every person on a gliding site to stop the launch if there appears to them to be the slightest risk of an accident if the launch continues.

Launching signals and procedure are standard in England, so that wherever you glide similar signals are in use and there is no risk of confusion. However, at some sites an instructor on the ground gives all the launching orders once the pilot has said he is ready to launch.

The launching signals are normally given by bats or flashing light signals. Obviously, for safe operation they must be clearly visible from the winch or tow car a mile or more across the airfield.

The signaller should repeat back the orders which he receives so that the pilot is certain that his orders have been correctly heard and that the signals are being given.

The signals used are, 'Take up slack', 'All out', and 'Stop' (see Fig. 7).

The 'Take up slack' signal gives the tow plane pilot, car or winch driver permission to select the gear for the launch and to take up the slack in the cable. The glider will not then be badly jerked when launched.

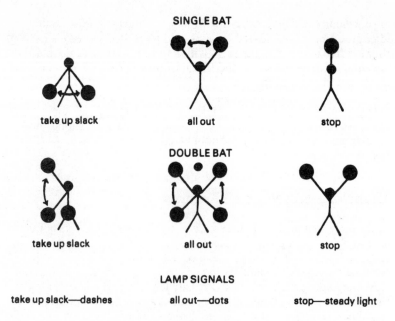

7. Standard British Gliding Association launching signals.

The 'All out' signal means that the slack is out of the cable and gives the pilot or driver permission to go ahead with the launch, and the 'Stop' signal tells them to stop the launch immediately.

If light signals are being used, the 'Dashes' and 'Dots' must be long enough to allow the bulb to light up clearly for the 'Dots' and for there to be a distinctive difference between the two signals. A definite difference in rhythm will also help to make the signals easier to read at a glance. The lamp is usually mounted on a stand so that it cannot be wrongly aimed while the signals are being given.

If it is necessary for the person holding the wingtip to give the launching signals at the same time, the single bat signals must be used. Signalling by rocking the wings is dangerous as there is no means of giving a 'Stop' signal after the glider has begun the take-off. A 'Stop' signal would be vital if, for instance, the glider overran the cable so that the parachute became entangled with the skid. This is a potentially dangerous situation because the pilot would be unable to release the cable. Obviously, whatever method of signalling is used, it must be possible to give the 'Stop' signal at any time during the beginning of the launch.

Ideally, all launching signals should be acknowledged by a light at the winch so that the pilot and signaller can see that the winch is receiving the signals correctly. This can save the signaller calling for the launch and wondering whether his signals are being received. If the winch is temporarily out of action, the winch driver should give a 'Stop' signal, as this will save unnecessary signalling at the launch point. A 'Ready' or 'Take up slack' signal can then be given from the winch as soon as it is ready to launch again.

On some gliding sites, the winch may be out of sight of the launch point and an intermediate signaller is needed to relay the signals in the middle of the field. This signaller must always face the launch point with his back to the winch as he signals so that he will see a 'Stop' signal immediately if one is given.

The use of a telephone and radio communication for signalling has been tried but it is neither cheap nor foolproof. With either of these methods, a failure of the system, or difficulty in hearing above the noise of the winch engine at full power, might result in the launch being continued despite a 'Stop' signal. Radio communication between the pilot and the winch can help to obtain the ideal launching speeds, and this gives an improvement of up to 20 per cent in most conditions. On aerotow, radio is a great advantage as the glider pilot is able to tell the tow plane where he would like to go.

The same single-bat signals are used for aerotowing but as the distance between the glider and towplane is so short, a hand signal can be used instead of a bat. A forward signaller standing to one side and ahead of the towplane should repeat the signals so that the tow pilot can see a 'Stop' signal should one be given after the 'All out' and when the tug has already moved forward.

3 Before your first flight

Gliding school or club?—When to go gliding—Sensations—Fitting a
parachute—Getting in—Cockpit checks

Gliding school or club?

In some countries glider training can be done at a commercial school.
They do not necessarily have better facilities or instruction than a club,
but you will be able to book your flying in advance. This makes it possible
to go to the gliding site and have a few flights and be back working or
doing something else for the rest of the day. Because gliding is so labour-
intensive and the utilisation of a glider is relatively low, at a commercial
gliding school it is usually more expensive than flying a light aircraft. In
a gliding club, the majority of the work is done by the members and you
will be expected to stay and help on the flying field and to play your part
as a member. But this is all part of the enjoyment of gliding.

When to go gliding

If you can choose on which days you are going to go gliding, always listen
to the radio or look at the weather forecast and try to avoid obviously bad
weather. For your first few flights, you need good conditions to make quick
progress. Do not go gliding if the forecast is for gales, rain or hill fog.
Strong winds usually mean bumpy conditions and these are best avoided
until you have done several flights and are used to handling the controls.
Rain makes gliding unpleasant, since everyone gets wet. You cannot see
clearly and the performance of all gliders is spoiled by the effect of water
on the wing, so gliders are not normally flown in rain. Any dry day with
a light wind and without low cloud will be ideal for learning.
Unfortunately, at a soaring club a really good day will attract all the more
experienced pilots—which leaves fewer launches for instructional flying.

If you arrive and the weather is too bad to fly, you can learn useful things
by helping in the hangar or by listening to the other pilots chatting over
a cup of tea. There may be talks and discussions by the instructors and
you will probably be welcome to join in and listen even if, as on weekdays,
they are primarily for course members. Go to as many talks as you can,
as this will save you time and money.

Remember that drinking and flying do not mix and if you do have any
alcoholic drinks, then you certainly should not fly solo. Whereas you may

26

be able to drive fairly safely after a few drinks, research shows that ability to fly is seriously affected by *any* alcohol and that the effects last 10 – 12 hours or more. So even if the weather looks hopeless at lunch time, it is best to stick to soft drinks in case of an improvement later on.

When you arrive at the gliding club, before you do *anything else* put your name on the flying list. If you are first to arrive, start a flying list yourself, even if the weather looks doubtful. The flying list is the order of flying, so no name—no fly!

The training at most gliding clubs is on two-seater gliders, but it can also be done on a motor glider, if one is available. Changing from one type of glider to another or from gliders to motor gliders from flight to flight will be like trying to learn to drive using a car for some lessons and a truck for others. It makes it all more difficult and confusing.

The motor glider is vastly superior for learning how to land and can extend its flights if required. Instead of a turn of 2 or 3 launches on the glider, you can get 8 landings in a 30-minute session in the motor glider and it is practice you need. Naturally you will be keen to progress to real gliders, but be patient because you will learn more quickly in the motor glider and an extra day or so on it can save you many days of training on the glider.

All two-seater training machines have full dual control so that the instructor can take over in an instant if you need help at any stage. In smooth air the glider will fly 'hands off' without assistance. It is stable and is not about to fall out of the sky, although it may feel like it.

If you have never flown before you will probably notice the change of pressure in your ears as the glider gains or loses height. If this becomes uncomfortable or makes you temporarily deaf, it can be cured by swallowing, or pinching your nose and blowing occasionally.

There is no need to worry about air sickness during your first few launches because the flights are too short to upset anyone. In any case, it is most unlikely that you will be one of the rare people who are affected in this way.

Sensations

On your first few flights you will experience some vivid and occasionally worrying sensations. This is quite normal and you will find that after a few flights the sensations become less and less noticeable. An aircraft is often tipped slightly by bumps in the air, so that even if you hold the controls still it does not continue in steady flight. This means that the pilot has to make some corrections on the controls to keep the glider in level flight. Eventually you will learn to recognise these bumps and to correct for them, when they happen, smoothly and automatically.

While you are still getting used to the controls, these bumps are rather disconcerting and it will be difficult for you to tell, for example, whether the glider is banking over rather quickly because of a bump lifting one wing or whether it is because of a movement you have made on the controls. Sometimes a bump will tip you one way, sometimes the other. A small movement on the stick to apply some bank for a turn may have no effect at all for a few seconds if a bump is opposing the control movement, whereas on another occasion a small movement may result in a rapid banking movement into quite a steep turn. This can be rather alarming and is bound to be confusing until the control movements have become more or less instinctive.

These sensations and how and why they occur are explained in the author's *Beginning Gliding* (A & C Black). Briefly, any nose-down pitching movement of the glider or any turbulence causing the glider suddenly to sink a few feet produces an unpleasant feeling, similar to that felt when driving over a hump-backed bridge or in an elevator or lift. After a few flights this feeling decreases because when we lower the nose and as we look ahead and see the movement against the horizon, our brain suppresses the sensation which by then we have learned to expect.

You will also notice that on some occasions as you bank the glider over into a turn you get a vivid feeling that the banking movement is getting out of control. This impression of overbanking and falling towards the lower wing can be very unnerving. This will not happen after a few more flights as it is caused by failing to use the rudder correctly at the start of the turn. Also with a little more practice, you can see that the angle of bank is not getting too steep. Once again your eyesight helps your brain to suppress the sensation and it ceases to be a problem.

We all have an inborn fear of falling, and our sense of balance is primarily to protect us from toppling over and hurting ourselves. Normally the sensations are suppressed by our eyesight, which confirms that all is well. After a few flights have made you familiar with the three-dimensional movements of an aircraft, the eyesight once again becomes the master of the situation so that as long as you can see what is happening the sensations are scarcely noticeable. Contrary to your expectations you will not experience the same sensation of height as when you look down from a cliff or high building. (I don't like looking down from a high window either!)

Fitting a parachute

Parachutes are required for aerobatics, cloud flying, and competition flying when there is a higher risk of overstressing the glider or of having a collision. They are not always carried for normal training flights. Parachutes are also worn as additional weight and packing for the smaller, lightweight pilots. (Most parachutes weigh about 15 to 18 lb.)

When not in use, parachutes should be kept in their carrying bags and not left overnight in the cockpit. They must not be allowed to get damp or contaminated with oil or acids.

Your instructor or pilot will show you how to put the parachute on and adjust the harness. It is extremely unlikely that you will ever need your parachute, or even see one used from a glider, but if you wear one you must know how to use it.

The harness should be tightened so that it is slightly uncomfortable to stand upright. (The straps will be looser when you sit down.) Notice the position of the ripcord handle. This may be in a different position on another type of parachute as they are not standardised.

In an emergency, the first thing is to jettison the cockpit canopy. Next release your safety harness, *not the parachute harness*, and get out of the cockpit as quickly as you can. If height permits, delay pulling the ripcord for a few seconds, then pull it *hard*. Otherwise, pull as soon as you are out of the cockpit.

For a safe landing you must keep your feet and knees together with your knees slightly bent so that you land and take the shock on both feet. If you are descending facing directly into the wind or downwind, try to turn yourself to land sideways and try to relax.

After landing the canopy can be deflated to stop yourself being dragged along the ground by pulling hard on any lines you can reach, or by running round the parachute.

It is best to put the parachute on before climbing into the cockpit and to practise getting out quickly with it on.

Getting in

Your pilot will show you how to climb into the glider.

It is always quite safe to step onto the centre of the seat and then onto the floor or foot boards on either side of the control column. You may find that you need some padding behind you in order to reach the controls and rudder pedals easily. In this case you should remember to find suitable cushions every time you come to glide so that you will always be sitting at the same height and position on instructional flights.

Your instructor will help to fasten the safety harness when you are sitting in the cockpit. The purpose of the harness is to prevent the pilot from moving in his seat in bumpy conditions in flight and to prevent injury which might occur in a bad landing through the pilot moving forward and striking the instrument panel. An efficient harness must, therefore, hold the pilot round the waist and shoulders. After getting into the cockpit it is best to lay out all four straps in position before attempting to fasten them.

With all types of safety harness it is most important to tighten up the waist straps first *before* tightening the shoulder straps.

It is also important to adjust the harness so that you are held firmly in position and feel as though you are really a part of the aircraft.

There is nothing more uncomfortable than having the harness too loose, so that you move in the seat. Even if your straps feel too tight when they are first adjusted, after a few moments they will ease off as you settle into the seat.

The next thing to do is to look round the cockpit at the controls and instruments. The cockpit layout for a typical glider is shown in Fig. 2.

The controls consist of the control column and the rudder pedals. The instruments generally include an airspeed indicator, altimeter, variometer, turn and slip indicator and a compass. These are unimportant on the first few flights. The release knob for the launching cable is painted yellow and is generally on the left of the instrument panel. There is also a blue lever on the left for operating the airbrakes or spoilers and probably a small green lever for adjusting the elevator trim tab.

Cockpit checks

A routine check ensures that nothing vital can be missed and that the pilot can take off without a nagging fear that perhaps he has forgotten something. In Great Britain this take-off check is standardised for gliders and is remembered by the mnemonic CB SIFT CB. Each letter stands for a particular item. Other countries have similar checks and you should ask your instructor for details. These checks *must* be learned by heart.

C – Controls – check for full and free movement of the stick and rudder and that these controls are all working correctly.

B – Ballast – check that the cockpit loads (pilot weight plus the weight of the parachute) are within the limits on the cockpit placard. Additional ballast is *vital* if the pilot's weight is less than the prescribed minimum (note: gliders of the same type do not necessarily have the same minimum or maximum cockpit loads).

S – Straps – check that your safety harness (and that of any passengers) is tight.

I – Instruments – check that there are no obvious errors or broken glasses in the critical instruments and reset the altimeter if necessary.

F – Flaps – set the flaps, if fitted, for take-off. (Flaps are not always fitted to training aircraft and this is sometimes omitted.)

T – Trimmer – the trim lever should be checked for full and free movement and set to the appropriate position for take off—on most gliders it is central for wire launches and slightly forward for aerotow.

C – Canopy – check the canopy lock and push up in the centre of the canopy to check that the whole canopy is secure.

B – Brakes – check by pulling the airbrake lever fully open and seeing that the airbrakes are open on both wings. *Then close and lock them.*

Once this check has been completed the glider is ready to be launched.

4 Early flights

The correct flying attitude—Using the controls—Trimming—Turns—To turn correctly—The landing—Points to remember

On your first one or two flights it is most probable that your instructor will do the launch and hand over control to you after he has released at height. If he has adjusted the trimmer correctly the glider should fly steadily in the correct attitude with no pressures on the stick. In fact in smooth air it will fly itself.

The correct flying attitude

During the early flights you must try to keep the glider flying in the correct attitude and speed for efficiency by looking ahead and learning to recognise the correct position of the nose in relation to the horizon. By looking ahead you can detect both nose up and down and banking movements. Do not look at the wingtips or you will find the nose position changing unnoticed. If the attitude is correct, the speed is correct, the glider is flying efficiently and the handling will be normal; if the nose is too high, the speed will be too slow, the controls will be sluggish and ineffective and the glider will mush down, losing height rather quickly. If the nose is too low, the glider will be diving at a high speed and losing height rapidly.

Notice that whereas any change in attitude (nose position) can be seen and corrected immediately, both the airspeed indicator and the sound of the airflow have a considerable time lag. This is because the glider gains or loses speed gradually, quite a few seconds after any change of attitude. (In the same way, a bicycle freewheeling onto a steeper slope takes time to gain speed.)

If you look ahead and see the nose dropping, it is usually possible to bring it back to the correct position long before there is any change in the airspeed. Notice that the speed is always controlled by the attitude. Even in the motor glider or a normal aircraft the engine power has little effect on the speed. If the nose is high the speed is low even at full power. Conversely, even with the engine switched off, a nose-down position results in a high speed. The attitude controls the speed and the power controls the rate of climb or descent.

Using the controls

On your first or second flight you will be shown how each control works. The stick movements are easy to remember. You press, or lean the stick

31

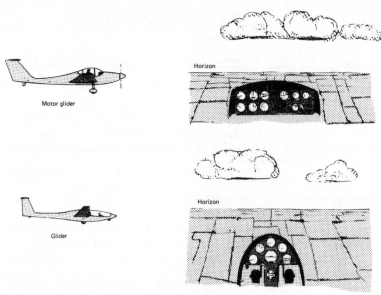

8. Judging the attitude by the position of the nose.

in the direction you want the aircraft to go, press the nose down, pull the nose up, lean the stick to the left and the left wing will go down, etc. However, the rudder movements (your foot pedals) are not instinctive; left foot forward swings or yaws the nose to the left and right foot forward yaws the nose to the right. Moreover, the rudder controls on most gliders have very little proper feel and do not tend to centre themselves. Car drivers often find that they fail to move the glider rudder sufficiently with their right foot, probably because in a car the right foot has the more delicate job of controlling the accelerator. A common fault at first is to brace both feet so firmly on the rudders that pressing on one pedal has little or no effect. As you push on one foot, the other foot must be moved back to allow the rudder to move.

There are several points to remember about the effects of the controls. Notice that any forward movement on the stick to lower the nose gives you that nasty hump-backed bridge feeling. Be gentle. The elevator is very powerful and sensitive. The size of a sideways movement of the stick controls the rate of roll and not the angle of bank—e.g. a small move to the left will result in a slow rolling movement to the left, with the angle of bank getting steeper and steeper until the pilot makes a countermove to stop it. A large move to the left will give a rapid rolling movement which again will continue until the pilot makes a countermove to stop it—in other words to bank to a certain angle the pilot initiates the banking by moving the stick, and then stops it with a countermove when it reaches the angle he wants. Turns can only be made by banking the glider.

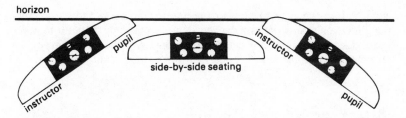

9. Side-by-side cockpits. The view ahead with side-by-side seating can be very misleading at first. Here, the instructor's part of the nose looks too low in a left turn and too high in a right turn.

Trimming

All gliders have some degree of fore-and-aft stability which means that if they are trimmed to fly 'hands off' at a particular speed, they will always tend to return to that speed after being disturbed. When the glider is correctly trimmed the pilot can relax without the need for constant corrections on the elevator.

The first essential is to adjust the attitude until the glider is flying steadily at the desired speed. Remember to make only small changes in attitude and to wait for the speed to settle down. Then relax your hold of the stick just enough to detect whether the nose is tending to rise or fall, but correct it immediately. Hold the correct attitude and readjust the trim lever a little at a time until there is apparently no forward or backward pressure remaining on the stick. Test the trimming by relaxing once again. If the glider is correctly trimmed it will fly 'hands off' with the speed and attitude remaining constant. It is useful to practise trimming at various speeds until you can do do it quickly. Always retrim at any time you notice any constant load on the stick; it is easier to fly a well trimmed glider. Never move the trimmer in flight unless your other hand is holding the stick. Nose heaviness is corrected by moving the trim lever further back; i.e. it works on the same principle as the stick movement.

Remember, do not attempt to retrim the glider exactly unless you have it flying at the correct speed and attitude. It must be in steady flight at the time.

Turns

Because of the low flying speed and large span of a glider, the rudder has to be used in conjunction with the stick movement (sideways) to apply and to take off the bank when entering and coming out of turns. During the turn, very, very little rudder is required, but a small backward move is needed on the stick to prevent the nose dropping and to ensure that the glider maintains the same speed. It is surprisingly difficult to make the rudder movements correctly in harmony with the stick movements and many beginners find it easiest to think aloud about the moves.

To turn correctly (see Fig. 10)

Look around and particularly behind in the direction you are going to turn; *then look ahead* and correct the position of the nose if it is too high or too low; apply the bank with the stick and rudder together (stick to the left with left rudder, i.e. left foot forward), check the bank with a countermove sideways on the stick just beyond the central position to stop the bank increasing, and *then* reduce the rudder to leave a very small amount of rudder in the direction of the turn (left rudder in a left turn). Finally ease back on the stick to prevent the nose dropping as the turn continues.

During a continuous turn use sideways moves on the stick to correct small changes in the angle of bank, and changes in forward or backward pressures to maintain the correct position of the nose in relation to the horizon. Look around several times in each circle. As you come out of the turn, take off the bank by leaning the stick the way you want the aircraft to go, using the rudder at the same time—i.e. stick to the right with right foot forward. As the wings come level relax the backward pressure on the stick so that the attitude remains normal and centralise both stick and rudder together.

Simplifying this: look around and behind, look ahead, stick and rudder together, check the bank with the stick *and then* reduce the rudder, ease back to stop the nose dropping. Check the angle of bank and nose position, check that you have reduced the rudder, look around. Take off the bank with the stick and rudder together, relax the backward pressure and centralise the stick and rudder as the wings come level. You could do far worse than learn these movements off parrot fashion and say them to yourself as you make each turn.

Note that the stick and rudder are moved exactly together as the bank is applied and taken off, and at any time you are bringing the wings level after being tipped by a bump. Small sideways movements of the stick need small rudder movements but larger movements of the stick (to apply or take off the bank quickly) necessitate larger rudder movements. However, you never need a large amount of rudder during *any* turn. Turns are really a matter of the bank and backward pressure on the stick and once established in the turn these are the essential movements. In gliders the rudder is used to stop any tendency to swing sideways as bank is applied or taken off.

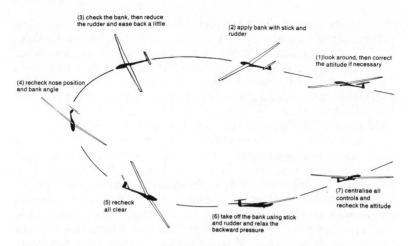

(3) check the bank, then reduce the rudder and ease back a little

(2) apply bank with stick and rudder

(1) look around, then correct the attitude if necessary

(4) recheck nose position and bank angle

(7) centralise all controls and recheck the attitude

(5) recheck all clear

(6) take off the bank using stick and rudder and relax the backward pressure

10. How to turn.

(1) Look around and behind for other aircraft, and re-check the attitude.

(2) Watching ahead, apply the bank with stick and rudder together.

(3) Check the bank with the stick and *then* reduce the rudder.

(4) Re-check the nose position and the angle of bank.

(5) Re-check it is all clear to continue turning.

(6) Take off the bank using the stick and rudder together and relax the backward pressure on the stick.

(7) Centralise the stick and rudder as the wings come level and re-check the attitude and speed.

The rudder movements are the real problem and continue to give every beginner trouble throughout his training.

Notice that you must relax one foot as you push the other. If you brace on one foot and push hard on the other it will feel as though you are moving the pedals, but in fact you are only stretching the cables and the rudder itself will hardly move at all. Everyone becomes very tense at times and most people find that they are not moving the rudder nearly enough.

If you fail to use the rudder or use very little movement as you start to turn, any reduction in movement will leave the glider turning with far too little rudder, i.e. with the wrong rudder on and a slipping movement. Reducing the rudder too soon also causes this slipping movement. This can be detected by a sensation of falling towards the lower wing and a feeling that the glider is tipping over into a steeper and steeper bank. Always check the banking movement with stick first, then immediately afterwards reduce the rudder to leave a little in the direction of the turn.

Some types of glider suffer from a tendency for the rudder to overbalance during inaccurate turns. This gives a beginner the confusing and misleading impression that the instructor is interfering with the rudder control. For example, if too little rudder is applied at the start of the turn, as the glider starts to slip the rudder will be moved over by the airflow so that the pedal pushes against your foot. Similarly if too much rudder is left on during a turn, it will tend to move further, with the same result.

These effects do not occur if the rudder is used correctly. Always push back against any tendency for the rudder to move as this will bring the glider back into accurate flight. I always brief my students to imagine there is an idiot in the rear cockpit who always pushes the rudder the wrong way.

On an early flight you should be shown exactly why the combined stick and rudder movements are necessary. There is a distinct tendency for the glider to swing to the right as the stick is moved to the left to apply bank to the left. This swing is called *adverse yaw*, and is the effect of aileron drag. (Fig. 11.) It occurs whenever the stick is moved sideways to apply or take off bank and is very noticeable in gliders because of their long wing spans and very low flying speeds. Aileron drag is scarcely detectable in a modern powered aeroplane and therefore the rudder is not required for turns in these aircraft. Whereas the amount of rudder movement needed scarcely varies for different angles of bank, the amount of backward movement on the stick needed in a turn *is* dependent on the angle of bank. It is the backward movement which pulls the wing to a slightly larger angle, and this produces the additional lift required for the turn. Gentle

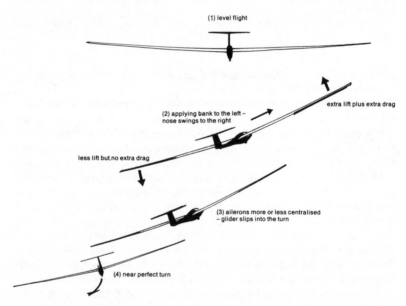

(1) level flight

extra lift plus extra drag

(2) applying bank to the left – nose swings to the right

less lift but no extra drag

(3) ailerons more or less centralised – glider slips into the turn

(4) near perfect turn

11. Adverse yaw. If the bank is applied without using any rudder, the nose swings the wrong way for a few seconds, causing a sideslipping motion towards the lower wing. As the angle is checked with the aileron, this sideslipping becomes an almost normal turn.

turns require very little extra lift, whereas steep turns need much more. You will notice that if you fail to ease back, the nose drops gradually in a gentle turn, but more quickly in a steeper one. Remember to relax forward again as you bring the wings level to straighten up, or when changing from one turn to another.

Judging the attitude during a turn is a relatively simple matter in a tandem-seater aircraft, whereas with side-by-side seating the position of the nose will appear to change depending on which direction you are turning. Look at your side of the nose as you apply the bank and try to ignore the apparent change of the vertical attitude of the nose. The width of the nose makes it easier to see any banking movements in a side-by-side trainer than in a tandem-seater. In fact, these differences become insignificant after a few flights.

The normal attitude and cruising speed is enough for turns using angles of bank up to about 40°, which is steeper than you will normally use. Very steep turns require an extra 5 knots or so because stalling speed is much higher in a steep turn.

The landing

With motor glider training it is usual to make a start on the landings after two or three trips of handling and practising turns. It is an easy matter to do 7 or 8 landings in a half-hour session, and you soon learn how to land.

With 'all glider' training most instructors begin to teach the landing straight after instruction on how the controls work as it is difficult to get enough practice. At first the instructor takes care of the circuit planning and the use of the airbrakes, leaving the student to concentrate on his turns and then on the landing itself. It is much easier for the student if the use of the airbrakes is not introduced until the landings are reasonably consistent.

It is quite normal to find that as you start to concentrate on the approach and landings, your co-ordination deteriorates for a while. This causes the glider to swing about instead of flying straight.

Later, when you start the circuit planning and the use of the airbrakes you will probably find to your dismay that you cannot get the glider to fly where you want it to go. This is quite normal and is caused by forgetting to use the rudder. Once again, after a few more flights you will overcome this problem, so do not feel discouraged.

Whereas everyone has a problem in learning to use the rudder correctly in conjunction with the stick movements, it is unusual to have much real trouble over learning to land. It is difficult and takes a great deal of practice to form the habit of using feet and hands together automatically, whereas landing is a normal learning problem.

No two landings are identical and the pilot has to learn to watch ahead and see how the aircraft is responding to his control movements. It takes practice, and this is more difficult to come by for a glider pupil who is doing 2 or 3 flights in succession and then not flying again for a long period.

The process of landing is very comprehensively explained in *Beginning Gliding*. The key points are as follows.

Look well ahead during the final approach, 100 – 200 yards ahead and not just over the nose.

Start the levelling out with a *minute* backward movement on the stick at about 20 – 30 feet so that by the time the aircraft is flying level it is 2 – 5 feet above the ground—*not* too close (see Fig. 12).

12. The round-out, hold-off and landing. At about 20 – 30 feet a very tiny, gradual movement is made on the stick to start the round-out. The glider is then kept just above the ground with a gentle gradual backward movement until it sinks slightly and lands.

The aim is then to keep the aircraft off the ground for as long as possible without gaining height. This is achieved by a gradual backward movement on the stick. If the aircraft begins to balloon (gain height) stop the backward movement and wait for a moment; as it begins to sink again you must stop it sinking by easing back gently. Eventually the aircraft will settle and touch down. It is an instinctive reaction at first to move the stick forward as soon as you see the aircraft ballooning up, but if you do so you will fly back heavily into the ground. It is only when you balloon up 15 – 20 feet that a small forward movement is needed and then you have time to ease back and stop the descent. If you are trying to get down on to the ground you will never make a good landing. However, if you find yourself up at 10 or 15 feet and flying level, do not make any further backward movement on the stick until the aircraft has started to sink and is nearer the ground (see Fig. 13).

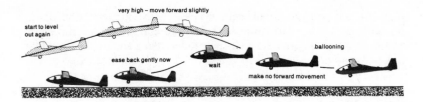

13. Corrections when ballooning or holding off too high. Unless the height is more than 10 – 15 feet, do not move forward on the stick. Hold the stick still and wait until the glider starts to sink again – then hold off with a gradual backward movement until it lands. If ballooning is very high a *small* movement forward should be made to start a fresh approach.

Landing is the knack of seeing and understanding what is happening and of responding appropriately on the stick. It takes some practice, because the sensitivity of the controls is different each time and because, as the aircraft floats along using up its excess speed, the controls become less and less responsive.

The airbrakes have nothing to do with the landing itself, but regulate the approach angle, and control where the glider will touch down. Regardless of the approach misjudgments, the glider must always be held off properly for as long as possible or the landing itself will be a bad one.

A premature landing means touching down at a higher speed in a more nose-down attitude and this leads to bouncing heavily unless the ground is exceptionally smooth.

During these early landings the instructor will be using the airbrakes for you, and if the glider balloons badly, he will reduce their setting to allow you another attempt at landing a little further up the field. Reducing the airbrake like this is a skilled business since if it is done just as the aircraft balloons up, it results in more lift and more height still. The correct moment to reduce the airbrake is just as the aircraft begins to sink again. This reduces the drag and gives a little more lift so that there is control for a further attempt at the hold-off.

Once your landings are fairly consistent and the instructor no longer needs to make these corrections, it is time for you to take over the operation of the airbrakes. Trying to start using the airbrakes too soon usually causes even more difficulties. Ideally the whole landing should be done without any need to change the setting of the airbrakes.

After touchdown, a gradual backward movement will keep the tail down, reducing the loads on the front skid. Do not relax, keep the wings level and keep the glider straight with the rudder, using the stick and rudder independently.

Points to remember

1. The correct attitude gives the correct speed and efficient gliding flight.
2. The attitude, controlled by the elevator, determines the speed; nose high—too slow and poor control, nose low—too fast.
3. Lean the stick the way you want to go.
4. Left foot forward applies left rudder and swings the nose to the left. Remember to relax your other foot.
5. Relax. If the glider is accurately trimmed it will fly itself.
6. Learn the order of the control movements for a turn.
7. Keep a good lookout for other aircraft but watch ahead as you apply the bank. Do not look at the wingtips.
8. Use the stick and rudder together to apply and take off bank.
9. Very little rudder is needed during any steady turn.
10. Do not forget the small backward movement on the stick during the turn.
11. Look about 100 yds ahead during the approach and landing.
12. Round out very gradually starting about 20 to 30 feet up, and aim to be flying level 2 to 5 feet above the ground, not too close. (These heights can be reduced as you gain experience.)
13. Keep just off the ground for as long as possible using a gradual backward movement on the stick.
14. Hold the stick still if the glider balloons up a few feet, then continue the hold-off as it starts to sink again. Do not move forward unless the aircraft balloons to 20 or 30 feet.
15. After touchdown keep the wings level with ailerons and keep straight with the rudder alone.

5 Launching by aerotow

Launching methods—Aerotow launching—The take-off—Positioning up and down—The low tow position—Turns—Releasing the tow rope—Boxing the wake—Towing speeds—Releasing in lift—Emergency signals on tow—Aerotow rope breaks, etc.—Towing accidents—Tugging

Launching methods

In most countries aerotowing has superseded winch and car launching, but if the cost of fuel continues to rise it seems possible that many more gliding clubs will revert to these very economical methods of launching.

Aerotow launching requires quite a high standard of handling and if your training is by aerotow, your instructor may well do the launch himself until you are well over halfway through your training. This is often better than attempting aerotow too early, and becoming disheartened at your lack of progress.

With winch or car launching, the launch is easier since the glider will more or less fly itself up the launch like a kite. The important things are to keep the wings level on take-off and to control the initial climb so that it starts gradually, and progressively steepens up into the full climb. Most modern gliders tend to come up into a steep climb by themselves and the pilot has to prevent this from happening too quickly by easing forward on the stick just after take-off, but not enough to stop it climbing normally. If the gliding site is a small one and it is difficult to get high launches or to reach soaring conditions, the instructor may assist or even fly the whole launch to make sure of getting high enough to give you a chance to practise your turns. On a longer site or in good conditions you may find yourself doing the whole take-off and launch on your third or fourth flight. When the initial climb is correctly done, there should be no particular hazard if the cable breaks at any stage of the launch. On your first few flights your instructor may take over or tell you what to do if this happens. Usually it just means a landing down the field and a long walk back.

In a motor glider the take-off is very easy. There may be a slight tendency to swing off to the right because of the effects of the engine and propeller slipstream, but if it is kept straight with the rudder, the aircraft will take itself off the ground when it reaches flying speed.

One distinct advantage is that you can practise turns and improve your co-ordination all the time you are climbing to height. On an aerotow you would be sitting as a passenger most of the time on the tow.

41

You may notice that while the aircraft is climbing the rudder is a little heavier to move and that errors such as forgetting the rudder do not cause quite such a noticeable swing of the nose as in a glider. The extra slipstream behind the propeller makes both fin and rudder more effective. When the power is cut off and the propeller is either windmilling or stopped, the motor glider handles much more like a normal glider, but still has rather heavier rudder loads. Changing the power also affects the fore-and-aft trim. Power off results in the aircraft becoming more nose-heavy, full power gives a slight nose-up pitching movement. (This does not happen where the engine and propeller are mounted high above the fuselage as in the Motor Janus.)

The advantage of the aerotow lies in its flexibility. The glider can be launched to almost any height and can be towed into a thermal or to a particular place before releasing. This is a great advantage on days with poor conditions when a series of winch launches to 1,000 feet or so would not have much likelihood of reaching lift.

If a launch height of 1,000 – 1,500 feet is required, a winch or autotow launch is quicker and cheaper.

The aerotow is one of the simplest forms of launching in smooth conditions as the pilot has only to maintain a steady position in relation to the tug. If glider training is carried out solely by aerotow, the average pupil may be able to handle the glider for most of the aerotow after five or six launches. However, aerotowing in smooth conditions is a very different matter to aerotowing on a turbulent soaring day or in rotor flow.

The take-off and initial climb of the tug-and-glider combination is comparatively poor in most cases and the effect of strong turbulence such as the curl-over effect behind a hill may prevent the combination climbing and make towing impractical at some gliding sites.

Another factor which must be considered is the result of an engine failure or premature release just after take-off. If the site is surrounded by wooded or rough ground the chances of a successful landing by either the tug or glider are slight unless some hundreds of feet are available for selecting and reaching a suitable landing area.

Weighing up the considerations for and against this kind of launch, it clearly depends upon the suitability of the site and the type of towing aircraft available. The initial cost of the launch is high because of the fuel consumption and upkeep of the aircraft, but the prospects for soaring are greatly improved. This makes aerotow launching well worth while for advanced soaring flights, from flat sites. Unfortunately it is a very expensive way of launching to a thousand feet or so for training in landings.

Aerotow launching

Although the additional height provided by an aerotow launch gives more time for practising turns, etc. and may make the circuit planning easier, the tow itself requires more skill than a car or winch launch. Until the student has considerable practice and can co-ordinate the stick and rudder movements smoothly, keeping exactly in position behind the towing aircraft is bound to seem difficult if not impossible.

Keeping position is a matter of spotting any slight change and correcting for it immediately; it is the knack of seeing the beginning of a movement and responding with a tiny correction on the controls.

Because the launching speed is greater than the normal cruising speed of the glider all the controls are more sensitive than normal. However, the aileron is also considerably heavier. This often results in a tendency for the beginner to undercontrol the aileron while overcontrolling with the fore-and-aft movements on the stick.

The take-off

Since the distance between glider and tug is short, the signals can safely be given by the wingtip holder to a signaller standing about twenty yards ahead and to the left of the tug, in a position clearly visisible to the tug pilot.

The tug is taxied forward slowly to take up the slack in the rope until the signal 'All out' is given.

The trimmer should always be set forward a little for aerotowing. After completing the pre-take-off vital action checks the tow rope is attached to the nose hook, if one is fitted. Before giving the order to 'Take up slack', make quite sure that it is all clear ahead of the aircraft; that there is no one in front or near the glider other than the wingtip man holding the wingtip level; and make sure that there are no gliders on the approach by asking if it is 'all clear above and behind'.

The stick should be held lightly with the right hand and the left hand should be kept near the release knob throughout the launch.

During any take-off run the wings must be kept level, while the glider is balanced on the main wheel with the tail just off the ground. If the main wheel is ahead of the centre of gravity, as in most modern single-seaters, this will involve easing the stick forward to get the tail off the ground. In gliders which have a nose wheel or front skid, a slight backward movement may be needed to get balanced on the main wheel. In either case leaving the ground with the tail wheel or skid touching means that the glider is flying at a very low speed and may be unable to recover safely if the tow fails a few feet up. If the glider is held with the tail just off the ground it will not leave the ground until it reaches a safe speed.

During the ground run the stick and rudder must be used independently because the glider may swing in either direction while at the same time dropping either wing.

Whatever type of launch is being made, the exact control movements on take-off depend, of course, on the type of glider being flown. If it is fitted with a front wheel or nose skid and sits with it firmly down on the ground, the pilot will need to lift the nose to get the glider balanced on the wheel for take-off.

On a glider which has the main wheel well ahead of the centre of gravity so that the tail skid or wheel is firmly on the ground, a forward movement will be necessary to avoid leaving the ground in a semi-stalled position.

In any case, the glider should be lifted off the ground as soon as possible and then flown at a height of 5 – 10 feet to allow the tug to accelerate quickly to take-off speed.

Since the towing speed is well above the normal cruising speed of the glider, it is necessary to increase the forward pressure on the stick gradually to hold the glider in position as it gains speed. It is vital to prevent the glider flying too high during the take-off or initial climb as this will pull the tail of the tug up and prevent it leaving the ground.

If the field is short, a slight advantage may be gained by moving down into the low tow position as the tug is just leaving the ground. This reduces the load on the tug for a few seconds as the glider moves down. Alternatively, the glider may be held down very near the ground all the time until the tug has taken off and climbed up to a correct position for the low tow position. (This is normal practice in Australia.)

Both of these methods, together with the use of a short tow rope, should be applied when the length of run available is critical. When considering the conditions for take-off the following factors should be borne in mind: the experience of the pilots, the weight and drag of the glider, power of the tug, wind strength, take-off run, slope and surface of the ground and possible down-draughts.

If the tug seems unable to climb, the cause is almost certain to be that the airbrakes have opened. Always recheck the airbrakes if the launch looks or feels abnormal and also, of course, if the tug gives the rudder waggling signal.

The glider pilot must always be prepared to abandon the tow if there appears to be any risk of the tug not being able to clear the far boundary. This decision must be made in plenty of time so that there is room for a safe landing. The glider pilot should always be able to anticipate the tug pilot jettisoning the glider and should cast off at any time when the tug appears to be in a difficult situation.

Positioning up and down

The normal towing position is with the glider flying just above the turbulent wake of the tug. The exact position depends upon the type and power of the towing aircraft but if a line is taken through the fuselage the glider should be just above that line. The propeller slipstream and

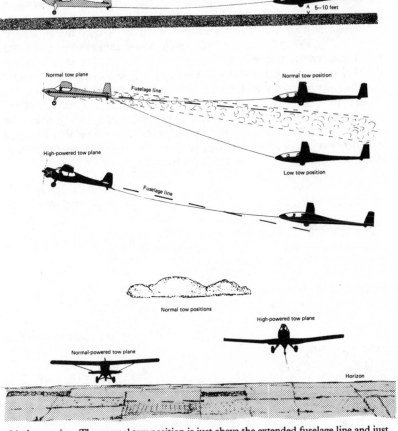

14. Aerotowing. The normal tow position is just above the extended fuselage line and just
clear of the turbulent wake.

wash from the wings is always deflected a little downwards. (See Fig. 14.)

There are several ways to judge this position. Once the position is known it can be maintained by keeping the same view of the tug. For example, on the Super Cub, the position should be approximately with the top of the fin in line with the top of the cabin or with the tailplane cutting just above the junction of the undercarriage and wing struts.

On a clear day the glider may be positioned so that the tug appears in a constant position relative to the horizon. For low-powered tow planes such as the Super Cub, Citabria, etc., the position is with the tug just about on the horizon. More powerful tugs will be above the horizon because of their much steeper climbing angle.

On some gliders it is a simple matter to choose a point at the top of the instrument panel or a suitable mark on the canopy well forward and keep it steady in relation to the tug. As soon as the tow plane appears to start to move up or down a small correction is required to stop it immediately. These tiny corrections need to be a small movement followed by a countermove to prevent too great a change. The secret is to detect the beginning of any movement of the tow plane and to move the control in time to prevent the glider from getting seriously out of position.

Care must be taken not to let the glider get too high or the tail of the tug will be pulled up, putting it into a dive. Within a few moments the speed will build up so that, unless prompt action is taken, this situation may become worse and it may be necessary for the glider pilot to release or for the tug pilot to jettison the glider.

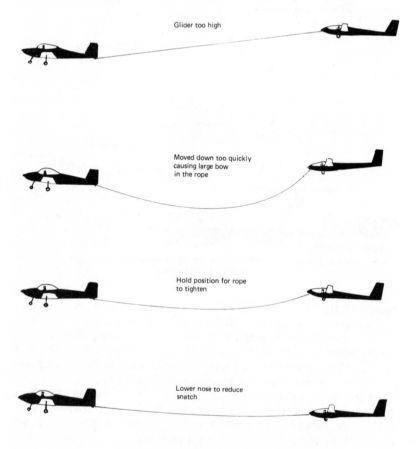

Glider too high

Moved down too quickly
causing large bow
in the rope

Hold position for rope
to tighten

Lower nose to reduce
snatch

15. Correcting for bows in the tow rope.

In smooth conditions a satisfactory tow will result if the glider pilot maintains the correct position accurately. This requires the undivided attention of the glider pilot and it is, therefore, essential that he is completely prepared for the flight before take-off. No attempt should be made to look at maps or make notes during the tow as a few seconds' distraction can result in the glider getting right out of position and may mean having to abandon the launch. The pilot must concentrate on holding the correct position, and any corrections should be made as gently as possible. At the comparatively high speeds on tow, the glider's ailerons are heavier than in normal flight and the elevators in particular are usually very sensitive, so that care must be taken in adjusting height. The movement of the tug gives a very good indication of the presence of a thermal since the tug flies into it first and is lifted before the glider. Smooth corrections are needed if any change in position occurs during the tow. The general tendency is for the glider to get too high because any relaxation on the controls will result in it climbing.

If it does, the nose must be lowered very gradually or the glider will gain speed, allowing the rope to get slack. A few seconds later, as the glider slows down and the tug accelerates without the drag of the glider, the rope will snatch tight giving both the tug and glider a severe jerk which may break the towing rope. If a nylon rope is being used, it will stretch and then catapult the glider forward again. The extra speed makes the glider climb up and slackens off the rope so that once this surging starts, prompt action is needed to prevent it developing further and causing a break. If the 'bow' in the rope is only a slight one, no action need be taken other than to hold the correct towing position as the slack comes tight. However, if the 'bow' is serious, the glider should be held in position until the rope begins to tighten up. The jerk can then be eliminated by lowering the nose slightly just before the rope comes tight. This increases the speed of the glider for long enough to prevent the jerk. When a correction is made in this way, it may result in the glider getting into the slipstream for a few moments but this is of far less importance than the risk of breaking the rope. (See Fig. 15.)

If a very bad 'bow' is allowed to develop, it is probably better to release than to endeavour to damp it out. Excess height in relation to the tug can be lost without gaining speed by making the change very gradually. The airbrakes should not be used unless it is absolutely necessary, as they cause so much drag that the combination may be unable to climb. Excessive use of the airbrakes has been the cause of several forced landings in the past and it is unnecessary to use them except on the rare occasions when a descent is made on tow.

The normal tow gives a good view of the ground ahead so that the pilot can see suitable landing fields just after take-off, when a forced landing requires immediate action to get down safely. It is also much better when flying towards the glare of the sun as the pilot is looking down on the tug and rope and can see them clearly all the time.

The low tow position

The low tow position is with the glider flying just below the slipstream of the tug. Before going down to the low tow position the glider should be lined up directly behind the tug in order to pass straight through the rough air of the slipstream until it arrives in the smooth air below in approximately the position shown in Fig. 14. If this is done smoothly no 'bow' will form in the tow rope. The correct position is easily determined by moving up very slowly until the buffeting of the slipstream is felt on the wing or canopy above the pilot. Having found the edge of the slipstream, the ideal position a few feet below the slipstream can be assumed.

The low tow position is less tiring to hold for long flights as the tug and rope can be more easily seen against the sky (except when flying towards the sun). It is easier to make corrections without getting the tow rope slack and the tendency to get a little too high does not upset the tug. It has also been suggested that the rate of climb is slightly better with the glider in the low tow position. The only disadvantage seems to be the risk of damaging the glider should the rope break over it and, for this reason, the high tow position should be resumed if there is any likelihood of this happening.

Turns

With an inexperienced glider pilot the tug should not exceed a gently banked turn except in emergency since it will make it difficult for the glider pilot to hold position. However, it is possible to tow in steeper turns (up to rate 2 indicated in the tug) and this may enable the tug pilot to make use of thermals to improve the rate of climb and save the need for full power all the time. No signals are given between the tug and glider during the tow so that the glider pilot must watch the tug all the time. The first indication of a turn is the aircraft beginning to bank, and the glider should begin to bank immediately so that it follows the tug round with the rope meeting the nose of the glider in line with its fuselage. An accurate turn should hold this position, and either the high or low tow position will keep the glider out of the slipstream. Steep turns in the normal position necessitate moving a little higher to keep the correct position. Unless rising air is being exploited to assist the climb, only gentle turns should be made since any turn seriously reduces the rate of climb. If the towing rope is at an angle to the nose, the glider is not in line with the correct path of the turn. This often occurs during a prolonged turn when, without realising it, the glider pilot may easily apply rudder so that the turn becomes inaccurate and difficult to maintain smoothly. It sometimes helps to remove the feet from the rudder pedals for a moment to relax them.

Do not get too low. If the buffeting or tipping of the slipstream is felt, move up a little to regain full control again.

Even in straight flight beginners usually swing from side to side violently. This is caused by their anxiety to get back into line behind the tug, and by overcontrolling and keeping the control movements on for far too long. To stop this swinging, do not try to get back into line. Just bring the wings level even if the glider is still out to one side. The rope will then gradually pull the glider back into line without your help. With more experience it is better to fly the glider back into the correct position using the normal co-ordination of the stick and rudder.

Releasing the tow rope

If the glider has been towed upwind of the gliding site, the decision to release can be made by the glider pilot at any time, or the tug pilot may be briefed to waggle his wings when he wants the glider to drop off. In this way an experienced tug pilot can wave off the glider in an area of lift so that there is little chance of it not soaring. The glider pilot should always release from the normal tow position and, once the rope has been seen to go, he should turn off immediately into a climbing turn* so that he is clearly seen by the tug pilot who can then fly back to the airfield. After the tow, the glider pilot may find himself flying too fast. This can be avoided by retrimming and bringing the glider near to the stall for a few moments after release. If, however, the flight is for a badge task such as a Silver or Gold 'C' height, the glider should lose height for at least 200 feet and hold that height for long enough for the barograph to record a short step before beginning to gain height. If the glider is already in lift, circling down with full airbrake may enable this to be done without losing the lift. The launch height will then be taken as the highest point on the step. The tug pilot must note the time, height, and position of the release for record attempts.

Boxing the wake

This useful exercise is intended as a check of towing ability and is used in the U.S.A. for the test for the Glider Pilot Rating. Occasionally a student

---

*In Great Britain the turn can be made in either direction but in most other countries, including the U.S.A., it is mandatory to turn off to the right.

learns to aerotow without experiencing any difficulties and without ever getting badly out of position. Boxing the wake gives the pilot practice and is a fair indication of how well he will manage in turbulent conditions.

It is usual to warn the tow pilot that you will be boxing the wake and to climb to about a thousand feet before starting.

The glider is first moved down steadily through the wake into the low tow position and then back up again. This acts as a warning that the next moves are intentional and not accidental and also reminds the student how far down he will need to go to keep out of the wake.

From this position the glider is banked gently to bring it out to the side of the tow plane and held there with a small amount of bank and rudder. It is then moved down smoothly into the low tow position, keeping to the side to keep clear of the wake. It is then moved across to the other side and back up and across into the original normal tow position.

It is a matter of opinion whether the whole manoeuvre around the wake should be done as one smooth movement or in stages, pausing for a few seconds in each corner.

Towing speeds

The normal maximum towing speed for the type of glider is indicated on the cockpit placard and this should be strictly observed in turbulent conditions.

However, in smooth air the loads on aerotow are very similar to those in gliding flight and it is common practice to tow at higher speeds when retrieving a glider from a cross-country flight in reasonably smooth conditions.

At too low an airspeed, under about 55 knots in a modern machine, the glider may become uncontrollable if it gets into the wake of the tow plane. It may be unable to move back up to the normal tow position. Towing speeds have to be increased 5 – 10 knots when the glider is carrying water ballast.

Releasing in lift

With an aerotow launch on a soarable day it is a bad policy to tow up to a set height such as 2,000 feet and then to release and start to search for a thermal. If the glider does not release in lift, it is almost certain to be in sink and it will often have lost 500 feet or more before some worthwhile lift is found.

Instead, the pilot should be prepared to release in any good lift he flies through within 300 – 400 feet of his target launch height. If the average rate of climb on the tow is 4 – 5 knots, the moment that the rate of climb

rises to 8 – 10 knots it will be worth releasing. At towing speeds any slight
delay will result in being a long way beyond the best lift and it generally
pays to release and immediately turn very tightly through a little more
than 180° to take the glider back towards the lift. Even so at normal gliding
speeds it will take many seconds to fly back into the lift.

Emergency signals on tow

The wave off signal (Fig. 16)
In any emergency, if the tug pilot wants the glider to release and there
is sufficient time available, he will signal by rocking the tow plane's wings
vigorously. This is an *order* to release and the glider pilot must obey it
immediately. Since engine failures are rare, it is always wise for the glider
pilot to check the position of the airbrakes and make quite sure that they
are closed immediately after releasing the rope.

The tug pilot can and will jettison the glider if he has a serious problem
such as an engine failure.

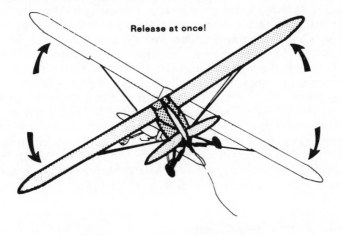

16. The wave off signal. Release at once.

The rudder waggling signal (Fig. 17)
In the event of the glider having the airbrakes open during a launch, if
time and height permits the tug pilot will signal to the pilot by rapidly
waggling his rudder from side to side. This signal tells the glider pilot
to check his aircraft for a problem and to close the airbrakes if they are
open.

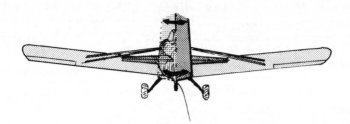

17. The rudder waggling signal. Check your airbrakes.

If the combination is able to climb, the tug pilot should always get the glider up to at least a thousand feet and over the gliding site before signalling, and higher still if the pilot fails to recognise the problem and has to be waved off.

The 'can't release' signal
In the event of the glider being unable to release the towing rope, the glider should be flown out to the left of the tug about one span distance in order to attract the attention of the tug pilot and then the wings should be rocked. The tug should then tow the glider over the field and release the rope from the tug end. From here the glider can make a high approach to ensure that the end of the rope does not catch in anything on the boundary. If the speed is kept above normal and the release is kept pulled, the rope should pull out of the release if it catches on anything during the landing.

If the glider is towed into cloud or very poor visibility for more than a few seconds so that the pilot loses sight of the tug, the glider will have to release since it is impossible to fly for long without getting badly out of position. Heavy rain or hail, particularly in an open glider, may make it impossible to see the tug and a considerate tug pilot will keep clear of conditions which make it difficult for the glider pilot.

Aerotow rope breaks, etc.

Since there is always a possibility of breaking the tow rope or engine trouble in the towing aircraft it is a wise precaution to take a careful look at all the fields just beyond the take-off area.

In normal conditions the angle of climb of the combination is bound to be steeper than the gliding angle of the glider flying downwind, which means that it will almost always be able to reach the take-off field for a downwind landing.

Typically, even a 150 h.p. Super Cub towing an ASK21 or Grob two-seater will have a rate of climb of 3 to 4 knots at a towing speed of 60 knots. This gives a climbing angle of 1 in 15 to 1 in 20 in still air and a much steeper angle against a wind. If the rope is broken at normal speed, virtually no height need be lost turning off to one side so that the situation can be assessed and a decision made whether to return to the field or land off the gliding site.

If it is decided to fly back, it is important to decide whether the height is sufficient to allow an abbreviated circuit with a landing into or across wind, or whether a downwind landing is safer.

There is no particular hazard in making a downwind landing on a gliding site or airfield unless it is very windy weather. However, the choice must be made *before* reaching the upwind end of the field so that any excess height can be lost by using the airbrakes. It is safest to aim to land in the upwind half of the field so that in the event of a misjudgment there is plenty of room ahead for a safe landing.

Select an absolutely clear landing path directly downwind if possible. Approach at a normal approach speed using the airbrakes normally and holding off fully to minimise the touchdown speed. Then take extra care to keep straight and to hold the wings level. Otherwise as the glider loses speed a wing will drop and cause a bad swing or ground loop.

Never land close to obstructions on a downwind landing and never attempt to land back at the launch point to save time. The distance that the glider will float and run after landing is always uncertain when landing downwind because the effects of the wind gradient (explained on pages 132ff) add to the airspeed in this special case.

In the event of an engine problem (or the airbrakes being open during the tow), the launching speed is likely to be abnormally low and the rate of climb poor. Always check your brakes if the launch seems abnormal in any way.

If you are waved off or jettisoned, do not turn off immediately. Check those airbrakes and make sure that you pick up a safe airspeed before turning. If height permits, turn sufficiently to assess the possibilities of getting back and if this is at all doubtful, choose a field ahead or slightly to one side and land into wind. Do not try to get down in the field immediately below. Your glider is not a helicopter and glides at an angle which is not very steep, even with full airbrake.

Towing accidents

Moving onto a more advanced type of glider is usually when towing incidents and accidents occur. In most of the single-seaters the elevator control is very sensitive compared with any two-seater and this makes it easy for an inexperienced pilot to start an up-and-down pilot-induced oscillation (P.I.O.).

Anxiety not to pull the tail of the tug up often results in the glider pilot attempting to keep within a foot or two of the ground. Then any correction to stop the glider moving up even a few feet will result in the start of a pitching motion which is difficult to stop and may result in flying into the ground.

Although it is vital not to get too high, it is quite safe to lift the glider up to a height of four or five feet. At this height the glider pilot can watch the tow plane instead of the ground and this prevents the P.I.O. developing.

Indeed there is some evidence to suggest that in many of the fatal towing accidents the initial fault lies in keeping too close to the ground just after take-off.

When the glider is launched on a c.g. hook on a windy day the effects of the wind gradient will be significant. If it is held very close to the ground the tow plane may be first to start to climb and to gain energy by moving up rapidly through the wind gradient, leaving the glider some way below it. Then when the glider pilot starts to move up, the glider leaps up in the wind gradient with the effect of the c.g. hook bringing the nose up as it would in a winch launch. Unless the glider pilot reacts very quickly the situation may be out of control in a few seconds with the glider far too high above the tow plane. This can be fatal for the tug pilot.

When flying an unfamiliar type of glider it is good advice to make the first few flights with the cockpit load well above the minimum and to make a point of lifting the glider well clear of the ground on take-off. Four or five feet is ideal and much safer than trying to keep a few inches up and so flying into the ground.

Unless the rope is very short the glider has to get up to about twenty feet or more before causing the tow pilot any worry. Above that height is definitely dangerous and must never be allowed to happen. Obviously a longer rope reduces the risk of tipping the tug but very long ropes seem to cause problems of big bows in the rope and constant jerking. 200 feet seems about the best for training flights.

Tugging

There is no doubt that being a tug pilot and towing gliders involves far more risk than just flying a light aircraft. The tow plane spends its whole life climbing at low speeds and full power and then descending with the engine cooling rapidly. This shortens the life of the engine and greatly increases the chance of an engine failure.

The tug pilot must also accept that his life is literally in the hands of the glider pilot during the initial climb away from the ground. If the glider gets too high on tow, the tug pilot will be unable to prevent the tow plane being tipped into a vertical dive with little hope of recovering in time. This can happen so quickly that the tug pilot has no time to release. The tug pilot should not hesitate to jettison the glider if it gets too high on tow. From time to time accidents like this do happen and a considerable amount of research has been done to produce a release system for the tow-plane which would work automatically if the glider started to get too high and pulled the tail of the tug up. So far no really practical solution has been found.

If either the glider pilot or the tug pilot is inexperienced, it is vital to have a talk before the flight to discuss the signals, etc., to be used. Ideally the tug pilot should also be a glider pilot. This should enable him to find strong lift to improve the rate of climb and so save fuel. However, should the tug pilot be new to the job it is important to make sure that he understands the following points:

1. The towing speed required and the maximum towing speed of the glider.
2. The need for full power for take-off and the initial climb and the need for turns to be gentle.
3. The need to check that the glider has its airbrakes closed before take-off and after starting to climb, and at any time if the tug does not seem to be climbing normally.
4. Where to climb, i.e. upwind of the field but within gliding range, unless otherwise stated, and the height required.
5. Whether it is intended to fly in the high or low tow position. (He should be ready for the change of trim and not assume that the glider has released if the tug suddenly starts to accelerate; this may be the glider changing position or jerking the rope.)
6. The signals to be used to indicate that the glider must release, that the glider is unable to release and that the glider has the airbrakes open.
7. That he must not enter cloud.
8. The necessary engine handling to avoid damage to the engine caused by rapid cooling during the descent, i.e. reduce the power gradually after release.
9. The position and operation of the release knob and when to use it.

6   Wire launches

There is nothing dangerous about these ways of launching a glider but
accidents do occur with pilots who are unfamiliar with wire launches or
who get out of practice. The winch or tow car driver also needs to know
what to do and it is dangerous to attempt these kinds of launches without
some previous experience, ideally dual with a competent instructor. The
launch must be abandoned if it becomes too slow or in rough air if it
exceeds the maximum winch launch speed. Excessive speeds and poor
launches are usually caused by the pilot holding the glider down instead
of making a smooth, progressive change into the full climbing angle.

Winch launching

Whereas car launching requires a smooth road or runway of at least 800
to 1000 yards and is usually only practical on a disused airfield, winch
launching can be done on relatively rough land provided that there are
adequate smooth areas for take-off and landing.

With winching, flexible multi-strand cable is usually used whereas with
car launching the abrasion and wear caused by towing the cable back along
the runway makes piano wire or plastic-coated heavy-duty cable more
suitable.

As the cable is pulled tight by the winch, the order 'All out' should
be given, just before the glider begins to move. Until the glider is moving
along the ground accelerating smoothly, the stick should be held well
forward, as otherwise any jerks can result in the tail skid banging heavily
on the ground. By the time that a running speed has been reached, the
stick can be allowed to find its own position by holding it very lightly
and allowing it to move back. The glider will run on the wheel and leave
the ground as a safe speed is reached. At first the take-off attitude should
be held as the glider gains speed and climbs away very gradually. It must
not be pulled up into the climb or pulled off the ground, and should not
be held down and flown level. (See Fig. 18.) A small forward pressure
is usually required.

After a few seconds a safe speed for the climb should be reached and
the gradual climb can then be steepened. The instructor will tell you the
minimum climbing speed or in the early stages may just tell you when
it is safe to climb. Most modern gliders tend to be pulled up into the full

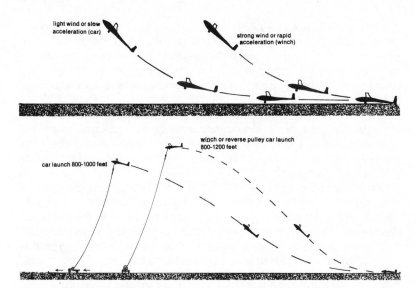

18. Car and winch launches. The rate at which the angle of climb can be increased after take-off depends on the acceleration and wind strength. Winch launches give better acceleration and greater height than car launches.

climbing angle as soon as they leave the ground. Unless the acceleration is very rapid, the pilot must prevent this from happening too quickly by moving forward on the stick. The climbing angle should be gradually steepened by relaxing this forward pressure so that the glider is at a safe height by the time it is in the full climb. The exact angle is not critical but a very steep climb may break the cable in turbulent conditions. The instructor will tell you if the angle of climb is correct and you will gradually learn to recognise the angle without his help.

Near the top of the launch, the cable pulls the nose down from the climbing position, and the ground comes into view again over the nose. If you know the position of the winch in relation to the airfield boundary, a glance at the ground will tell you whether you are nearly over the winch.

The cable should always be released so that it will drop well inside the boundary of the field and in front of the winch. However, it is really the winch driver's responsibility to shut off the power completely when the glider is about 80° to the winch and, if this is done, the reduction in power can be felt in the glider and the nose will tend to rise.

At this moment the nose should be lowered below the normal cruising attitude before releasing, so that the cable is not under tension at the time. The release is then perfectly smooth with the glider flying off the cable without any jerk. The release knob should be pulled firmly twice and if there is any doubt whether the cable has fallen, look out to check it.

If the cable is released under tension, the glider will probably zoom into a climbing attitude as the weight or pull of the cable is released. The nose should be lowered immediately to avoid stalling the glider. When the cable is released under tension, the cable may be thrown in a loop round some part of the winch, resulting in damage to the cable and causing a delay.

The moment when the cable is released near the top of the launch is not critical. If the cable is released prematurely, the maximum height will not be gained on the launch, whereas, if you fail to release the cable altogether, the cable will release itself by operating the automatic over-ride part of the release.

Obviously, it is vital to keep the wings level during the take-off run or a wingtip might touch the ground and swing the glider badly. Particularly on calm days, full aileron control will not be gained until the glider has run some distance. The correction for a wing dropping must, therefore, be a very prompt and large movement of the control while the speed is low. As flying speed is reached, the controls become more effective and normal movements are all that are required. Provided that the take-off run is directly into wind and the cable has no large bow, the glider will be kept straight by the pull of the cable and little or no rudder will be needed.

As the climb is assumed, it is helpful to look ahead for a cloud to keep heading towards so that any swinging of the nose can be seen immediately. If the wings are held level, the climb will normally be straight towards the winch. Corrections for keeping the wings level in the climb must be made by the co-ordinated use of the ailerons and the rudder. Otherwise the glider will swing off to one side as the correction is made. This effect is caused by the 'aileron drag' which is explained in detail on page 103ff.

If the airfield is narrow or the launches are being made slightly out of wind, look down at the ground to see if the glider is still in line with the take-off run and the winch. A slight bank towards the wind will bring the glider to a position on the upwind side and prevent the possibility of dropping the cable out of the field.

The most common faults in the take-off and climb are the failure to keep the wings level and making too steep an initial climb. These faults are easily overcome as the pilot gains experience.

Difficulty in keeping the wings level is often caused by the pilot making a correction to bring them level and then failing to take off the correction at the right moment just before they become level. This fault will be accentuated if the rudder is not used to assist the aileron during these corrections.

The need for a gentle initial climb cannot be over-emphasised and however great the desire for a good high launch, the first part should be identical. It does not suddenly become safe to steepen the climb at a certain height and, therefore, the climb should be a gradual curve until the full climbing angle is reached.

If the cable breaks, you should lower the nose of the glider immediately and release the end of the cable. Your instructor will then advise you where to land or what to do if this happens on an early flight.

Car launching

Some gliding organisations launch by towing the cable by car instead of using a winch. This method is ideal where it is necessary to operate from runways, and saves the expense of a winch. From the pilot's point of view the launch is very similar to a winch launch except that extra care must be taken to keep the wings level and to climb away gently.

This is because the acceleration is not so rapid as on a winch launch so that for a considerable time after leaving the ground the glider has only a small reserve of flying speed. A cable break at this stage needs prompt action and could not be safely dealt with if the glider was climbing steeply near the ground. This danger is accentuated by the breaking properties of the piano wire which is usually used instead of stranded cable. If the wire has been kinked, it will always break on the following launch. However, unlike winch cable, which takes a big load to break it, a kink in piano wire will often break during the take-off run or the initial gentle climb before a big load is applied. The pilot must, therefore, be especially alert for this possibility.

It is sometimes necessary for the towing car to change gear just after the glider leaves the ground, and this causes a momentary loss of speed which could be disastrous in a steep attitude. Since the wire is not being wound in, there is no hurry to gain height at first and with car launching the glider continues to climb all the time until the moment that the car slows down at the end of the run.

Since piano wire is very easily kinked or tangled, special care must be taken in light winds to release it promptly when the car slows down. Then the car has room to continue towing until the cable parachute touches the ground with the wire laid out straight.

A powerful truck with an automatic gear change is ideal, and Ford F100s have been used at Lasham for many years. For the maximum rate of launching two wires and two cars are used. Another variation is to take the wire round a large pulley mounted at the end of the runway so that the car drives towards the launch point and has the whole length available. After the glider has released, the car continues to the take-off point to drop the wire ready for the next launch. (Parachutes, etc., are fitted to both ends of the wire.) This method, which is known as 'reverse pulley', gives much higher launches with little additional trouble.

Experienced pilots visiting England should note that our launching weak links are often only 1,000 lb breaking strain. This will not allow for the very steep angle of climb used with winch launching on the Continent, where a much stronger weak link is used for two-seater gliders and heavier solo machines.

Cable breaks and launch failures

With any kind of launch the possibility of mechanical failure must always be borne in mind. At all times, the climbing angle must be such that there will be plenty of height and speed to recover into normal gliding flight and make a safe landing.

The immediate action is to lower the nose, to drop the cable and to decide quickly if there is room to land ahead or whether a turn must be made. Speed must always be regained *before* using any airbrakes and if the failure happens close to the ground and there is insufficient time to check the air speed indicator, the airbrakes must not be used in case the speed is too slow.

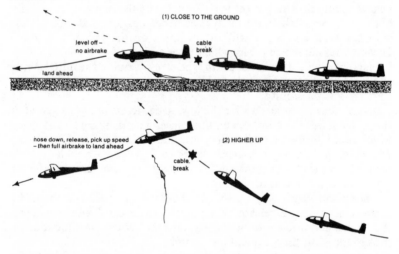

19. Cable breaks and launch failures near the ground. Level out, release the cable end and land ahead *without* airbrake. Higher up, nose down, release the cable end. If there is room to land ahead, pick up speed and then use the airbrakes.

However, if the trouble occurs at a greater height, once you have checked the airspeed indicator to ensure that the approach speed has been reached, full airbrake should be opened immediately to prevent any risk of flying out of the field. If there is plenty of room to glide down and land ahead, this is always the correct thing to do. It is not really the height alone which matters but also the amount of room remaining ahead for a landing.

There can never be hard-and-fast rules about the maximum height from which to glide ahead since so much depends on the wind strength and the shape and size of the gliding site. A rather slow launch on a calm day will leave far less room ahead at any stage of the launch. Furthermore, on a calm day the glider will glide and float much further up the field.

If, after lowering the nose and releasing the cable, there is any doubt about there being room to land ahead in the space available, or if there is obviously insufficient room, after flying speed has been regained the glider must be turned off to one side or the other. On a small gliding site the direction of this turn may be critical and the various factors involved, e.g. the wind direction and strength, and the shape of the field, should always be considered *before* getting into a glider at the launch point.

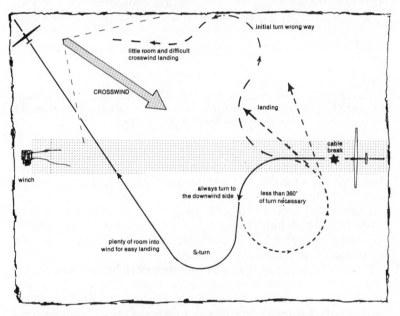

20. Cable break procedure in a crosswind. Turning off to the downwind side gives more room. Less than a complete circle is needed to land into wind. Use a well-banked turn, checking the A.S.I. frequently. A gentle turn uses up more height – perhaps too much.

There is usually a definite advantage in making the initial turn to the downwind side of the field since it allows a longer approach into wind. Also if a continuous turn is made in this direction a full circle is not required and less height is needed.

If the landing areas ahead are wide it will be easiest to turn off, fly across wind and then to turn back into wind (known as an S-turn). On a narrow strip, however, the choice is between going straight ahead or making a complete circle. This is because an S-turn on a narrow strip involves at

least as much turning as a full circle, and results in extra problems if there
are trees or obstructions along the sides of the strip.

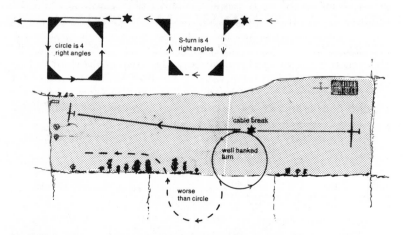

21. Cable breaks on a narrow airstrip. Note that an S-turn is a bad choice as it involves
as much turning as a 360° turn and obstructions on the boundary cause problems. The
choice is straight ahead or a 360° turn.

Once you have decided that there is insufficient room to land ahead
it is important to turn off as soon as a safe speed has been regained. Any
delay results in a rapidly worsening situation with less height and far less
room available ahead for landing.

A snap decision as to whether to make an S-turn or a full circle is not
required. After the initial turn it again becomes a case of looking up the
field and considering 'Can I turn back into wind and land in the space
now available, or must I keep turning?'

It cannot be too strongly emphasised that a well banked turn must be
used and that the bank, speed and height relative to trees and any other
obstructions must be monitored throughout any turns. After turning off
to one side it may become obvious that there is ample height to make an
abbreviated circuit. In this case maintain the approach speed and keep
rechecking the airspeed indicator so that there is no risk of running out
of height and speed if strong sink or turbulence is encountered. In smooth
air 150–200 feet may be lost in a well banked 360° turn.

The most critical situations usually occur in light winds after a slow
launch, as this leaves the glider still climbing slowly further up the field
without much height and without room for a landing ahead. In these cases,
if the cable does break or the car or winch engine fails altogether, the choice
of action becomes very limited, but there is sometimes the possibility of
landing downwind if the field is large enough.

On most of the larger gliding sites cable breaks are simple enough to deal with and are an inconvenience rather than a real hazard. Cable break practice is a very essential part of pre-solo training, and where there are special problems due to the small site, early solo flying has to be limited to ideal conditions and a higher standard of airmanship is essential.

Remember that a launch failure or cable break can happen on any flight. Before *every* take-off, plan your actions in the event of a cable break—taking into account the wind direction and strength, obstructions and the shape of the airfield.

Points to remember

On aerotow

1. Try not to overcontrol, use firm movements on the ailerons and very tiny movements on the elevator.
2. Try to stop any change of position immediately.
3. Try to keep your wings level with those of the tow plane.
4. Stop any swinging by holding your wings level and let the glider find its own way back into line.
5. See that the tow rope has released before turning off into a climbing turn.
6. Always check your position relative to the gliding site immediately after release.
7. Ask your instructor about the launching signals and emergency procedures and learn them.
8. In the event of an abnormally poor launch or wave off always check that your airbrakes are closed and locked.

Car and winch launches

1. Control the climb so that it changes gradually into the full climbing angle as a safe height and speed is reached.
2. Abandon the launch if the speed drops below the minimum cruising speed or above the placard speed in turbulent conditions.
3. Correct for drift by banking slightly into wind throughout the launch.
4. Lower the nose before pulling the cable release twice hard to drop the cable.
5. Think before you fly. In the event of a cable break which is the best direction to turn off? Is an S-turn practical or is a full circle the only alternative to going straight ahead?
6. Never use the airbrakes until you have confirmed that you have regained a normal approach speed. If landing ahead and speed and height permit, use plenty of airbrake without delay.
7. Turn off promptly if you are uncertain whether there is room to land ahead, then decide what to do.
8. Use well-banked turns and plenty of speed.

7 Stalling and spinning

Stalling—The symptoms of the stall—Why it happens—Incipient spins—
Full spins—Recovery from a full spin—Low 'g' sensations—Points to
remember

Stalling

Stalling is a very important lesson in gliding because in normal cruising
flight the glider is flown with a comparatively small margin of speed above
the stall. In relation to this margin, the effects of turbulence are large and
can easily result in an unintentional stall which could have serious
consequences near the ground.

During your training you will practise stalling the glider and recovering
to normal flight until you can recognise the approach of the stall without
reference to the instruments. Recognising the stall and making a prompt
recovery must become almost instinctive, because your attention may be
distracted by other gliders nearby, or by the ground.

There is nothing dangerous about stalling unless it occurs too near to
the ground. For this reason, we always practise stalls at a safe height and
we always fly at a higher speed than the normal cruising speed below a
height of 400–500 feet.

If the glider is flown with the nose above the normal cruising position
(by easing back very gradually on the stick to keep the nose up), the first
obvious change is the quietness as the airspeed decreases. After a short
while, the nose drops and height is lost rapidly. A further backward
movement on the stick will not prevent the nose from dropping as control
has been lost for a few moments.

This is the stall.

A relaxation of the backward pressure on the stick, allowing it to find
its normal position, is sufficient to help the recovery and, after a few
seconds, the nose can be brought back to the normal cruising flight
position. The stall is very gentle unless the nose is pulled right up.

It should be remembered that, if the nose is above the normal cruising
position, the glider will stall unless prompt action is taken to lower the
nose. Prevention of the stall is just a matter of lowering the nose or relaxing
forward on the stick.

64

The symptoms of the stall

In straight flight	*While turning or pulling out of dives*
1. Low airspeed	Speed may be up to 2 times normal stall
2. Quietness	No, noise depends on speed
3. Poor control response	Good response until stalled
4. Buffet	Yes, more buffet
5. Nose drop inspite of backward movement on stick	Yes
6. Uncontrollable wing drop	Yes
7. Rapid loss of height	Not always
8. Nose high attitude It soon will be stalled!	No, nose can be down
9. Rearward position of stick	Feeling of excessive 'g'

Many of the newer two-seater gliders have such docile stalling characteristics that they are almost unsuitable for serious training. Instead of having a definite nose drop at the stall they usually reach a semi-stable state, buffeting badly and mushing through the air with the nose a little higher than in normal flight but losing height rapidly. Since many of the single-seaters have a normal stall and will spin, some experience in a two-seater which stalls more completely is highly desirable.

Why it happens

The lift from the wings of an aeroplane depends on the airspeed and the angle at which the wing moves through the air (angle of attack). The faster the speed the more lift the wing creates and the greater the angle of attack the more lift is created. So to support the weight of the aircraft when it is flying at low speed the wing has to be at a large angle of attack, whereas at high speed the wing angle is very small.

The maximum angle of attack at which the air flows smoothly over the top of any wing is limited to about 16° or 18°. Beyond that angle the air over the top surface becomes very turbulent and breaks away, causing very high drag and a loss of lift. (Fig. 22.) When this happens the wing is said to be stalled.

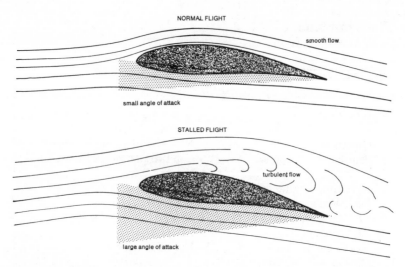

22. Normal and stalled airflow. As the air flows over the wing, pressure is reduced above it and is increased below, creating the lift. At an angle of attack of about 15° – 18°, the airflow breaks up causing a loss of lift and high drag. This is the cause of stalling.

In normal flight the wing is kept at relatively small angles to produce the necessary lift with low drag. At too low a speed or during manoeuvres, if the angle of attack exceeds the stalling angle the aircraft cannot continue in steady flight. The nose or wing drops and height is lost for a few seconds until the wing becomes unstalled. (Fig. 23.)

Stalling happens therefore because the angle of attack becomes too great. This can be caused by the pilot pulling back on the stick too much or too sharply and pulling the wing to too large an angle, or by the pilot allowing the aircraft to lose too much speed so that it sinks rapidly. This sinking results in a larger angle, thus causing the stall.

Unlike some modern jet airliners, when a glider stalls the nose drops automatically and the wing tends to unstall itself by meeting the air at a reduced angle. The normal recovery in a glider is to relax the backward pressure or to ease forward on the stick gently to allow it to recover.

It is vital for the pilot to recognise the stall, because any further backward movement on the stick to attempt to stop the nose dropping will delay the recovery and accentuate the loss of height.

In straight flight the symptoms of the stall are mainly those associated with flying very slowly—the low airspeed, quietness, poor response and lightness of the controls. The actual stalling speed in straight flight (about 30 knots in most training gliders) is raised during the turns and other manoeuvres or if a heavier load is being carried (such as a very heavy pilot or water ballast). During steeper turns these symptoms may not be present because of the higher stalling speed, and the stall is then recognised mainly

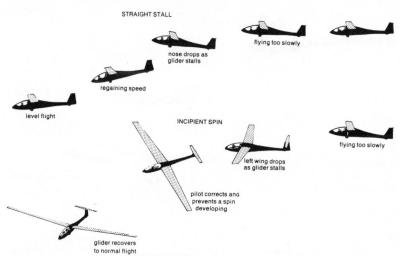

23. Stalls and incipient spins. At the stall the nose drops and the glider loses height for a few seconds until it regains normal flying speed. If one wing stalls before the other, that wing drops. This is called an incipient spin.

by the distinctive buffeting of the stick and the nose or wing dropping in spite of any attempt to stop it. If the nose drops regardless of a backward movement on the stick, this is a sure sign that the wing is stalled. When the backward pressure on the stick is relaxed for a few seconds, the wing unstalls and the glider can be levelled out into the normal gliding attitude almost immediately.

Incipient spins

If the glider is turning and the wing is stalled, the inner wing will usually drop, causing a slightly greater loss of height. (Fig. 23.) At or near the stall the ailerons are very ineffective and therefore it is better to unstall the wing by moving the stick forward a little while applying opposite rudder (right rudder if the left wing drops) to prevent the aircraft swinging further. After a few seconds the ailerons *should* be used to control the bank again and the glider can be brought back to level flight or into the original turn.

This dropping of a wing at the stall is called an incipient spin, and knowledge and experience of recovering quickly from incipient spins is an important part of learning to glide.

If as the glider stalls and drops one wing the pilot fails to recognise the situation and tries to stop the nose dropping by holding the stick hard back the glider may drop its nose still further and start to spin. This is a downward near-vertical spiral in which the wings are still stalled.

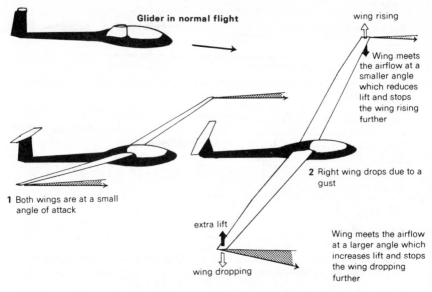

Glider in normal flight

wing rising

Wing meets the airflow at a smaller angle which reduces lift and stops the wing rising further

1 Both wings are at a small angle of attack

2 Right wing drops due to a gust

extra lift

wing dropping

Wing meets the airflow at a larger angle which increases lift and stops the wing dropping further

24. Lateral damping in normal flight.

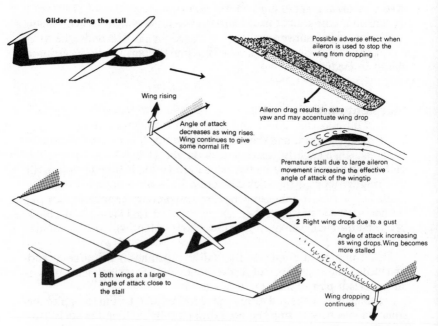

Glider nearing the stall

Wing rising

Angle of attack decreases as wing rises. Wing continues to give some normal lift

Possible adverse effect when aileron is used to stop the wing from dropping

Aileron drag results in extra yaw and may accentuate wing drop

Premature stall due to large aileron movement increasing the effective angle of attack of the wingtip

2 Right wing drops due to a gust

Angle of attack increasing as wing drops. Wing becomes more stalled

1 Both wings at a large angle of attack close to the stall

Wing dropping continues

25. Lateral instability during stalled flight. This is the start of auto-rotation and a possible spin.

There is a very important change which takes place as an aircraft begins to stall. In normal flight any banking movements are heavily damped so that an aircraft is fairly stable and does not tend to tip over very far. (Fig. 24.) However, when the stall occurs this damping effect disappears and the aircraft becomes laterally unstable, tending to roll over. Since it also drops its nose in the stall, the rolling turns into a steep downward spiral known as a spin. (Fig. 25.)

If, however, the wing becomes unstalled, the spin stops immediately as the lateral damping comes back into force. At the incipient stage of the spin, therefore, a movement forward on the stick which unstalls the wing prevents any risk of a full spin developing. Failing to ease forward on the stick may result in a full spin or a second stall or incipient spin, losing even more height.

Full spins

Most gliders show a marked reluctance to enter a full spin if they are stalled in well banked turns whereas from a gently banked turn, particularly if too much rudder is applied, they will spin one or two turns losing several hundred feet in a few seconds. Some training and experience at entering and recovering from full spins is essential before going solo, although it is obviously more important to learn to recover from incipient spins and to prevent full spins developing.

Recovery from a full spin (Fig. 26)

The standard recovery action for a full spin is as follows:
1. Full opposite rudder and then with the aileron central,
2. stick steadily forward until the spin stops,
3. centralise the rudder and ease out of the dive.
This should be learned by heart and applied as a drill.

On some occasions the application of the full opposite rudder may be sufficient to stop the spin but the stick must *never be kept back* or a spin in the opposite direction may occur as the wing restalls. If the spin does stop immediately, relax the backward position of the stick to about the normal flying position, centralise the rudder and ease back to level flight.

If the spin continues, move the stick progressively forward until the wings become unstalled, stopping the spin, and then centralise the rudder and recover to level flight.

There is no mystery about the causes of spinning. The aircraft has to stall, drop a wing and remain stalled. Any recovery from the stall at this point prevents a spin. In fact it is always the forward movement on the stick which is the vital action to recover from stalling and to prevent spinning.

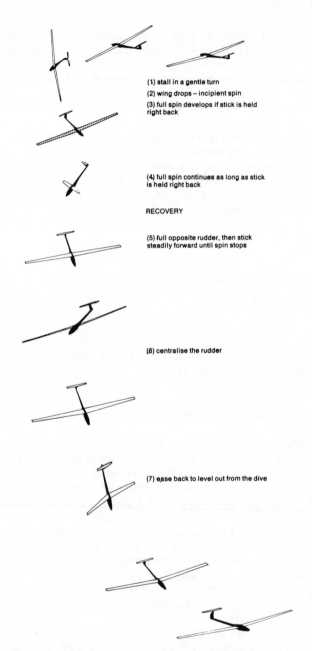

(1) stall in a gentle turn

(2) wing drops – incipient spin

(3) full spin develops if stick is held right back

(4) full spin continues as long as stick is held right back

RECOVERY

(5) full opposite rudder, then stick steadily forward until spin stops

(6) centralise the rudder

(7) ease back to level out from the dive

26. The fully developed spin and recovery action. The incipient spin can only develop if the stick is held right back. Recovery takes less than one turn and is simple.

With an unintentional stall near the ground, however, the pilot will instinctively pull right back on the stick to attempt to stop the nose dropping—the worst possible reaction. If the stick is moved back and hits the back stop without any response, it is a sure sign of stalling and of the need to ease forward for a few seconds before bringing the aircraft back into level flight again.

Stalling, and spinning, is only really hazardous because of the rapid loss of height. It is caused by flying and manoeuvring at too low an airspeed, usually at a time when the pilot is distracted. It is therefore particularly important to monitor the airspeed indicator readings repeatedly every few seconds during the base leg, final turn and approach and indeed any time when the aircraft is within 500 feet or so of the ground.

It does not take much practice to become accustomed to detecting the approach of the stall with its distinctive buffeting and to learn to recover quickly and prevent any tendency to spin.

Low 'g' sensations

On some occasions as the stall and recovery is made the beginner will feel a low 'g' sensation similar to driving over a hump-backed bridge. This feeling is not an indication of stalling and must not be mistaken for it. It occurs whenever an aircraft pitches further in a nose-downwards direction (including levelling out from a steep climb), or momentarily if it flies into strong sinking air or from strong rising air into more normal conditions. A large forward movement on the stick in normal flight or during a recovery from a stall will always make this feeling more pronounced.

Since most beginners associate this sensation with falling there is a tendency to assume that the aircraft is falling out of control when it occurs. This is not so. The recovery from a stall is almost instantaneous as the stick is moved forward and there is never any need to hold the aircraft in a steep dive. Any marked low 'g' feeling is an indication that the pilot has overdone the forward movement.

With further practice most beginners learn to overcome their natural dislike for the low 'g' sensation, but until then an unexpected stall or other pitching movement could result in a delayed or even an incorrect recovery response.

Points to remember

1. The elevator controls the angle of attack of the wing in flight and any excessive backward movement on the stick can pull the wing beyond the stalling angle.

2. Unless you recognise that the glider is stalled you will attempt to stop the nose dropping by pulling back on the stick. This will delay or prevent any recovery.

3. Easing forward on the stick allows the wing to unstall.

4. Stalling in a turn, the inner wing will usually drop.

5. If a wing drops, ease forward and apply opposite rudder. Then bring the wings level with the ailerons and return to normal flight.

6. To enter a spin the aircraft must be kept stalled after it drops one wing and starts to spiral downwards. Any relaxation of the backward movement of the stick will normally allow the wings to unstall. This stops the spin immediately.

7. Learn the full spin recovery action by heart, word for word.

8. Always maintain extra speed below 500 feet. Do not attempt to judge your airspeed but monitor the airspeed indicator every few seconds and correct any loss of speed immediately.

9. Keep alert at all times and remember that you cannot spin unless you stall.

8 Control of the approach

Airbrakes—Approach speeds—Uses of the airbrakes—Points to remember

Airbrakes

There are various types of airbrakes, but those in general use have two effects. They spoil the lift over a portion of the wing and they create extra drag.

Spoiling the lift is similar in effect to reducing the wing area. With less wing to support the same weight, the glider must fly a little faster. In other words the minimum flying speed or stalling speed is increased. In most gliders this increase is 2 – 3 knots, a small but—as you will see—most useful effect.

The drag increase depends on the type of airbrake. Spoilers, which are a simple hinged flap on the top surface of the wing, are least effective. These are used on the older Schweizer 222, K4 two-seaters and some motor gliders. They require a progressive pull force to open them, are spring loaded and have no positive lock to indicate to the pilot that they are properly locked. They often cause a slight nose-down trim change so that the nose tends to drop if they are opened quickly. This may be almost sufficient to prevent the glider losing speed.

Most other types of training gliders have the type of airbrakes shown in Fig. 27. These have geometric overcentre locks to keep them closed in flight because the airloads tend to pull them open once they are unlocked.

Whereas spoilers require a pull to hold them open at high speed, most airbrakes require a firm grip and a positive push force on the lever to hold them in the desired setting and to prevent them opening themselves fully. Form the habit of keeping your left hand firmly on the airbrake lever all the time during the final stages of the circuit and approach. Otherwise you may find the airbrakes opening themselves fully so that you come down short of the airfield.

With both spoilers and airbrakes the nose position must be lowered as they are opened or the extra drag will cause a loss of airspeed.

Before learning how to use the airbrakes it is important to understand how they affect the approach speed needed for a satisfactory round-out and landing.

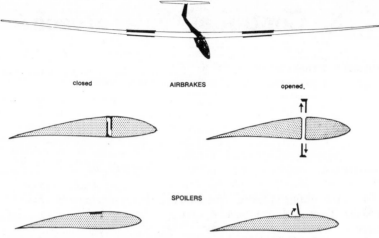

closed AIRBRAKES opened.

SPOILERS

27. Airbrakes and spoilers. Airbrakes create large amounts of drag with some loss of lift, and a definite nose-down movement is needed to maintain speed. Spoilers have a similar but weaker effect and usually cause a slight nose-down change of trim as they are opened.

Approach speeds

Although the rise in stalling speed is only 2–3 knots, a satisfactory approach with full airbrakes requires an extra 10 knots. This is because the drag of the airbrakes starts to slow the glider down very rapidly as it is levelled out for the landing. The table shows how the approach speeds need to vary with the amount of airbrake.

Type of glider	Normal cruising speed, in knots	Minimum approach speeds for calm air, in knots		
		Full airbrake	Half airbrake	No airbrake
ASK 13	42–43	52 (allow 55)	48	below 40
Schweizer 233	35–38	45	42	below 35
Falke motor glider	45	52 (allow 55)	50	below 45
Grob G103	45	52 (allow 55)	50	below 45
ASK 21	42–42	55	50	below 45
★........................				
★........................				
★........................				

*Complete for your own training machines.

Note: These speeds may seem a little high but are necessary if the nose is lowered an extra amount late in the approach so that the final part is steeper than normal.

If an approach is being made at 55 knots with full airbrake in either the Falke or K13 there will be adequate speed for a proper round-out and float before touchdown. If the speed drops to 50 knots, the pilot must either regain 55, or if that is not possible, reduce the airbrake setting to about half. Otherwise he may not be able to avoid a heavy landing. If after a slow approach he balloons, it may be safer to reduce the airbrakes still further or to close them altogether to allow a safe landing to be made. Provided that the final approach was started with the airbrakes out and at a suitable speed, there will be a reserve of energy available to help if you balloon badly or lose a little speed unexpectedly near the ground. You can close or reduce the airbrake setting at any time since this gives more lift and less drag. However, if you have reduced the amount of airbrake because of ballooning or loss of speed *never* try to open them again until the glider is on the ground. If the airbrakes are opened the glider will rapidly drop 5 – 10 feet as it loses lift. If it is flying too slowly, opening the airbrakes will cause a very heavy landing.

Do not be afraid to use full airbrake if you have plenty of speed, but use caution and limit the amount of airbrake if the speed is marginal. Always move the airbrakes smoothly and never jerk or snatch them.

Uses of the airbrakes

Airbrakes may be used in various ways and situations and it is very important to understand how and why they are used since they are essential for safe and accurate landings.

(1) Using up excess height. On some occasions it will be obvious that the glider is far too high and your one thought will be to get rid of some or all of the surplus height. Opening the airbrakes is a good way to do this because at any moment you choose you can close them again to check your rapid descent. If it is obvious that the final turn will be unnecessarily high, it is the normal procedure to get rid of excess height by using the airbrakes on the base leg. (The base leg is the last part of the circuit before turning onto the final straight approach for the landing.) However, in windy weather, when it is very unwise to get much behind the downwind boundary of the gliding site, the final turn into wind is made much higher than normal and the airbrakes are opened to throw away the excess height on the approach. Because of the strong wind the approach is very steep and little attempt is made at a precision landing because the landing run will be very short and errors will be small.

At any time the approach is started in a position where it is obvious that there is too much height always use *full* airbrake straight away to lose the excess height quickly. Then if the space allows the airbrakes can be partially closed to reduce the rate of sink and make the landing easier. A common error in such a situation is for the beginner to be far too cautious about opening the airbrake, with the result that it becomes necessary to land with full airbrake or run out of the landing area altogether.

(2) Controlling the approach angle. In normal conditions, on the final approach the angle of descent is controlled by the airbrakes. Full airbrake steepens the approach and closing the airbrakes results in returning to the flatter glide. With practice the approach path can be very accurately adjusted with the airbrakes to give a landing within a few feet of a given spot. Small changes in attitude are of course needed to maintain the same approach speed when the airbrakes are varied.

Using an aiming point. The expert is able to make adjustments to the airbrakes to control both the approach and the length of the float before touchdown. Adjustments during the hold-off need special care because it is not safe to open the airbrakes further unless the speed is adequate. This can only be assessed by judging the response to small movements of the elevator since there is no time to check the airspeed indicator. Most beginners are unable to do this with any degree of certainty, so the inexperienced pilot is well advised to freeze the position of the airbrakes lever at 20 – 30 feet and to limit any changes to reducing the amount of airbrake to extend the float when necessary. In the same way it takes practice to be able to see the subtle changes which indicate whether the glider is approaching accurately.

The final turn and approach is a busy time for the beginner and it is only some time after soloing that he learns to organise the thinking and flying so that there is enough time for refinements. There are very few gliding sites where an overshoot of even 200 or 300 yards is serious, and therefore perfect judgement and complete control are not necessary at this stage. It is important to realise that diving the glider on the approach does not prevent an overshoot. The height lost is turned into extra speed which must be used up during the hold-off and this results in a very long float before landing, so that an overshoot still occurs. When the airbrakes are used, height can be lost rapidly without gaining excess speed and the extra drag also reduces the float.

Fig. 28 explains why it seems so difficult at first to gauge exactly where the glider will land. The flight path is seldom along the axis of the fuselage, especially in a strong wind. The more experienced pilot uses the 'aiming point' method, as illustrated, to detect whether he is under- or overshooting.

Just after the final turn onto the approach he selects the amount of airbrake he thinks will suit his position and height, and settles at his chosen

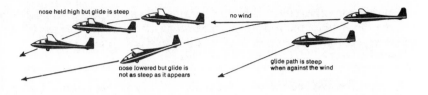

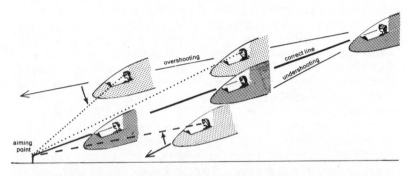

28. Aiming point technique. *Top:* A glider seldom flies exactly in the direction of the fuselage axis. *Bottom:* An object on the landing area ahead moves down relative to the nose if the glider is overshooting it, or moves upwards if it is undershooting.

approach speed. He chooses an aiming point some 50 – 100 yards short of the desired touchdown point to allow for the round-out and float before touchdown. A convenient mark on the ground, such as a path, is easiest to see. By noting the position of this object in relation to the top of the nose or some other obvious point on the canopy or fuselage ahead, any tendency to under- or overshoot can be seen.

If the aiming point is seen to be moving downward in relation to the nose, the glider is overshooting and will pass over the point. More airbrake is needed, together with lowering the nose a little to maintain the approach speed. This, of course, necessitates noting the new position of the nose in relation to the aiming point before watching again for the trend. With practice an experienced pilot can guarantee to bring the glider down over the aiming point so that the landing is within a few yards of the chosen spot.

If the glider is tending to undershoot even slightly it is disastrous to attempt to stretch the glide by raising the nose as this results in a loss of speed and falling short of the landing place. The immediate action is to *close* the airbrakes as this extends the glide without losing speed. When using the aiming-point method on the approach it is a common error at first to watch the aiming point for too long, so that the glider almost flies into the ground. Do not forget to look out well ahead once the glider is getting down to 20 – 30 feet and is nearing the moment for rounding out.

Many approaches are too short to allow time for an inexperienced pilot to use this method but it does take the guesswork out of the business of making accurate approaches, and it is the only way to guarantee spot landings.

(3) Speed control. The airbrakes are seldom used as a speed control, but it is important to realise how they affect the speed. If the glider is approaching at an excessive speed (say 60 – 65 knots on a calm day), the extra speed will give a very long float above the ground before touchdown. This will result in overshooting and a long push back to the launching point after the landing. If the speed is excessive, full airbrake will help to slow the glider down and shorten the long float before touchdown. Normally it is necessary to lower the nose to overcome the extra drag of the airbrakes so that the approach speed is maintained. However, if the speed is already excessive the attitude may be held constant as the airbrakes are opened.

The pilot must learn to read the airspeed indicator very quickly during the approach, to check that the speed is adequate. If the speed gets a little slow and height permits, the nose must be lowered to regain speed. This cannot be done during the final 50 feet or so and the only alternative is to reduce the amount of airbrake. This helps to prevent a further loss of speed and allows a safe round-out to be made at a lower speed than with full airbrake. (Fig. 29.) It should always be remembered that an extra 5 knots merely gives you a slightly longer float before touchdown, whereas 5 knots too little results in poor control with the probability of a heavy landing.

Similarly with rounding out a little too high or ballooning up during the landing, the loss of speed can result in a heavy landing. If the airbrakes are in use, the setting can be reduced *just as the glider starts to sink again* so that the reduced drag and improved lift will enable a normal landing to be made a little further down the field. However, if the airbrakes are closed partially or fully to avert the possibility of a heavy landing, on no account should they be reopened until the aircraft is firmly on the ground. Opening the airbrakes raises the stalling speed and always causes rapid loss of height for a few seconds, making it difficult to avoid a heavy landing.

On the approach the nose must be lowered to maintain speed as the airbrakes are opened. However, if the airbrakes are closed or partially closed because of a tendency to undershoot the landing area do *not* try to lift the nose of the glider to avoid the resulting increase in speed as the airbrakes are closed. The increase in speed will seldom be serious and is of more benefit in helping the glider to penetrate against the wind to get to the landing area.

The ideal position for an approach in light winds is to finish the final turn at a safe height (about twice the height of tall trees as a minimum) and at an angle to the landing area which allows a spot landing using most

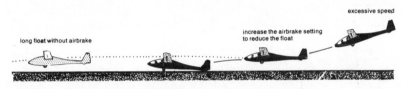

29. Using the airbrakes. If the glider loses speed on the final stage of the approach, close the airbrakes as necessary to avoid a heavy landing. Excessive speed results in a long float, which can be reduced by opening more airbrake.

but not all of the airbrakes. This gives a little adjustment either way and allows for the possibility of turbulence or sink causing an extra loss of height. An approach which requires little or no airbrake is potentially dangerous because there is no means of extending the glide path if any height is lost unexpectedly. In windy weather use the airbrakes cautiously, because the approach angle is very steep, making the moment to start the round-out very critical.

Points to remember

1. Consult your instructor and then complete the table on page 74 for the types of glider you will be learning on.
2. Use caution and limit the amount of airbrake if the approach speed is slow. Do not be afraid of using plenty of airbrake if you have plenty of speed.
3. Check the airspeed indicator readings on the approach and remember that 5 knots too fast is better than 5 knots too slow.
4. The airbrake setting can be reduced at any stage of the approach or landing. Use caution or avoid opening them close to the ground.

5. Lower the nose to maintain the airspeed as the airbrakes are opened but maintain the attitude when closing the airbrakes to prevent undershooting.

6. If the approach becomes slow, reduce the airbrake to prevent a heavy landing.

7. Never reopen the airbrakes if they have been closed or partially closed because of ballooning or a slow approach.

8. Try to arrange the approach so that the airbrake setting is constant for the complete round-out and hold-off.

9. Avoid landings with little or no airbrake.

9   Circuit planning

Circuit planning—Preparing to land—Pre-landing checks—Never low and slow—The final turn—S-turns—Windy weather—Points to remember—First solos

Coming back from a soaring flight or any launch by aerotow, the ideal is to arrange to join the circuit at the upwind end of the field and off to one side at about 700 – 800 feet. It is better not to pick an actual ground feature, as some instructors suggest, because the same feature will not be there away from the home site or if the circuit is in a different direction. Also, if you pick a landmark there is a tendency to fly to that point regardless of what is happening and this may lead you into trouble. If you are a little higher than usual, you will need to be further out and if you hit bad sink on the way you will want to fly directly back towards the landing area ignoring the normal entry point for the circuit.

After a good car or winch launch, unless the glider is released in the middle of a thermal, it should be flown away from the release point to allow other launches to take place. The direction of the circuit should be determined by the direction of the first turn, since it is very undesirable to fly across the launching line again during the flight.

A common mistake is to turn off at right angles to the launch line. In windy conditions this results in the glider drifting quickly downwind so that it is difficult to avoid arriving back at the launching area much too high. Ideally, in both calm and windy conditions, any search for thermals should be made upwind and to one side of the release point. This leaves more time for circling and gaining height before drifting downwind of the landing area. However, if there are any obvious indications of thermals, such as other gliders soaring or cloud forming, fly directly to that area.

During the search for lift, you may fly more or less where you like but you must constantly check your position and height in relation to the landing area.

When learning to glide you will find it helpful to say aloud your assessment of the launch before looking at the altimeter to check your judgement. If this is done, there is no chance of having a bad launch and not being aware of it. Also if you can, it will save you many launches if you think aloud, so that your instructor knows *why* you are doing things, rather than having to guess. What and how you think is of vital importance in gliding, where awareness and anticipation are so important.

81

Circuit planning

The aim in circuit planning is to get the glider back to the final turn at a safe height and in a position from which the landing can be made at the chosen position in the landing area. This is made simpler by arriving at one side and opposite the landing area at a height of about 500 feet, so that there is time to assess the situation and to adjust the position and height of the final turn. If the glider is kept too close to the landing area there is little time for assessing or for repositioning before the final turn on to the approach. Whenever the height allows it is best to keep well to one side to allow for a proper *base leg*. Some instructors may refer to making a 'square' circuit since the glider circuit can be related to the 'square' circuit used by powered aircraft. This consists of flying straight and level at a constant height parallel with the landing run on the downwind leg, and of flying exactly at right angles to the landing run on the base leg before turning finally on to the actual approach. However, with the glider descending but meeting unexpected rising and sinking air, the downwind leg may have to be moved in or out to keep within safe reach of the landing area, yet not too close to it.

Similarly, the base leg is not often made exactly square to the approach. Even a small patch of rising air encountered on the base leg will necessitate moving a little further back for the final turn, or an overshoot would

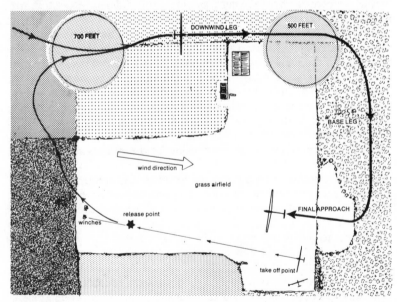

30. Basic circuit planning. A glider leaving the upwind end of the airfield at about 700 – 800 feet will arrive opposite the landing area at about 500 feet ready to start the base leg.

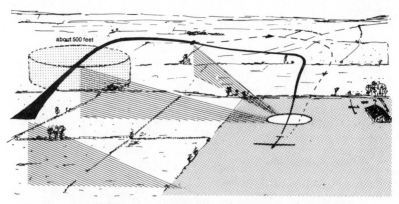

31. Planning the circuit. Watch the angle to the landing area, particularly during the final stages of the circuit. Aim to arrive opposite the landing area at about 500 feet and always complete the final turn by a safe height.

become inevitable. Trying to make a square circuit may even result in getting into a dangerous situation.

A little experience soon shows approximately how much height is lost in normal conditions in flying down from one end of the gliding site to the other, i.e. on the downwind leg. It is usually 150 – 300 feet depending on the performance of the glider and on the wind strength. But remember that on a calm day without the help of the wind behind you, the final turn will need to be further back so you will have a greater distance to fly. Particularly on a long field more height will be necessary for the glider to arrive back, at about 500 feet, opposite the landing area. Look across to your landing area and try to assess your angle to it as in Fig. 31. It needs to be about 20° – 30° unless you are short of height. A steep angle indicates that you are either too close or too high and that you will probably overshoot your landing point. Any excessive loss of height which results in arriving back too low is a very real embarrassment, since whatever happens the final turn must be completed by a safe height. This will necessitate cutting the circuit short, keeping closer to the field and making a 180° U-turn onto a final approach before the glider gets desperately low. The glider pilot must learn to recognise this type of situation before it gets serious and abandon his original plans. (Fig. 32.) In this case, move in to an angle of about 45° to the nearest safe landing area for the rest of the circuit.

Once the basic pattern of the circuit is properly established *the key things for successful circuit planning in a glider are to think ahead and to be decisive.* Flying downwind, for example, the glider pilot should not be checking the exact height so much as thinking ahead and considering his angle to the edge of the field and whether he will arrive back opposite the landing area with too much or too little height. If immediate action is taken,

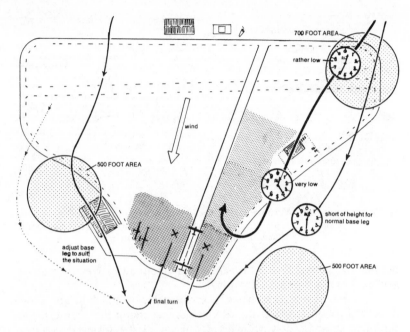

32. Procedure when the glider is running short of height on the circuit. Close in to the landing area. At about 500 feet pick up speed and prepare for landing. Turn in to land in the middle of the airfield if necessary. Do not leave the final turn too late; compare your height with trees or buildings and turn in to complete the turn by a safe height. Note that in the left-hand circuit shown, the turn onto the base leg has been made early to conserve height.

whether it is moving out a little or closing in, it will usually mean that the final turn-in point can be reached for a normal approach. By the time the glider is opposite the landing area the pilot should begin to consider the position for the final turn. If there is excessive height some must be used up by adjusting the base leg to put the final turn further back and by using the airbrakes.

Preparing to land

The really important thing about the circuit planning is the decision to abandon all attempts at soaring and to prepare for landing. It is only too easy to go on searching for lift, or attempting to soar at low altitudes leaving insufficient time and height to position the glider properly for a landing. The beginner must take this decision at about 600 feet, but local rules may dictate higher or a little lower than this for a particular site where special conditions prevail. For example, in tropical weather it is normal practice to pick up extra speed on joining the circuit at the upwind end of the airfield at 800 – 1000 feet. This takes the glider through any strong sink quickly so that less height is lost and the planning is scarcely affected. (This is common practice in the U.S.A.)

In order to reduce the effects of turbulence and of lift or sink on the glider, extra speed is essential during the last parts of the circuit.

With most training gliders this extra speed should be maintained for the whole base leg, final turn and final approach. With types which require rather lower approach speeds, the extra speed will have to be lost again after the final turn to stop the glider floating a very long way after the round-out. This is only necessary when the airbrakes of the particular type of glider are rather weak and ineffective.

Pre-landing checks

The preparation for landing is often made in the form of a definite cockpit routine as an aid to memory.

However, most of the items included are a matter of general airmanship. If the wheel is retracted, this is lowered ready for landing and the flaps, if fitted, are set as required. (These items are not always found on training gliders.) The nose is lowered and the trim is adjusted to help maintain the approach speed. As far as possible the proposed landing spot should be chosen and the whole approach area should be checked and re-checked for other gliders and approaching aircraft. Most important, because of the probability of altimeter errors, the readings of the altimeter should be completely ignored for the base leg and final turn.

In a more advanced type it may be wiser to use a definite check list and memorise it. (There will seldom be time to read anything properly in the air.)

There are various recommended checks, all of which have their merits. Apart from checking that the undercarriage is down and properly locked, most of the items are really airmanship points which are fundamental to safe flying. This is the reason that there is so much controversy over them.

Here are a few of the well-known check lists:

Britain—UFSTAL Undercarriage, Flaps, Speed, Trim, Airbrakes, Lookout.
Australia—FUST Flaps, Undercarriage, Speed, Trim.
New Zealand—SUFB Straps, Undercarriage, Flaps, Brakes.

Unable to agree about a definitive check list, at Lasham we have always insisted that the student prepares for the approach by: picking up speed, re-trimming, getting a hand ready on the airbrake, disregarding the altimeter.

Other things not mentioned in any of these check lists, but which are wise to do, are as follows:

Checking the wind sock for changes in the wind.

Checking which landing areas are clear enough for landing.

Checking for other traffic.

Checking the angle to the landing areas and the height in relation to trees, etc. nearby.

All of these things need to be done by the time that the glider is down to about 500 feet.

At this stage it is wise to unlock and open the airbrakes momentarily to check that they are not frozen up. If they are held closed but not re-locked the tendency for the airbrakes to snatch open is greatly reduced. From this point onwards the pilot should be constantly glancing at the landing area in order to assess the height and positioning. The airspeed must also be constantly monitored by quick glances, since it is difficult if not impossible to judge speeds and altitudes accurately during this final stage of the approach.

Never low and slow

If you are running rather short of height on the downwind leg, you will find yourself instinctively trying to get back by flying slowly in order to take advantage of the following wind. However, there is a very serious risk incurred by gliding slowly during the last few hundred feet. Any sudden loss of height caused by flying into unexpected sink or turbulence will result in being too low to gain the extra speed that is vital for a safe turn at low altitude. Within seconds the pilot may be faced with an impossible situation. If he attempts to convert his remaining height into speed there will be no height left for the turn. Alternatively, if an attempt is made to turn without the extra speed, the glider may easily become stalled and spin in the turbulent air near the ground. Once the glider is low and slow there is no solution and an accident is almost inevitable.

These disastrous situations can only occur if the pilot fails to make a clear-cut decision to get ready for the landing at a reasonable height. 300 – 500 feet is perhaps the lowest safe height to make this increase in speed. However, it is more usual to make this speed change at about 500 feet just before turning onto the base leg. In windy or very unstable conditions much more height is desirable and on airfields where power flying and gliding go on together, or where all launching is by aerotow, it is not unusual to gain the approach speed at the upwind end of the field at about 800 feet. In this case no circling or attempts to use lift are permitted below this height. You will be told about the local rules and how you should plan your circuit by your own instructor when you start to learn circuit planning.

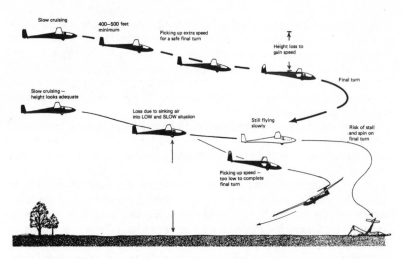

33. Never low and slow. Extra speed is essential when flying below 300–400 feet. It is only too easy to forget that while the glider is still flying slowly you have far less *real* height and may already be desperately low for a safe final turn.

The final turn

The final turn should be completed by at least the height of very tall trees, or about two complete wing spans of height and normally much higher. Provided that the base leg is not too short, you should have plenty of time to look across at the landing area and any nearby obstructions such as trees or buildings in order to compare your height with them. You must decide whether, by the time that you have flown into the position for the final turn, you will have enough height to allow the necessary minimum of straight approach. Normally, it should be necessary to use some airbrake at this stage to lose height down to the ideal turning height.

Provided that the decision to use the airbrakes is taken in reasonable time, it is possible to use up any normal excess of height by using full airbrake. In this way, it should *never* be necessary to make an **S**-turn. At the same time, if there is a choice of landing areas, the circuit should be extended by landing in the farther one. Also, the base leg could be made a little farther from the landing area in order to give a longer approach.

If there is no excess height, special care must be taken to keep within easy reach of a landing ground, and the final turn must be made before the glider gets dangerously low. In this case it may be impossible to land in the chosen landing area and any attempt to do so may only result in an unwarranted risk being taken.

There is absolutely no excuse for making a dangerously low turn as it is always possible to compare your height with something on the ground and start the turn before the glider gets too low. The most common reason for such an incident is the pilot relying upon the indications of the altimeter and making no attempt to judge the height by looking out. You cannot fail to see that you are getting dangerously low if you look outside the cockpit and use your judgement.

Obviously, the airbrakes should only be used on the base leg or final turn when it is clear that there is no possibility of undershooting the landing area and when there will definitely be sufficient height for a safe final turn.

The position of the final turn usually determines how far up the field the glider will land. Fig. 34 shows the effect of the strength of the wind and other factors on the final turn. Ideally, the final turn should be completed well behind the boundary in light winds. Notice that a gentle turn, or a turn at too high an airspeed, will result in the turn being completed too far into the airfield. A gentle turn will take much longer to complete than one with a steeper angle of bank and, therefore, will use up much more height. If you are already getting rather low on the base leg, turn into wind immediately, using a well-banked turn. Do not start a gentle turn or attempt to edge the glider round gradually or you will find yourself still turning when you reach the ground.

The commonest error is to forget to allow room for the final turn and for a reasonable length of straight approach. Most beginners keep the base leg far too close to the landing area so that, when the final turn is made, they find themselves right above the landing area and the actual landing

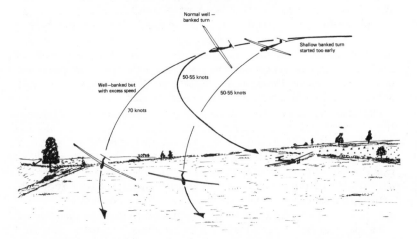

34. Final turns. Use a well-banked turn and control the speed. A low final turn and overshoot can be caused by allowing the speed to become excessive or by using a gradual turn.

is then a long way up the field. Of course, in very strong winds this is not a bad error since the approach is bound to be very steep and the glider does not float far on the landing. In light winds, however, the final turn needs to be completed several hundred yards back and there is virtually no risk of undershooting.

During the final turn the pilot should reassess the position so that he is ready to use the airbrakes immediately if the approach needs to be steep. Here a delay of even 10 seconds will mean an extra 300 yards' overshoot.

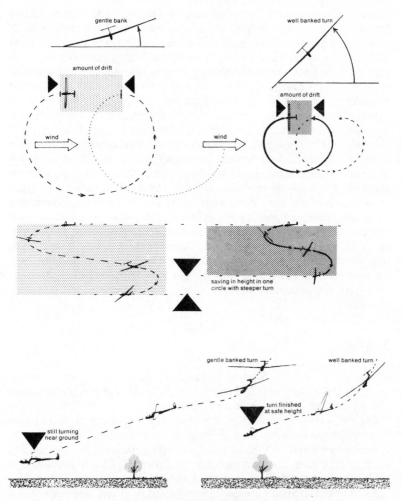

35. Circling and the effects of drift. A well-banked turn uses up less height and reduces the distance the glider drifts with the wind. Use well-banked turns.

If the angle to the landing area is steep, start by opening full airbrake. It can always be reduced a few seconds later if desired. At first, every beginner tends to get left behind with the speed and apparent complexity of needing to position the glider in the right place and at the right height for the approach, but with a little practice the idea of thinking ahead becomes established.

Provided that the final turn is in approximately the right place at the right height it will be a simple matter to adjust the final approach for an accurate landing in the chosen area.

The planning and manoeuvring necessary to arrive opposite the landing area at about the right height can be resolved into a few simple rules. It is always far easier to arrive back with extra height than to try to be precise and perhaps to run short of height owing to sinking air. Extra height is only an embarrassment if the glider is kept too close to the landing area. It is usually an easy matter to use up an extra 200 feet by opening the airbrakes fully at the start of the base leg.

If it is intended to use up some height by circling, it is important to use a well-banked turn to minimise the time taken to complete the circle. A gentle turn will use much more height and will also result in the glider drifting downwind much further. In sinking air a circle will usually result in a loss of about two hundred feet. It is wise, therefore, to consider whether this will be just an embarrassment or whether it will be dangerous. Once the glider is opposite or downwind of the landing area, circling to use up height is not safe and is bad airmanship. In one circle the glider may lose so much height and drift so far back that it may be out of safe gliding range of the landing area. (Fig. 35.) *Never* circle to use up height on or near the downwind boundary of the field. The height can easily be used up by widening the circuit and by using the airbrakes straight away. Moreover, the pilot has complete control over the situation if it is done this way.

S-turns

Although the use of S-turns is normally discouraged, an S-turn is preferable to making a circle downwind of the landing area to use up height and so turning your back on the landing area.

Fig. 36 shows how to make an S-turn. If the glider is far too high to be brought into a reasonable position for a normal final turn and approach, it is flown on past the turn-in point, dropping back behind the landing area slightly. A turn is made *towards* the airfield (*NEVER* away) so that the aircraft is in a position to start a new base leg from the other side. This time the airbrakes are used promptly, if required, to ensure that a normal final turn and approach can be made. It is most undesirable to make a further S-turn and it is always a sign of poor planning to do so.

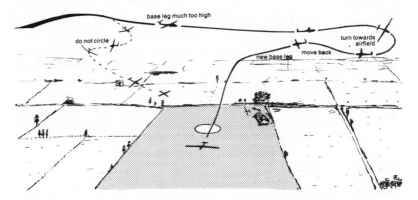

36. The S-turn. Never turn or circle away from the field to use up height on or near the base leg.

S-turns create a traffic problem on a busy airfield and should not be necessary. It is, however, important to understand that they are the only safe way of dealing with a situation like this which has been allowed to get out of hand. It is the safe alternative to making a 360° turn to use up height. However, during the rest of the circuit planning it is quite acceptable to circle towards or away from the field. On the base leg, if your position is rather too close and too high, turn out and away, but do not circle.

In the case of winch or car launches the actual height achieved dictates whether the circuit consists of flying straight back for a landing, or whether there is time for a few turns in search of a thermal or for some practice stalls, etc. The experienced pilot assesses the whole circuit by looking at the angle to the landing area and so judging whether the gliding angle will enable him to reach it with plenty of height. The whole problem of circuit planning is made far easier by ensuring that a little extra height is kept in hand for the base leg. This enables a longer base leg to be made, leaving more time for assessing and adjusting the height with the airbrakes. Remember that, unless the wind is directly down the airfield, the glider will tend to drift closer or further from the field on the downwind leg unless it is headed off at an angle slightly to counteract this effect. The base leg will also have a head or tail wind component reducing or increasing the ground speed at this point.

The beginner is strongly advised to search for his lift at the upwind end of the field so that he can have a proper downwind leg if he fails to find any.

However, the more experienced pilot may even decide to go downwind to a promising area, especially if there are other gliders soaring and marking the lift there. But he will be aware of the risks involved and able and prepared to make a satisfactory approach and an accurate spot landing from any position he gets himself into. This would be risky for an early solo pilot and quite rightly would result in strong criticism.

This kind of understanding and experience is essential to avoid hazards when flying cross-country. Then, on some occasions, a last-minute realisation that the chosen field is unsuitable may necessitate quick and clear thinking to get down safely into an alternative field nearby.

Whenever the airfield traffic will allow, every student needs experience at rejoining the circuit from every possible direction and position. From this he will have learned how far he can safely go when he is solo and how best to get back into the circuit for landing.

Windy weather

There is always a tendency to lose flying speed and sink further when approaching to land in windy weather. The friction between the ground and the air above it reduces the wind strength so that at one moment the glider is flying against a very strong wind, whereas a few seconds later it is flying against a much lighter wind nearer the ground. This causes a drop in airspeed and there is insufficient time for the glider to regain the lost speed.

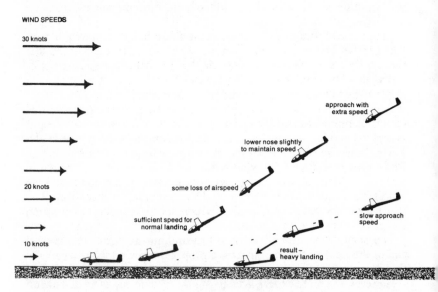

37. The wind gradient. In strong winds there is a rapid decrease in wind strength near the ground. This causes a serious loss of flying speed during the final stages of an approach. Use extra speed in windy weather.

This *wind gradient* effect can be accentuated in the lee of trees and buildings and in the vicinity of hilly ground. The air remains turbulent for half a mile or more behind obstructions, sometimes reinforcing the wind gradient effect for a few seconds and at other times almost cancelling it out in a completely random manner.

More speed is essential to ensure that even with a loss of 5 – 10 knots there will still be sufficient speed for a satisfactory round-out and landing. Even with adequate speed there will always be a rapid sinking as speed is lost during the last 100 feet or so. If the sinking seems severe, close or reduce the amount of airbrake being used to prevent a heavy landing.

In very gusty conditions it may be wise to let the glider land a little earlier than normal instead of holding it off for the slowest possible touchdown. If the airbrakes are opened fully just as the glider lands, this will prevent any gust from lifting it off the ground again.

A cable break during the first few hundred feet of the launch can be particularly critical since the wind gradient causes a loss of airspeed delaying any recovery from a slow launch. Always check the airspeed indicator and ensure that adequate approach speed has been reached *before* opening the airbrakes.

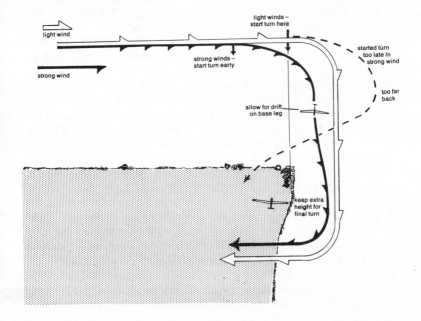

38. The base leg in windy conditions. Always start the turn onto the base leg earlier in windy conditions. Allow for drift and make the final turn with extra height.

It is very unlikely that you will be allowed to fly solo in windy weather until you have 30 – 40 solo flights in gliders. Even a slight error of judgment can result in serious damage to the glider, and instructors realise that early solo flying in bad conditions is not worth the risk.

Points to remember

1. Try to join the circuit well to the side and upwind of the landing areas with adequate height in hand. Check the wind direction and consider how it will affect the circuit planning.
2. Do not circle to use up excess height, unless you can afford to drift and lose 200 feet. Otherwise move out, using up the height by extending the base leg.
3. As you fly back downwind, check that the landing areas are clear and look out for other aircraft landing, so as to assess where it will be safe to land.
4. If the circuit looks marginal for height do not let yourself get low and slow. Keep checking your speed and make sure that you pick up extra speed in time.
5. At 500 feet, or opposite the landing area (whichever happens first) prepare for landing: undercarriage down, lower the nose, gain speed and retrim, unlock the airbrakes and disregard the altimeter. No more circling to use up height. Think ahead.
6. If it looks as though the final turn will be much higher than necessary, use the airbrakes and move back to reposition the final turn to give a longer approach.
7. Constantly check the airspeed, the angle to the landing area and your height in relation to trees or buildings wherever possible.
8. Lower the nose to maintain the correct speed as the airbrakes are opened. If the speed is adequate, do not be afraid to use full airbrake—if the speed is slow, be cautious and limit the amount of airbrake.
9. Correct for any drift on the final approach. Always bank away from any obstruction if you start to drift towards it.
10. Do not land close to other gliders or obstructions. Remember, the glider always swings or tends to swing into any crosswind. Allow plenty of room for drifting or swinging during the landing.
11. In windy weather always allow extra height in your circuit planning and especially for the base leg and final turn.
12. Always use a higher speed for both the base leg and final approach.
13. Always turn onto the base leg earlier in windy conditions. Never risk running short of height so that a low final turn becomes necessary.
14. Do not fly solo unless you have flown in worse conditions before and are quite sure that you understand all the risks.

First solos

Learning to glide is much more than a matter of learning how to handle the glider. To be safe a pilot must be confident about his ability, yet fully aware of his limitations. He must understand what he is doing and must have had sufficient practical experience at dealing with emergencies and awkward situations to be confident about his own ability to cope with them unaided. This requires an honest and mature outlook which we do not all possess when we start learning to glide. If a beginner is overconfident, the first solo flight should be delayed. Unless a pilot develops an honest judgement of his own ability and shows discretion in his flying at all times, sooner or later he will have an accident. On the other hand, underconfident beginners have a different problem. It is not safe for them to solo until they have overcome their lack of confidence with extra flying experience and a real understanding of how and why things happen. In some cases this may take months or years and it is irrational for an instructor to try to raise the student's confidence by artificially boosting his morale with 'pep' talks. Unless the student is confident in his *own* ability any false confidence will quickly vanish if a difficult or unexpected situation arises. This can be the cause of panic and disaster. The beginner who already possesses a tidy, methodical and well-disciplined way of thinking has a distinct advantage since these qualities must otherwise be taught or assimilated during training.

At many clubs it is difficult to arrange to fly regularly with the same instructor and this can slow down your progress and hold up your first solo. An instructor needs to get to know you and your flying over a number of flights to judge if you are really ready for this step. If each dual flight adds further proof of your inability to fly consistently and safely without help, you are certainly not ready to solo. In this case if you persist in asking when you can go solo, the instructor will assume that you are grossly overconfident and in need of more training.

Before going solo you must prove that you can plan your circuits and deal with any contingencies, such as cable breaks, running short of height and stalling and spinning, without advice or help from the instructor. Most clubs have a list of mandatory items like these which must have been done recently and which the instructor must sign off as completed. It must never be forgotten that getting off solo quickly is of far less importance than becoming a competent pilot able to fly safely in all conditions.

Statistically, first solo flights are safer than most other flights because the pilot has recently revised all the critical situations and is in good flying practice. You will not be sent solo until you are quite safe and the weather is suitable.

On your first few solo flights you will learn faster if your instructors watch your flying and landings and criticise each one. You are bound to make some mistakes and unless they are clearly explained they can easily lead to bad habits.

This is also the stage at which many students give up altogether. Very often, after their first few solos, the weather or lack of opportunity make it impossible to fly again for a period. This can result in a growing lack of confidence and to their worrying whether they will still be able to fly safely. This is particularly liable to happen if they have been sent solo with a bare minimum of experience.

Try to avoid any break in your flying once you have soloed and make sure that you fly dual again each day before re-soloing. During these daily check flights, ask to repeat any exercise at which you do not feel absolutely confident such as launch failures and stalling and spinning.

In most cases you will be making your first five or ten solo flights in the two-seater before converting to a single-seater. It will take a few flights before you feel at home and confident in the new type and, therefore, on the first few occasions that you fly it, you should have a daily check flight.

SECTION II

Further training and soaring

10   More about turning

Why bank—Forces in the turn—The variation in stalling speed with angle of bank—Aileron drag—Co-ordination—Efficiency in turns—The yaw string and slip indicator

Why bank

Turning is by far the most important phase of gliding flight and is the basis of good thermal soaring. It is well worth while trying to learn something about the theory of turning in order to understand how to turn a glider efficiently.

In order to make anything change direction, a force must be applied acting towards the centre of the turn. The size of this force depends on the mass of the object, its speed and the radius of the turn; for instance, with a glider the force required for a turn of 300 feet radius at 40 knots is equal to nearly half the weight of the glider. This is provided by the lift from the wings when the glider is banked.

Many pilots find it difficult to understand that the rudder plays only a minor part in making a turn. In fact it does not materially affect the rate of turn and is only used to produce the slight yawing force which balances the turn.

Fig. 39 shows what happens if the wings are kept level and full rudder is applied in an attempt to produce a rapid turn. Notice that the force produced by the rudder acts outwards, away from the direction of the turn. When the rudder is applied, the fuselage yaws until the power of the rudder is balanced by the weathercocking tendency of the aircraft (i.e. the tendency for the fuselage to swing back into line with the airflow). This leaves the fuselage at only a small angle to the relative airflow, which will result in a small force being developed in the direction of the turn. The fuselage moving sideways through the air creates considerable extra drag which reduces the speed and steepens the gliding angle. Flying with too much rudder on is therefore likely to lead to a critical semi-stalled condition from which a spin may develop. In this case the stall will occur without having the nose high.

Clearly the rudder is incapable of producing a force equal to half the weight of the aircraft.

In order to understand the need for a combination of movements from all three controls, it is easiest to consider a turn with no bank, one with the wings vertical and then a normal turn of 45° of bank. (See Fig. 40.)

A turn with no bank would be entirely a yawing movement. A turn with vertical bank would be entirely a pitching movement and would resemble a loop on its side. It follows, therefore, that any normally banked turn must be a combination of both yawing and pitching movements.

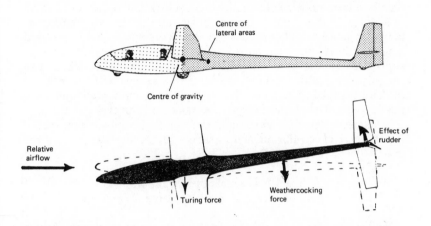

39. The effects of applying rudder only. The aircraft yaws until the power of the rudder is exactly balanced by the weathercocking tendency. The only turning effect is the result of the fuselage acting as an aerofoil.

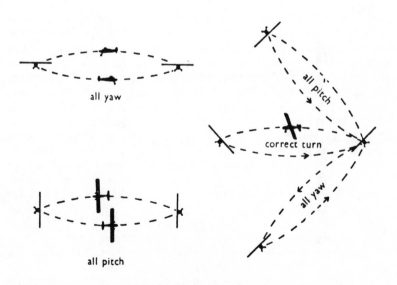

40. Yawing and pitching movements in turns.

Forces in the turn

Before explaining the forces acting on an aircraft in a turn I should explain that for this purpose it will be easier to consider a powered aircraft instead of a glider. This is because a powered aircraft can turn without loss of height, whereas the glider turns in a downward spiral. In the powered machine, the weight is supported by the lift alone, whereas the glider is supported by the resultant of the lift and the drag. These two complications, which scarcely affect the issues involved, do make it difficult to explain a turn in a glider simply and concisely without some inaccuracies. The conclusions are the same for both types of aircraft.

When an aeroplane is in straight and level flight at a constant speed, it is in a state of equilibrium and, therefore, all the forces acting on it are exactly balanced. (Fig. 41)

The lift L equals the weight W.
The thrust T equals the drag D.

Similarly, a glider in steady, straight flight is in a state of equilibrium and all the forces acting on it are exactly balanced.

The resultant R of the lift and drag exactly balances the weight.

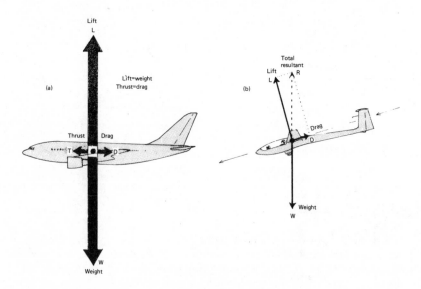

41. The balance of forces in steady straight flight. (a) On a powered aircraft in straight and level flight and (b) on a glider in a steady straight glide.

Fig. 42(a) shows the effect of applying bank alone. Weight still acts vertically downwards (this is always so) but the lift is now inclined. Since the lift force is still the same as the weight, there is insufficient vertical component of lift to support the aircraft and it must, therefore, accelerate downwards and lose height. The resultant of the lift and weight, *S*, causes the sideslipping movement towards the lower wing. More lift is required if a level turn is to be made. This can be obtained by flying faster or by increasing the angle of attack of the wing. (Fig. 43.) If the extra lift is obtained by increasing the angle of attack there will be more drag and a resulting reduction in speed. This is acceptable in a powered aircraft, but in gliders because of the small margin between the stalling speed and normal cruising speed, and because of the need to keep the wing at an efficient angle of attack, the speed is maintained or even increased slightly in the turn.

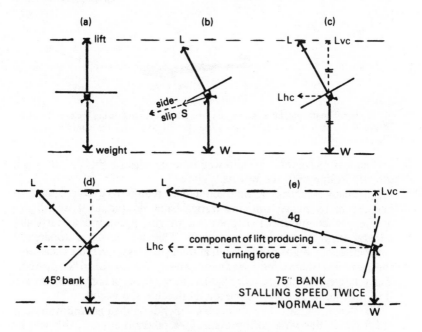

42. The forces acting on an aircraft in a turn.

Fig. 42(c) shows the lift force considered as two components, Lvc, the vertical component of lift opposing the weight, and Lhc, the horizontal component of the lift. It is the horizontal component which provides the force needed to turn the aircraft. Unfortunately, these diagrams cannot show the need for the yaw in the direction of the turn explained in Fig. 40. Without this yaw, the turn would still be unbalanced even if there

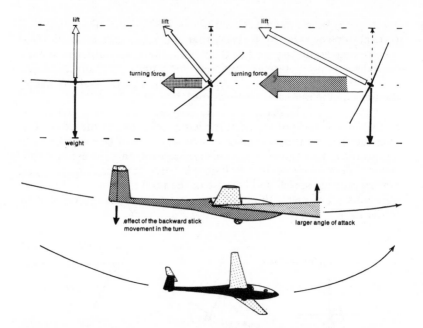

43. Turning. The turning force is provided by banking over and easing back on the stick. This pulls the wings to a slightly larger angle of attack to provide the extra lift required.

was no loss of height. The slip would occur because the aircraft is not directly in line with the relative airflow.

If the bank is increased, the amount of lift required for an accurate turn becomes much greater, until in a vertical bank, no amount of lift will give any vertical component to support the weight. A continuous vertically banked turn is therefore impossible. This fact is often apparently contradicted by high-speed aircraft at flying displays. On these occasions, the turns are seldom continued for long enough for any slip to be apparent. The very great inertia of a heavy fighter aircraft flying at high speed enables it to turn for some time before any noticeable slip occurs.

The steepest steady turn obtainable depends on the maximum amount of lift which the wings will provide. In a powered aircraft, this will be obtained with full power (to maintain the speed) and with the wing at the critical angle of attack just below the stall. At this angle of attack the wing gives the maximum lift.

In a glider, extra speed in a turn is provided by steepening the spiral and this results in a greater rate of descent.

Figs. 42(d) and 42(e) show that the amount of lift required for an accurate turn increases very rapidly when the bank gets beyond 45 degrees. This means that during the turn the wings are supporting an extra load. They must support the weight and provide the necessary force to turn the aircraft. In level flight if extra weight has to be lifted, the aircraft must fly faster to obtain the extra lift. The stalling speed is therefore higher. Similarly, in a turn, the extra lift required means a rise in the stalling speed.

The increase in stalling speed in a turn depends on the increase in the load carried by the wings. This is known as the load factor or loading in the turn and is proportional to the secant of the angle of bank. A loading of twice normal is known as a load factor of two, or commonly as a 2g (twice gravity) turn.

If the loading is four times normal (4g), the stalling speed will be twice normal. (The stalling speed increases in proportion to the square root of the load factor.)

The variation in stalling speed with angle of bank

Angle of bank	Load on glider 'g'	Increase (%) in stalling speed due to loading
0°	1	0
20°	1.1	1.05%
30°	1.18	8%
45°	1.4	18%
60°	2	40%
75°	4	100%

Aileron drag

A further complication to the problem of accurate turning is caused by the aileron drag already briefly explained in Chapter 6.

'Aileron drag' is the term given to the unequal drag of the ailerons while the aircraft is being rolled, for example when initiating a turn. The effect of this drag is to yaw the aircraft in the opposite direction to the banking movements, an undesirable occurrence when the pilot is attempting to turn the glider. This effect of aileron drag is known as 'adverse yaw'.

A movement of the control column to the left to initiate a bank and turn in that direction moves the left aileron up and the right aileron down. Since the whole wing is at a positive angle of attack, the movement of the aileron up reduces both lift and drag on that wing tip by reducing the effective angle of attack and camber. At the other tip, however, the lowered aileron results in greater lift and consequently greater drag. The differences in lift created by the ailerons bank the aircraft, but, at the same time, the unequal drag causes a yawing movement in the opposite direction. At first this adverse yaw affects the aircraft as a swing of the nose away from the direction of bank. Then, as the aircraft begins to bank, this yawing becomes a swing of the nose above the original attitude. (Fig. 11 on page 36.) A sideslip occurs towards the lower wing, and then the airflow striking the keel surface of the fuselage when the nose is yawed out of the line of flight overcomes the aileron drag and produces a yaw in the direction of the bank. This sequence of events is most undesirable since it means that the rudder must be used with skill to make accurate turns.

The amount of aileron drag varies with the type of aircraft, but is more marked on gliders than on most modern aircraft.

The large wing span of gliders results in any aileron drag having a large moment about the centre of gravity. Aileron drag is unimportant in most modern aircraft because of their relatively short wing spans.

Directional stability also governs how much yaw will occur for a given amount of aileron drag. Many older gliders lack directional stability and rudder movements are needed mainly to overcome aileron drag. Modern powered aircraft are now so stable in this way that normally no rudder is required to turn. This greatly simplifies the problem of handling the aircraft and particularly of learning to fly.

Since the ailerons bank the aircraft by varying the amount of lift developed by each wing, it is inevitable that each wing will develop a different amount of drag. More lift cannot be produced without creating more drag and hence some aileron drag must remain however carefully the aircraft is designed.

The aileron drag can be reduced considerably by arranging for the upward moving aileron to move through a much larger angle than the one which is moved down. (See Fig. 44(a).) This arrangement is known as *differential ailerons* and is used on almost all aircraft. Since the down-going aileron moves through only a small angle, it produces some increase in lift but without a very large increase in drag. In practice, the rate of roll is only slightly reduced by the loss in lift caused by restricting the movement of the control surface, but any slight loss is far outweighed by the ease in initiating the turn smoothly.

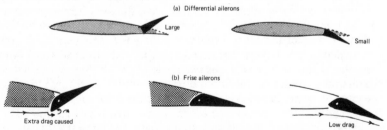

44. (a) Differential ailerons and (b) Frise ailerons, both methods of reducing the adverse yaw.

Frise ailerons are another method of reducing aileron drag. Fig. 44(b) shows the principle involved. The aileron is so designed that when it is in the central position or lowered, it fairs into the main aerofoil so that the drag is low. When the aileron is raised, the specially shaped leading edge of the aileron protrudes below the lower surface of the wing, disrupting the flow and creating extra drag. This additional drag helps to balance out the drag of the other aileron and minimise the adverse yaw. The load on the protruding leading edge of the aileron also acts as an aerodynamic balance and reduces the force required to apply full aileron. This helps to make the aileron control pleasantly light and effective. The main disadvantage of Frise ailerons is the risk of ice formation on the protruding leading edge of the aileron. This might jam the control surface or upset the balance of the aileron. The adjustment of this type of aileron is also much more critical.

The amount of aileron drag depends on the amount of aileron applied. This varies with the rate of roll required and not with the angle of bank. If the pilot is content to apply the bank very gradually, he will use only a small amount of aileron, which will cause very little aileron drag and need little or no rudder to overcome it. However, if the same angle of bank is applied rapidly, a large movement of the aileron will be used and a large amount of rudder will be needed to counteract the effect of the aileron drag. When the glider is in a steady turn, there is no aileron drag and the amount of rudder must be reduced after initiating the turn.

Similarly, when the glider is coming out of a turn the amount of rudder required will depend on the rate at which the bank is being reduced.

Aileron drag also has an undesirable effect at or near the stall since any attempt to prevent a wing dropping by using the ailerons results in a yaw in the direction of the dropping wing. Also, a large movement of the aileron when the wing is nearly stalled may even cause the airflow over the wingtip to break up and stall, with the result that the wing will drop instead of responding normally. Both of these effects will help to start a spin.

Co-ordination

Now, it is possible to see why all three controls are required to produce an accurate turn. When the bank is applied, the rudder must be used to overcome the aileron drag and to produce the slight yawing movement needed in the turn. As the angle of bank is checked, this rudder must be reduced. A gradual backward pressure is also needed as the bank gets steeper in order to increase the angle of attack of the wing to provide the extra lift required for the turn.

Any correction on one control will necessitate movements on the other two controls to maintain a steady turn, e.g. if more rudder is applied to correct slip, the yawing movement will lower the nose and tend to cause a further steepening of the bank. A backward movement on the stick will be needed to prevent the nose from dropping and a check movement will be needed on the ailerons to hold a steady angle of bank.

For a steep turn, the speed must either be increased before the turn is initiated or allowed to increase as the bank gets steeper. The backward movement will need to be considerably larger in a steep turn than for a gentle one.

Several other minor effects occur during gliding turns. The outer wing in a turn is always travelling slightly faster than the inner one and develops more lift. However, the inner wing travels less distance for the same loss of height and this results in that wing meeting the air at a larger angle of attack than the outer one. These two effects tend to cancel each other out and are not important. In most gliders it is necessary to prevent the bank from increasing in a steady turn. It is easiest to consider the ailerons as controlling the angle of bank without worrying whether in fact it is necessary to hold off the bank during a turn.

Care must be taken to maintain a safe speed for turning steeply. The steeper and tighter the turn, the higher the stalling speed and the greater the speed required for a safe turn. An extra 5 – 10 knots should be sufficient for turns of about 50 degrees of bank.

If the glider stalls while turning steeply, the wing and nose will drop. Attempts to tighten the turn or raise the nose will be ineffective until the glider has become unstalled by allowing the stick to move forward. Recovery from the stall will then be immediate but height may be lost bringing the glider back to straight flight. For this reason, steep turns should not be practised below about 700 feet except by experienced pilots. Steep turns are an excellent test of piloting ability and should be practised whenever possible.

In a very steep turn, very little rudder is required to provide a properly balanced turn. Almost all the turning movement has become a pitching movement controlled by the backward pressure on the stick. If this backward movement is insufficient to bring the wing to a large enough angle of attack to develop enough lift for the steeply banked turn, a sideslip will occur. This can only be overcome by providing the extra lift required or by correcting the slip with more rudder in the direction of the turn and accepting a downward spiral. Any attempt to raise the nose by using 'top' rudder will only create a greater slip and after a few seconds the nose will fall farther in spite of the rudder. This is because the directional stability is much stronger than the power of the rudder. As the aircraft slips towards the lower wing, the airflow strikes the side of the fuselage. The weathercocking action of the fuselage swings the nose down in spite of the rudder. Additional lift is needed to prevent the slipping, and if that is unobtainable the angle of bank must be reduced before it will be possible to raise the nose by easing backwards on the stick.

Contrary to the information in many gliding and flying manuals it is a fallacy to consider the controls as changing their function in a steep turn. Each control keeps its normal effect in relation to the pilot in the cockpit and each control has a proper function in a turn.

The angle of bank is always controlled by the ailerons. The position of the nose in relation to the horizon is always controlled by the elevator, and the sole function of the rudder is to balance the turn by eliminating slip or skid. However, in very steep turns the bank must be reduced before the nose can be raised.

Efficiency in turns

The glider pilot must always attempt to fly his aircraft efficiently if he is to make the most of any lift he encounters. In a turn this means keeping the aerofoil at an efficient angle of attack and minimising any losses caused by unnecessary drag. Any inaccuracies such as slipping or skidding will

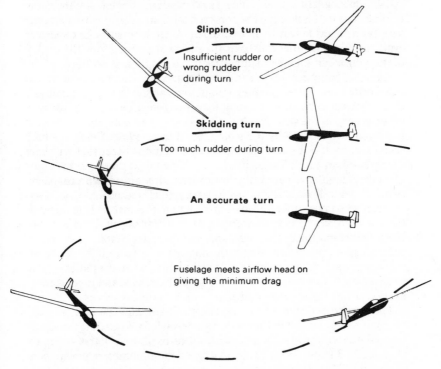

45. Slipping and skidding in the turn. Any inaccuracy causes extra drag and a greater loss of height. In skidding turns there is a marked tendency for the bank to increase.

cause an increase in the drag and this will steepen the glide and thereby increase the rate of descent. If the glider is slipping or skidding, the whole side of the fuselage is moving sideways through the air and, in effect, the pilot might just as well be flying along with the airbrakes fully opened.

There are few actual flight test results available for gliders in circling flight to confirm how the performance is affected by turning. Disregarding other factors, to keep the wing at the most efficient angle the speed will need to be increased to keep the same margin of speed above the stall as in straight flight, i.e. if the turn raises the stalling speed by 3 knots, the best turning speed for that angle of bank would be 3 knots above the normal cruising speed. Because of the need for this extra speed, the sinking speed is increased in a turn. The steeper the turn, the greater the sinking speed.

Most gliders have a fairly wide range of speeds over which the rate of descent is almost unchanged and a variation of one or two knots will not upset the performance. However, it does not help to fly very slowly because the glider will become stalled by any gusts and it will be much more difficult to maintain a steady circle. Good handling is essential if the glider is to be kept in the best part of the thermal. Particularly with a laminar flow type of aerofoil, it is more efficient to fly with sufficient speed to avoid the pre-stall buffet caused by the airflow separating from the surface of the wing at large angles of attack than to try to fly as slowly as possible.

A further complication arises from the size and distribution of the lift in a thermal. Again this is rather a vague and varying factor, but obviously if the thermal is small and strong it will pay to circle in steep turns in order to keep in the strongest lift. In this case, the higher rate of descent in a steep turn is offset by the strong lift. A heavy glider flying at a high speed will be at a disadvantage in these conditions because it will have a large turning radius. The radius of turn depends on the speed and angle of bank. A high-speed aircraft takes a large radius of turn whereas a low-speed glider will be able to turn in a very small radius.

Often when two different types of glider are thermal soaring together the one with the highest performance is outclimbed by the slower but less efficient machine. The lower speed of the latter enables it to turn in the stronger lift inside the turn of the high-performance glider. However, this advantage is far outweighed in straight flight, when the flatter gliding angle of the better machine takes it a greater distance and gives it more chance of finding another thermal.

The best advice is to adjust the angle of bank and speed to give the maximum rate of climb in the particular thermal. Avoid circling too slowly or at an unnecessarily high speed, i.e. for turns of up to 45° of bank, fly at about 2 – 3 knots above the normal speed for minimum rate of descent in straight flight. Increase the speed still further if a very steep angle of bank is being used or if the air is very turbulent and it is difficult to maintain a steady speed and angle of bank.

Thermal soaring is excellent practice in handling the glider in turns. In normal thermal conditions it is quite easy for an instructor to get the most inexperienced student to make turns in or near any thermal they may encounter and, even if no height is gained, the additional flying time is always valuable. Since thermals are nearly always turbulent, almost constant corrections are needed to maintain a steady turn and speed. This is good practice and also helps the student to realise that a high standard of flying is required. The extra time in the air and the height gained (if any) allows the student time to settle down and fly the glider without having to be worried so much about his position relative to the circuit and approach.

If through an error of judgement it is necessary to make a turn near the ground, the aim should always be to complete the turn quickly, and the greater rate of descent in a steep turn is outweighed by the reduced time which the turn will take to complete. A gradual turn will take much longer and, therefore, much more height will be lost. However, unless there is sufficient speed to make the turn, a steep angle of bank will only result in a stalled turn with disastrous results. There must always be sufficient speed for the angle of bank being used. A turn with an angle of bank of about 45° will give the minimum loss of height for a complete circle. Too much rudder will *not* increase the rate of turn and will only create extra drag which will result in a loss of speed and a steeper glide path.

The yaw string and slip indicator

Whereas the ball in the Turn and Slip or Turn Co-ordinator is perfectly adequate as a slip indicator for ordinary aircraft, small errors of slip and skid may be insufficient to register on the slip ball in a glider. However, any slight slip or skid will be detected by the yaw 'string' on the canopy which is dependent on the direction of the airflow instead of the very slight sideways forces.

The yaw string should always stream along the line of the fuselage unless the glider is being sideslipped deliberately.

Opinions differ on the use of the yaw string during early training. In the same way that a student pilot will often chase the airspeed if the use of the instrument is over emphasised in the early stages, it is only too easy to spend too much time watching the yaw string and making little corrections to re-align it. This results in a constant pedalling of the rudders and a constant slight weaving instead of smooth turns. It seems to be human nature to want to rely on an instrument rather than judgement and most people will over-concentrate on both the airspeed indicator and the yaw string if they are introduced too soon. If this is allowed the rudder will always be used as a corrective control and the basic good co-ordination will not be established.

My own opinion is that during the basic training it is most important to form the co-ordination habits needed without any aid. Later, perhaps not until after solo, the use of the yaw string should be explained and the yaw string referred to as a check that the turn is absolutely accurate.

However, it is even more important for eliminating slight errors in straight flight. With a modern machine which has a best gliding angle of about 40 : 1, any error will probably increase the drag sufficiently to reduce the glider to under 35 : 1. So the yaw string should always be checked on straight glides or any calculation for the distance which can be covered will be thrown badly out.

Some pilots and instructors are under the impression that if the yaw string is straight, the glider cannot spin. Although excess rudder will amost guarantee a wing drop at the stall, one wing can drop for a variety of other reasons. More important than the position of the yaw string is the need to maintain an adequate airspeed so that there is no risk of stalling. Remember that to spin, the glider must first stall and drop a wing and then it must be kept stalled.

It is true that almost all stall and spin accidents occur from a badly over-ruddered turn. Usually they start with the pilot getting low on the circuit and failing to make a turn into land before the height becomes critical: then because of the shortage of height the glider is flown too slowly without realising it. Instead of turning in earlier and being able to use a well-banked turn, the nearness of the ground makes the pilot use only a gentle bank. Quite unconsciously he may then use extra rudder to try to get round without more bank. This looks successful as the nose swings a few degrees but it causes much more drag and a rapid loss of airspeed as the fuselage batters its way sideways through the air. Without realising it the pilot will then try to stop the nose from dropping and the bank increasing and this will result in the glider stalling with a very violent incipient spin, with no possibility of recovery.

11 Better car and winch launches

Launching speeds—Pitching on the launch—The too fast signal—Slow launches

Although it is easy to fly the glider on the launch, it requires considerable skill and practice to get the maximum height possible on each launch.

Thermals are seldom of sufficient size or strength below 700 feet for an inexperienced pilot to use successfully. A 900 feet launch gives the pilot 200 feet of height to use in search of a thermal which is very little unless the gliding angle is very flat, as on a high-performance sailplane. An increase in launch height to 1,100 feet will at least double the chance of finding a thermal and a difference of this amount can be obtained with skill.

Launching speeds

The maximum launching speed is printed on the data card inside the cockpit, and the minimum safe speed for good control is about one and a half times the normal stalling speed or about normal cruising speed.

The ideal launching speed varies with the wind strength. In windy weather, the glider will climb up with very little assistance from the winch and the minimum launching speed will give a higher launch because less cable will be wound in. Also, at this speed, the cable and weak link will not be overloaded by the glider climbing steeply through turbulent air, so that the risk of a cable break is reduced.

In calm conditions a higher speed gives the best launch and a poor winch or tow car may have insufficient power to give the ideal launch in these conditions.

Two systems of speed control are possible. In the old system the car or winch driver judged the speed by the bow in the cable. More recently a power governor or tension measuring device has been used to control the load in the cable. With such a device the techniques are different. The winch or car driver varies the power output to keep the correct tension for the type of glider being launched.

If the launch is too fast, for example, the glider pilot pulls back more, increasing the tension. The driver then reduces the power slightly to re-establish the correct value.

This is an excellent system which takes a lot of the skill and judgement out of the launches. It also reduces the chances of overloading the weak link and causing a cable break.

Otherwise the speeds are judged by the way in which the glider is climbing together with the amount of sag in the cable. Surprisingly, it works well unless the glider pilot fails to get up into the climb properly.

The value of accurate launching speeds can be demonstrated by fitting both the gliders and winch with two-way radio. Perfect co-operation is then possible and improvements of 20 per cent increase in launch height in calm weather and 30–40 per cent in high winds have often been obtained even with inexperienced winch drivers. This is largely because of the small time taken to inform the winch of the correction needed. Prompt signalling on the part of the pilot, together with an alert winch driver, can effect similar improvements which are of great value on a flat site.

Steepening the climb may result in an increase in launching speed. This is explained in Fig. 46. However, reducing the angle of climb merely results in a worse rate of climb. A good driver soon settles down to launching

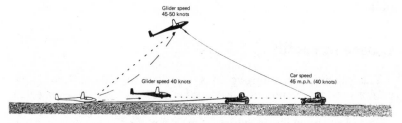

46. Effects of steepening the climb on a car or winch launch. The glider travels much farther in the same time.

at the desired speed and then signals are seldom needed unless conditions change.

The initial climb should always be gentle, becoming steeper gradually as height is gained. If the launching speed is correct, there should be no fear of breaking the cable provided that no sudden jerks are made in assuming the climb. Naturally, a large two-seater glider or heavy sailplane will put a greater load on the cable than a small solo aircraft and, therefore, on gusty days with a large machine it is wise to reduce the angle of climb slightly to avoid unnecessary cable breaks. Quite a large number of breaks, which waste valuable flying time, are caused by climbing very steeply at too high a speed instead of signalling and getting the correct launching speed. This can lead to a rather selfish state of affairs where one pilot obtains plenty of practice at cable breaks while the rest spend their time repairing cables.

A very large percentage of cable breaks are caused by poor piloting and it is noticeable how few cable breaks occur to experienced pilots.

Quite often the glider will pass through, or be launched directly into a thermal on the launch and this can be felt as turbulent air. It will show on the instruments as an unusually high rate of climb and launching speed at the top of the launch. If the launching speed is already too fast, the cable will often break when the glider is lifted by the thermal. It is usually best to complete the climb and then turn back to find the thermal again because, with the additional height, the thermal will be larger and probably stronger. If you do this, remember that other gliders may be waiting to take off. Unless you are climbing quickly above the launching height in the thermal, you must leave the area over the winch without delay.

Pitching on the launch

Some types of gliders have a tendency to pitch unpleasantly near the top of the launch. This pitching motion often begins when the glider flies through bumpy air or if the pilot makes jerky movements on the stick during the full climb. Unless the pilot stops the pitching, it will usually become worse with each successive movement until, finally, the cable breaks.

During the full climb, the elevator is holding the glider in the climbing attitude in opposition to the pull of the cable downwards from the nose. If the cable becomes slack for a moment, the elevator will raise the nose. By this time, however, the slack in the cable will have been taken up and a jerk will occur. This will pull the nose down and slacken the cable. Again the elevator will raise the nose and a second but more severe jerk will occur as the cable pulls tight. In this way, the pitching will get worse and worse as long as the pilot keeps the stick back and tries to keep climbing. (Fig. 47.)

To stop the pitching, the pilot must relax the backward pressure on the stick and reduce the climbing angle for a few moments. Time must be allowed for the oscillations of the cable to die out and for the winch or

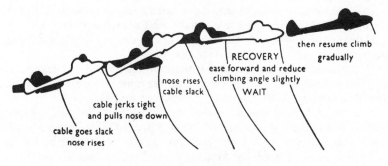

47. Pitching on the launch.

tow car to stop surging and take up the slack in the cable. Then the full climbing angle can be resumed carefully and the launch continued normally. If the climb is resumed too soon, while the cable is still oscillating, the pitching motion will begin immediately and corrective action will have to be taken again.

This pitching or 'bucking' as it is sometimes called, is much more severe when the cable release hook is near the extreme nose of the glider. It is also more marked with tow car launches than with winch launches and is made worse if the launch is too fast.

The too fast signal

Where the cable load is limited by the winch or car, steepening the climb will automatically reduce the launching speed. However, with other systems if the launching speed is high, the glider should be yawed from side to side by using alternate rudder with the wings level. Care should be taken not to steepen the climb at the same time or the load will probably break the cable. The signal must be clear, so that it cannot be confused with the swinging about which occurs when a beginner is carrying out a launch. Alternate rudder should be applied once or twice before continuing the climb. If the speed is above the maximum permissible and conditions are turbulent, the launch should be abandoned by releasing the cable since it is not safe to yaw the glider at higher speeds.

Slow launches

If the launch is too slow and the glider is not up to a safe climbing height (100 – 150 feet), the launch should be abandoned while there is still the opportunity to land straight ahead (remember that it may be a mechanical defect in the winch causing the slow launch or the winch driver may already be giving you full throttle).

It is important to realise that if the nose is lowered much from the climbing angle in use, the cable may become completely slack and the glider will lose *more* speed. This has been a common cause of stalling and spinning accidents from slow launches.

If the launch is much too slow it must be abandoned and treated as a cable break. In this case, of course, the nose must be lowered to at least the normal gliding attitude and the cable released at once.

It is very tempting to assume that the launching speed will improve so that more height will be gained. Since a power failure or cable break could still occur, there is a very real risk that the glider may be left in a position where it is too low for a circuit and yet has insufficient room for a safe S turn or a landing straight ahead. Do not wait for this to happen!

12 Landing out of wind

**The effects of a crosswind—The crabbing method—
The wing-down method**

Frequently, when landing in a restricted area, it is advantageous to be able to land out of wind in order to obtain the longest run of the field or an approach clear of obstructions.

The effects of a crosswind

If the glider is flown across wind, it will not track over the ground in the direction in which it is pointing but will 'drift' off to one side. If the glider is being flown accurately with no slip or skid, there will be no cross-draught in the cockpit. The glider is flying in a mass of air moving at the speed of the wind and is carried with it. (Fig. 48.) If the landing is made while the glider is drifting sideways over the ground there will be a severe sideways load on the main wheel and landing skid. This may easily break the skid or, if the landing is a bad one, the main wheel fixing and bulkheads may be broken.

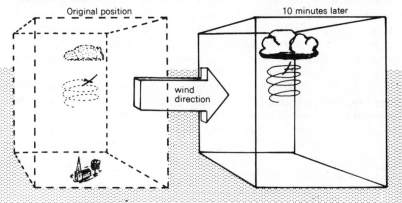

48. Circling in a strong wind. The glider circles under the cloud while the block of air is moved over the ground at the speed of the wind.

After landing, the glider will tend to swing into wind because of the weathercock action of the fuselage. (This is the tendency for the glider to swing into line with the airflow because of the larger amount of side area of fuselage and fin and rudder behind the centre of gravity. This causes the glider to behave in the same way as a weathercock.)

115

There is also a tendency for the wind to get under the windward wingtip and once the other wing touches the ground it will cause a bad swing.

There are two methods of making a crosswind landing. Both must be mastered eventually. However, the wing-down method is particularly important because it is the one which has to be used if the glider starts to drift towards an obstruction during the landing. The glider *must* be banked away from it as the rudder will only swing the nose but will not change the direction of flight.

If the landing area is wide enough, it is often possible to avoid landing out of wind by approaching diagonally into the available space. When this is not possible a crosswind landing has to be made. The object is to land the aircraft with no sideways drifting movement, since this creates large side loads which could easily damage the main wheel or skids.

The crabbing method

The final turn is completed with the glider heading slightly into the wind and tracking down the required line towards the landing area.

The wings are held level and the glider is flown accurately with the rudder central. For the last 20 – 30 feet the wind strength begins to decrease because of the wind gradient, and the drift correction can usually be reduced a little. The round-out and hold-off are made normally, but *just* before the glider touches down, the rudder is applied firmly to swing the nose into line with the aircraft's path over the ground. This ensures that as it sinks onto the ground there is no drift. At the moment of applying rudder it is also necessary to apply some opposite aileron to prevent the into-wind wing lifting as the glider is yawed. Once on the ground the into wind wing should be kept down slightly to prevent the wind getting under the wingtip and lifting it. Otherwise the other wingtip will touch the ground before the glider has stopped running. There is a very definite tendency for all gliders to swing into the wind when they are on the ground.

The wing-down method

After the final turn the approach is made with the into-wind wing down a small amount. The tendency for the glider to turn is counteracted by applying opposite rudder and this results in a gentle sideslip towards the wind. The angle of bank, which is never more than 5° or 10°, is adjusted to make the glider track along the desired landing run, keeping the glider pointing straight with rudder. Again at about 20 – 30 feet, the drift correction needs to be reduced until, as the glider is being held off, only 1° or 2° of bank will be needed. In this method, there is no last-moment action. The landing is made quite normally in the slightly banked position.

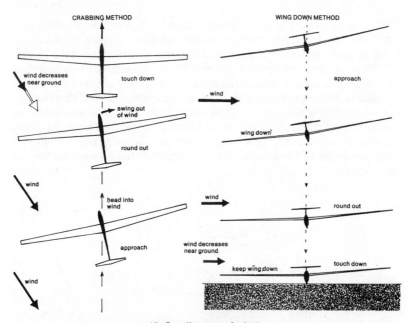

49. Landing out of wind.
Left: The crabbing method. The glider is pointed slightly into the wind with the wings level. Just after the round-out the out-of-wind rudder is applied to swing the aircraft into line with the landing direction.
Right: The wing-down method. The glider is banked slightly into the wind using the *opposite* rudder to prevent it turning. The approach is continued, gradually reducing the bank for the hold-off and touchdown.

As before, after landing the into-wind wing is held low and the out-of-wind rudder is required to prevent the glider from weathercocking round into the wind.

Notice that with both methods the pilot ends up holding the into-wind wing down and applying the out-of-wind rudder. Above all the glider must not be allowed to bank even slightly out of wind or it will drift very rapidly indeed.

Pilots have their own personal preferences as to methods but it is important to realise that if the glider begins to drift towards an obstruction during the last stages of the approach, the drifting must be stopped by banking away from it, *not* by using the rudder. If the area is smooth and clear the failure to correct for drift will seldom cause damage provided that the landing is properly held off. Most pilots use a combination of both methods.

Sooner or later you are bound to misjudge a crosswind landing and land with drift. If the landing happens to be a heavy one, the chances of damage can be greatly reduced by making sure that the initial touchdown is made on the main wheel as this will stand all but the heaviest sideways load without damage. If the landing is made with drift, a swing into wind will usually occur and must be prevented by immediate firm use of the rudder.

When landing out of wind, avoid approaching near to obstructions or other gliders so that even if the drift is not fully corrected, there is no danger of drifting too close to them or swinging towards them after landing. In very strong winds it is wise to allow the glider to turn directly into wind at the end of the landing run, as it is then possible to balance the wings level until help arrives. This is much safer than finishing out of wind with the possibility of the downwind wing going onto the ground and the risk of blowing over.

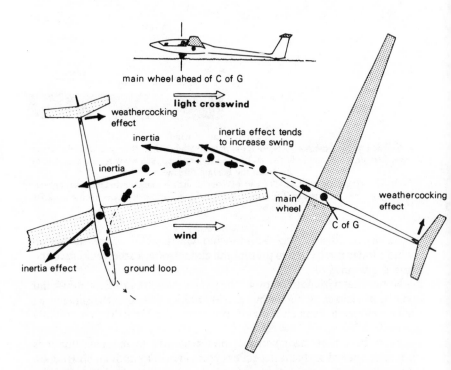

main wheel ahead of C of G

light crosswind

weathercocking effect

inertia

inertia effect tends to increase swing

inertia

weathercocking effect

main wheel

C of G

wind

inertia effect

ground loop

50. During the ground run. The inertia effect tends to accentuate any swing when the main wheel is ahead of the centre of gravity, as in modern gliders. In light winds the inertia effect becomes relatively more powerful than the weathercocking effect.

In a light crosswind, a normal approach may be made allowing for the glider drifting and then the drift can be eliminated by yawing the nose out of wind so that a landing is made without drift.

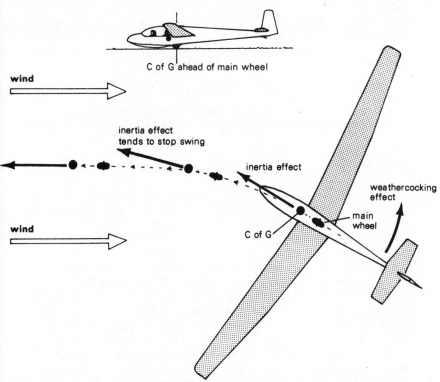

51. With the main wheel behind the centre of gravity the inertia effect tends to reduce the swing on the ground run and the weathercocking tendency is less, because more side area is ahead of the wheel.

There is always a tendency for the glider to bank when the rudder is applied to yaw the glider straight. This must be prevented by using the ailerons to keep the wings level or slightly wing-down into the wind. The glider will start to drift seriously if it banks out of wind and a fresh correction would then be required on the rudder to swing the nose of the glider farther out of the wind to eliminate the drift. If the crosswind is strong, it is easier to keep the 'into wind' wing low if the landing is made with a slight over correction of drift.

Gliders with the wheel mounted well forward of the centre of gravity have a much stronger tendency to weathercock into wind. If a swing does occur, the mass of the glider being behind the wheel accentuates the situation. Whereas on a windy day these gliders will just swing into the wind, in very light crosswinds, once a swing has started the glider will skid right round in a ground loop. Special care must be taken with these machines as, once a serious swing has developed, the rudder may be quite inadequate to keep control.

13 More about stalling and spinning

Stalling—Stalling speeds—Incipient spins—Auto-rotation and spinning—
Spiral dives—Recovery actions—The effect of the ailerons—Inverted spins

Stalling

If the nose of a glider is raised above the normal gliding attitude the increase in the angle of attack of the wing will at first produce more lift and drag. For a few moments the lift and drag may be greater than the weight, and the glider may even gain height. Then the extra drag will slow the glider down, and this loss of speed and the inefficient angle of attack will result in a steeper glide path and a high rate of descent. At this moment, there is often a tendency for the nose to fall and for the glider to try to resume normal flight. A further backward movement on the control column will result in a further increase in the angle of attack and a further fall in airspeed. Eventually, the wing will stall and the sudden reduction in lift will cause the glider to lose height very rapidly with the nose dropping.

At small angles of attack the airflow is smooth, and the speeding up and slowing down of the flow above and below the aerofoil creates good lift for only a small amount of drag. However, as the angle of attack is increased beyond the critical angle (generally about 15° for conventional aerofoils), a change takes place in the flow over the top surface of the wing near the trailing edge. The airflow breaks away from the surface, leaving a turbulent wake with large eddies. The flow over the upper surface is now turbulent and, near the surface, the air may even be moving towards the leading edge in places. (See Fig. 22, page 66.) If the angle of attack is reduced to below the critical, or stalling angle, the airflow will change back, immediately, to the normal smooth, unstalled airflow.

Experiments show that the stalling angle is not dependent upon the speed of the airflow. The glider will stall at any speed if the airflow meets the aerofoil at the stalling angle. Unfortunately, the glider is not fitted with an instrument which indicates angles of attack and the pilot must, therefore, know by experience the feel of the glider near the stall. If the glider is stalled by a very gradual backward movement on the control column, the stall will occur when the nose of the glider is only slightly above the normal gliding position. At the moment of stalling, the glide path will be steep and the rate of descent very high. A more rapid backward movement will result in the glider maintaining height until the stall occurs or, if the movement is very harsh, the glider may stall while climbing.

In a steep attitude the stall will usually occur at a lower speed and will be more complete. The nose will drop abruptly into a much steeper attitude, although the recovery takes about the same amount of height. If the glider is loaded so that the centre of gravity is well forward, the elevator may not be sufficiently powerful to stall the glider except by moving the stick back very quickly. A gradual backward movement on the stick, in this case, results in the glider mushing along at a very low speed, sinking rapidly. If the glider is pulled up into a very steep attitude, its inertia may keep it climbing until it loses all its speed. It may then fall backwards for a few moments in a tail slide. This is very undesirable and can be dangerous but is only likely to happen during aerobatics.

Stalling speeds

The speed at which the glider will stall in straight flight, when the control column is moved back gradually so that the speed is reduced at not more than 1 knot per second, is known as the *normal* or *basic* stalling speed for that glider. This speed will vary with the load carried, or with pilots of different weights.

For example if the stalling speed of a glider which weighs 500 lb empty is 30 knots when it is flown by a 120 lb pilot, it will stall at about 32 knots if flown by a 220 lb pilot. The indicated stalling speed will be within 1 or 2 knots of the correct value unless the instrument has been damaged or has faulty connections.

Small errors in the airspeed indicator can usually be safely ignored, but if the instrument overreads by a large amount, there is a danger that an inexperienced pilot may inadvertently fly the glider too slowly for safety.

During turning or looping manoeuvres, the loading on the glider is increased. This causes an increase in the stalling speed. In a very steep turn or a rapid recovery from a dive, the stalling speed may be more than twice the normal stalling speed for level flight. In this case, the loss of control generally associated with the approach to the stall will be absent, because the glider is not suffering from a low airspeed. However, the pilot will feel the 'g' and usually a buffeting of the controls, followed by a lack of response to any backward movement on the control column. Then one wing and the nose will drop, and height will be lost rapidly until a recovery is made. The recovery from a high-speed stall is, however, immediate once the backward pressure on the control column has been relaxed.

Incipient spins

During even a gentle, straight stall, one wing may stall slightly before the other so that the wing drops. If this occurs and the controls are

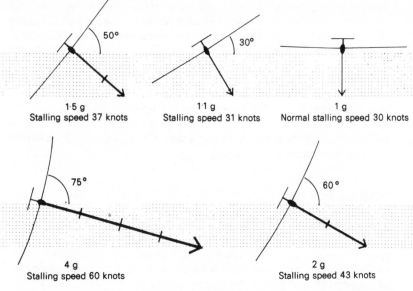

1·5 g
Stalling speed 37 knots

1·1 g
Stalling speed 31 knots

1 g
Normal stalling speed 30 knots

4 g
Stalling speed 60 knots

2 g
Stalling speed 43 knots

52. Stalling in turns. The variation in stalling speed with the angle of bank in accurate turns.

mishandled, the aircraft may fall into a spin. There are many causes of wing dropping at the stall.

1. Stalling while the aircraft is turning, is banked, or is yawing.
2. The aircraft being tipped by turbulence during the stall.
3. One wing having a slightly greater incidence than the other because of a warp in the structure.
4. The inherent tendency for a tapered wing to stall at the wingtip first unless some measure is taken to avoid this such as incorporating 'washout' at the wingtip.

Most gliders are designed to have gentle stalling characteristics and seldom drop a wing unless the controls are mishandled. The outer sections of the wings are designed to remain unstalled until the last possible moment so that the ailerons will be effective throughout any gentle stall. This can be done by decreasing the incidence of the aerofoil at the wingtips (known as washout), or by using an aerofoil at the tip which stalls at a greater angle of attack than the rest of the wing or has a very gradual breakaway.

If the ailerons are used excessively when the wingtip is nearly stalled, the effective angle of attack of the wingtip is increased by the aileron moving down and this may be sufficient to precipitate a stall at that wingtip. It is, therefore, important to avoid using the ailerons when trying to stop a wing from dropping at or near the stall. In any case, aileron drag will yaw the glider towards the lower wing and this will help to start a spin.

In almost any accidental and unintentional stall, the pilot is bound to react instinctively by pulling further back on the stick and attempting to prevent the wing dropping further by using the aileron and rudder in the normal way. For this reason there is not much point in an instructor insisting that you avoid using the aileron as a wing drops because unintentional stalls only occur when the pilot has failed to recognise the symptoms. The stall itself can almost always be prevented if the symptoms are recognised in time.

Auto-rotation and spinning

If a wing drops when the aircraft is stalled or nearly stalled, the downward movement of the wing results in a change in the direction of the relative airflow. The angle of attack of the down-going wing will be increased and this may cause it to become stalled, or more seriously stalled than the other wing. The reduction in the lift developed by the dropping wing will help to make it drop farther. The rising wing will have a reduced angle of attack and be almost or completely unstalled and will be developing much more lift than the one which is falling. The result of these differences in lift is an unstable rolling movement which is known as 'auto-rotation'. If no other factors were involved, the aircraft would continue to roll until the wings were unstalled. This horizontal spinning manoeuvre is known as a flick or snap roll. However, the effect of the force of gravity acting on the aircraft, together with the nose-down pitching moment at the stall, causes the auto-rotation to change from a horizontal rolling motion to a steep diving one.

Fig. 53 shows why this happens. In normal flight the wings are meeting the air at a small angle. If the aircraft is tipped so that the left wing drops, this movement results in a slight change in the direction of the airflow relative to the wing. The slight increase in angle results in a little extra lift which tends to damp out or stop the wing dropping further. The upward moving wing is also affected and makes less lift, helping to stop the banking movement. When the wing is stalled or nearly stalled, however, a similar tipping movement may take the dropping wing beyond the stalling angle so that lift is lost instead of gained. This results in a further dropping of the wing, making the angle even greater. The aircraft then tends to roll over out of control.

The uneven stalling of the wings which causes the auto-rotation also results in the wings developing unequal drag. The badly stalled wing has much more drag than the other one. This causes a yawing movement towards the dropping wing, which pulls the aircraft into the steep spiral descent which is the first stage of a spin. In most modern gliders, this yawing effect is insufficient for a full spin to develop. Additional yaw caused

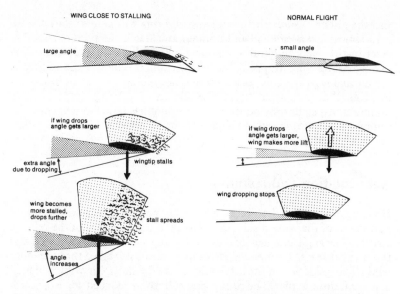

53. Lateral damping and auto-rotation. In normal flight the aircraft is resistant to rolling movements. In stalled flight if a wing drops it tends to continue dropping until the wing is unstalled. A stalled wing is laterally unstable and tends to auto-rotate.

by applying the rudder or creating a large amount of aileron drag by using a large movement of the aileron may cause a spin to develop.

Whenever the aircraft is stalled and one wing drops, auto-rotation will begin. It is sufficient for only one wing to be stalled to start an incipient spin. If the rate of yaw is sufficient to maintain the spiral and the wings remain stalled, the incipient spin will develop into a full spin. The angle of attack of both wings becomes much greater and the rate of rotation increases. The angle of attack of the wings in a fully developed spin is usually $30° - 40°$, so that it is much more difficult to unstall them once the spin has developed. Some gliders spin erratically, some steeply, fast or slow. However, most gliders need to be held into a spin or they will recover by themselves.

The spinning characteristics of all gliders are tested during the flight trials, and using the standard method of recovery the glider must stop spinning within one turn, and it must be possible to recover to level flight within 300 feet of initiating the recovery action. Most gliders are very loath to spin beyond the incipient stage, and will often recover if the controls are centralised or released. The correct recovery action is, of course, much more rapid and certain in its effect.

It is important to learn the spin recovery action and to sit in a cockpit on the ground and practise it as a drill of movements. The standard method of spin recovery is as follows:

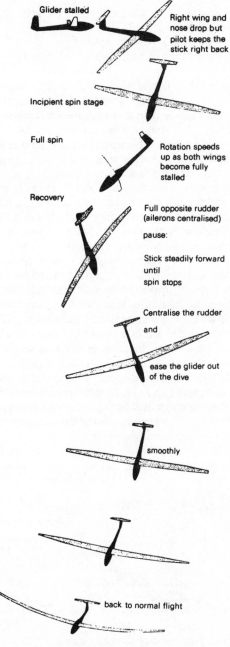

Glider stalled

Right wing and nose drop but pilot keeps the stick right back

Incipient spin stage

Full spin

Rotation speeds up as both wings become fully stalled

Recovery

Full opposite rudder (ailerons centralised)

pause:

Stick steadily forward until spin stops

Centralise the rudder

and

ease the glider out of the dive

smoothly

back to normal flight

54. The full spin and the recovery.

1. *Full* opposite rudder to the direction of the spin and then, with the ailerons central,
2. Stick steadily forward *until* the spin stops.
3. Centralise the rudder and *ease* out of the dive.

It is not unknown for individual aircraft to have slightly different spinning characteristics. Recovery action should be taken immediately if there is any tendency for the nose to rise progressively during a prolonged spin. Recovery from a flat spin is slow and unpredictable. It is wise to wear a parachute and to have sufficient height to use it if you intend to make any prolonged spins. (There is seldom any reason to do this unless you are the test pilot testing a new type of glider.)

If the centre of gravity is too far aft, it will be easier to put the glider into a spin and much more difficult to make it recover. In effect the extra power of the elevator will enable the wings to be stalled to a greater angle and the spin will become flatter. However, when it comes to the recovery, the elevator will have to overcome the tail-heaviness and, therefore, the recovery will be more difficult. In some gliders, the position of the centre of gravity is critical and on no account should the glider be flown with too light a pilot or it may be impossible to recover from a spin. The placard in the cockpit states the minimum load which may be carried. Usually this is about 140 lb for a solo glider but it may be as high as 175 lb in some.

A large yawing force provided by a powerful rudder or a large amount of aileron drag, will speed up the rotation and this will tend to flatten out the spin. Any flattening effect will increase the angle of attack of the wing and make the recovery more difficult. Fig. 55 shows why an increase in the rate of yaw flattens the spin. As the rotation increases, the centrifugal force produces a nose-up moment which prevents the nose from dropping and unstalling the wings. Conversely, during the recovery, any reduction

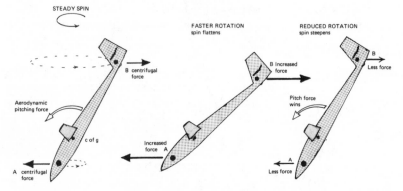

55. Inertia effects during a spin. If the glider is considered as if its weight is concentrated at A and B, the effect of an increase in yaw becomes clear.

in the rate of yaw will help to allow the nose to drop, which will help to unstall the wings.

The effect of having the spoilers or airbrakes out during the spin will vary with each design of glider. Usually, they help the recovery and prevent an excessive speed being reached in the dive. Airbrakes should always be opened immediately if a spin occurs or control is lost in cloud.

Spiral dives

Unlike a steep diving turn, or spiral dive as it is generally known, the speed remains low in a spin. This is the most distinctive feature when recognising a spin. But remember that the airspeed indicator gives false readings with large angles of yaw.

Sometimes the elevator is unable to keep the wing stalled beyond the incipient stage of the spin. In this case, as the nose and wing drop, the wing will unstall and the speed will increase with the glider in a spiral dive. (Fig. 56.) This can be recognised by the rapid increase in 'g' caused

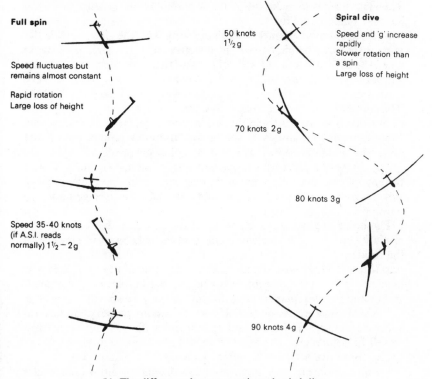

Full spin

Speed fluctuates but remains almost constant

Rapid rotation
Large loss of height

Speed 35-40 knots (if A.S.I. reads normally) $1\frac{1}{2} - 2$ g

50 knots
$1\frac{1}{2}$ g

70 knots 2 g

80 knots 3g

90 knots 4 g

Spiral dive

Speed and 'g' increase rapidly
Slower rotation than a spin
Large loss of height

56. The differences between a spin and spiral dive.

by keeping the stick back. To recover, relax the backward pressure on the stick, reduce the bank and level out using the controls normally.

Recovery action

Prompt action is the key to making a rapid recovery from an incipient spin and this is largely a matter of keeping in practice.

The opposite rudder is used to check the tendency for the glider to yaw towards the dropping wing. Unstalling the wing will eliminate any possibility of auto-rotation and prevent a spin. The wings must be brought level quickly if the minimum of height is to be lost and, since by then the wings are unstalled, the ailerons should be used for that purpose. The rudder will not pick up the wing at this stage as the glider is sideslipping steeply and the weathercocking action of the fuselage overpowers the effect of the rudder. Note also that the rudder is not used to raise the dropped wing in the recovery action. It merely checks the yawing tendency slightly. The order of control movements is unimportant at the incipient stage. The vital thing is to make the forward movement on the stick to get the wings unstalled quickly.

It is better not to attempt to raise the wing with the aileron while the wing is stalled. The increase in the effective angle of attack of the wing when the aileron is lowered will tend to stall that wing more and help the auto-rotation. The aileron drag will also help the yawing and, at the very least, this will delay the recovery and cause precious height to be lost. The correct use of the controls at this time is not instinctive, and plenty of practice is needed if the right action is to be taken in an emergency. Prompt action can always prevent a spin from developing, even if the corrective action is applied after the wing has dropped.

The recovery from a fully developed spin is important, but it should be remembered that only gross mismanagement of the controls and very slow reactions on the part of the pilot will make the average glider go beyond the incipient stage.

The order of the control movements is important. It is arranged to minimise any possible blanketing effects of the tail plane and elevator on the rudder. The amount of forward movement on the stick required to stop the spin varies with the aircraft and the stage of the spin. It is best to think of the forward movement as being a steady, progressive movement continuing *until the spinning stops*. In most gliders, the spin may stop after only a small forward movement. However, in many powered aircraft, no apparent change will occur until several turns after the stick has been moved fully forward. The ailerons should always be centralised.

The corrective action takes effect as follows:

1. *Full opposite rudder.* This tends to slow the rate of spin, which results in a nose-down pitching movement helping to unstall the wings. As the

rate of spin is reduced, the auto-rotation is also reduced because the wings become more equally stalled. The slight pause is to allow the rudder a moment to take effect before taking any further action.

2. *Stick steadily forward.* This pitches the nose down and unstalls the wings. Immediately the wings become unstalled, the auto-rotation must cease, and the spin has stopped leaving the glider in a dive. The rate of spin may actually increase just before it stops and this, or any other change, is a sign that the spin is stopping. The speed up in the rate of spin is caused by the governor effect of the mass of the aircraft while it spins. When the spin steepens, the radius of the spin is reduced and the inertia in the governor effect speeds up the rotation.

3. *Centralise the rudder.* Since the spin has stopped, the rudder is no longer required. The aircraft is in a steep dive or diving turn and the controls should be used normally to bring the glider back to level flight. If necessary the airbrakes should be opened fully to prevent the speed from becoming excessive. Failing to centralise the rudder may result in overstressing the fin, which is only stressed for sideslipping up to about 75 knots.

Note that the slight pause after applying the full opposite rudder is not intended to be a pause until the spin stops. In some types of aircraft the spin will not stop until the stick has been moved forward to unstall the wings. In others, the spin may stop immediately the opposite rudder is applied. In this case, the stick must *always* be moved forward sufficiently to ensure there is no risk of re-stalling. Because of the stability, the glider will try to recover from any dive by itself. Therefore, little if any pull force will be needed to bring it out of the dive. The moment the spin stops the recovery to level flight should be started.

No mention has been made of any action to be taken if the glider does not seem to be recovering from a spin after the correct recovery action has been taken. Any other action may only hinder the recovery and it cannot be too strongly emphasised that *on no account should the full opposite rudder be relaxed* until the spin has stopped. Provided that the glider is correctly loaded and is undamaged the normal recovery action will be effective.

The effect of the ailerons

The position of the ailerons can have a marked effect on the characteristics of the full spin and recovery, but it varies with the type of glider. Usually in modern machines, aileron applied in the direction of the spin (known as 'in spin' aileron) increases the rate of rotation and delays the recovery slightly. 'Out spin' aileron then helps to stop the spin and tends to turn it into a yawing, spiral dive. With some older designs the aileron has little effect except to help a full spin to be achieved when the full 'out spin' aileron is applied.

These effects may vary slightly with different loading and the ailerons should always be centralised at the start of the spin recovery action.

It is interesting to recall the effect of aileron during the incipient spin. Then any attempt to stop the dropping wing may even result in the wing falling further. It should also be noticed that a rapid movement of the ailerons near the stall can roll the glider so quickly that the dropping wingtip stalls in spite of that aileron being up at the time. This can easily occur during a very slow winch launch and is the reason that the 'too slow' signal given by rocking the wings is now discouraged.

Inverted spins

Unintentional inverted spins on gliders are almost impossible because of their inherent stability. If the glider is stalled while it is upside-down, it will fall away to one side by dropping the nose or one wing; there is no tendency to spin upside down. It may possibly fall into a normal spin, in which case, a normal spin recovery should be made.

14 Safe flying in high winds

Ground handling precautions—Wind gradient effects—Winch or car launching—Turbulence—Special precautions—Penetration—Conclusions and points to remember

Pilots who have been trained and sent solo in good conditions may often reach quite an advanced stage without ever having flown in a high wind, and they may unwittingly be sent solo in conditions which they have neither the experience nor the skill to manage safely.

Errors such as a slow approach or a low final turn and approach become more dangerous in windy and turbulent conditions.

The instructor in charge of flying is responsible for insisting that only really competent pilots fly solo when conditions are very rough. In most cases even experienced pilots can benefit from dual flying in such weather.

It is difficult to lay down any definite strength of wind which limits safe operating. However, it is seldom worth taking any risks unless soaring flights are possible. On the ground, the greatest care is needed to operate safely in winds of over 25 knots. In the air, the limitation is more often set by the amount of turbulence near the ground. It may seem strange that gliding usually continues in winds which ground most other light aircraft but it is only possible with careful ground handling.

Ground handling precautions

If the glider is facing into a strong wind with insufficient weight on the nose, it will be blown over. This can happen very easily if the tail is down, giving the wing a large angle of attack to the wind.

Once the glider leaves the ground there is little that the ground crew can do to prevent it from blowing over backwards. This type of accident always does extensive damage, often costing several thousand pounds to repair. It can easily be avoided by ensuring that there are always plenty of people available to hold gliders down and that they are well briefed, and positioned where their weight will be most effective. The tail men in particular should be experienced glider crews. The airbrakes or spoilers should be opened to reduce the lift of the wing, and the pilot's seat should be occupied all the time. Frequently, blow-over accidents occur through lack of supervision when in fact there are ample people to hold the glider safely. In windy weather, an instructor or a very experienced person should take control of the crew and ensure that they all know exactly what to do.

It is usually safer to push the glider by hand downwind rather than risk towing it behind a car as it may tend to overrun and collide with the back of the vehicle. Across wind the wingtip men have the safety of the glider in their hands, and must be particularly careful to keep the upwind wingtip low so that the wind helps to hold the glider down instead of blowing it over. Extreme care must be taken in turning the glider to ensure that the correct wingtip is held all the time. It should always be remembered that the cost and frustration of a damaged glider far outweigh the value and pleasure of flying in a very high wind. At most clubs the risks are assessed by the C.F.I. or instructor in charge who makes the decision to carry on or cease flying. It is very easy for him to put off the decision until conditions become dangerous for taking the gliders back to the hangars.

He is always right in stopping flying before an accident happens and always to blame if an accident occurs when flying continues in bad weather.

Since fairly strong winds are required for satisfactory hill soaring conditions, flying at hill sites is carried out in any weather in which the gliders can be safely handled on the ground and launched. The trainee at such places usually receives plenty of experience in windy conditions and soon becomes used to flying in the turbulent air near the hillside.

On flat sites situated in open country, severe conditions may be extremely rare and this may result in fairly experienced pilots being unable to fly safely in really rough conditions.

Wind gradient effects

The 'wind gradient' is the change in wind speed with height and is caused by the slowing down of the lower layers of the air as they pass over the ground. The 'wind gradient' is said to be steep or pronounced when the change in wind speed with height is very rapid and it is in these conditions that extra care must be used when taking off or landing in a glider.

Fig. 57 shows an example of a 'wind gradient'. The friction of the ground reduces the wind speed near the surface just as skin friction reduces the speed of the lower layers of the airflow over an aerofoil. If the surface is very rough, the friction will be greater and the lower layer will be slowed to a greater extent. This occurs when the area upwind is rough or covered with trees or houses.

The steepest 'wind gradient' is to be expected in high winds and to the leeward of rough ground. In these conditions, precautions must be taken to minimise its effects. It will be seen that the change in wind speed is very pronounced near the ground and up to 100–200 feet and then becomes less, until at about 1,000 feet it is negligible. In light winds, the wind gradient effect will be too small to affect a glider landing.

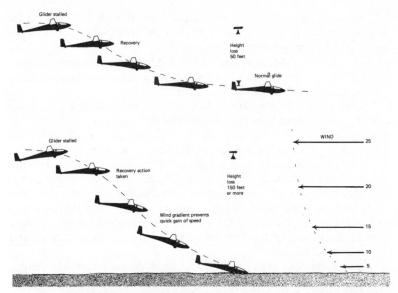

57. The effects of the wind gradient on the recovery from a stall near the ground.

A glider coming in to land takes only a few seconds to lose the last 100 feet or so of height. When there is a steep 'wind gradient' this means changing quickly from flying against a strong wind to flying against a much lighter wind. The glider, however, has considerable inertia and tries to maintain its original speed over the ground so that the reduction in wind speed causes a sudden drop in airspeed. In extreme cases the glider may even become fully stalled as a result of this sudden drop in airspeed, particularly if it starts the approach at a low airspeed.

The reduction in airspeed will cause the glider to sink rapidly and this effect is cumulative as height is lost. Finally, when the glider gets near the ground, since it is almost stalled it will need almost the full movement on the controls to level off for landing. In most cases a situation like this results in, at best, a heavy landing. Unfortunately the instinctive reaction to finding the glider sinking rapidly during the approach is to try to check the descent by easing back on the stick. This will only reduce the airspeed further and so increase the risk of stalling, and in any case will result in a higher rate of sink after a few seconds' delay.

It should be noticed that this is an occasion when the stall can occur with the glider in the normal gliding attitude. It is not necessary to have the nose high as in most cases of the stall, as the rapid sink of the glider increases the angle of attack of the wing.

The correct action during the approach through a steep 'wind gradient' is to come in at speed well above normal (at least cruising speed plus 15 knots) and to lower the nose to maintain this speed as the last 100 feet of height are lost. This will ensure that, when it is time to level out for landing, there is plenty of speed in hand so that normal control is available to correct for any gusts near the ground.

Alternatively, if the approach is made a little faster, a constant attitude can be held which will result in a normal aproach speed being reached by the time the glider is near the ground.

In conditions of high wind and gustiness near the ground, it is advisable for an inexperienced pilot to restrict the airbrake setting to about half for the last 20 – 30 feet of the approach and landing. Any tendency to level off the glide too high or to balloon up because of a gust will result in a rapid loss of speed. This effect, together with the drop in speed caused by the 'wind gradient' as the glider sinks onto the ground, may end in a heavy landing. A reduced amount of airbrake allows the pilot more time to correct any faults and is, therefore, a wise practice for inexperienced pilots. If a bad approach or landing is made in these conditions, the pilot's first action should be to move the brakes in to allow himself more time to control the situation.

The rapid sinking of the glider on the final approach in windy weather is often wrongly assumed to be the result of a down-draught or area of sinking air. In fact, this effect can be found anywhere when approaching to land in a strong 'wind gradient'. If the approach is badly judged so that there is a tendency to undershoot, any attempt to stretch the glide or check this sinking by holding up the nose will result in a more serious undershoot and possibly a fully stalled approach. This is the most dangerous action the pilot can take, particularly in a high wind.

Winch or car launching

The initial part of the launch is also in the steepest part of the 'wind gradient' and this results in a very rapid increase in speed as the glider gains height. The winch or car driver compensates for this by throttling back as the glider begins to gain height.

In order to prevent the winch engine stalling at the low speed needed in high winds, it is sometimes necessary to launch in a low gear. The take-off may then require full power to reach a safe speed because the wind speed on the ground is much less than its speed at height. Frequently, in these conditions, the initial launching speed tends to be slow and, for this reason, particular care is needed. If the winch fails or the cable breaks during the climb to a safe height and while the speed is low, a very critical situation arises. The slightest delay in lowering the nose will result in a stall, and even if this is recognised as such and the nose is lowered farther to regain speed, the rapid loss of height through the wind gradient prevents a quick recovery and may result in the stall becoming more complete.

Recovery from a semi-stalled situation below 150 – 200 feet in these conditions takes an abnormal amount of height, and only very prompt and deliberate action can prevent serious damage being done to the glider. (See Fig. 57.) It is particularly vital that the airbrakes are left alone until normal approach speed is obtained if the cable breaks during the first part of the climb. If the glider is already almost stalled, the high drag and loss of lift occurring when the airbrakes are opened may stall it. There is always plenty of room to land ahead without using the airbrakes if the cable break occurs near the ground.

Turbulence

The severity of turbulence in the air depends on several factors. The most vicious turbulence will generally occur in conditions when the air is unstable and the wind strength high. Obstructions such as hills, trees or buildings will all help to break up smooth airflow and cause difficult and even dangerous conditions for the glider pilot.

In very turbulent air, gusts in all directions of 5 – 10 knots or more are quite common. These can stall the glider or roll it over out of control into a steeply banked attitude particularly if it is flying too slowly at the time.

Turbulence can often be avoided by bypassing the likely areas caused by surface obstructions and irregularities. The area in the lee of a hill is usually one in which severe turbulence will be found in windy conditions. The 'wind gradient' is usually abnormally steep because in some places the surface wind may even be reversed near the ground just behind the crest of the hill and the air may be very violent for several miles downwind.

Areas in the lee of trees or other obstructions will also be particularly turbulent up to a height of several hundred feet and should be avoided whenever possible for approaches and landings. As a matter of principle, approaches should never be made over obstructions if there is an alternative clear approach which can be used.

Experience shows that maintaining a reasonably high speed will not necessarily prevent loss of control in turbulence. Frequently, when gliding in high winds, the glider is rolled over by a gust against the use of full aileron and rudder even though flying at twice the normal stalling speed. In straight flight the risks of losing a critical amount of height in this kind of situation are not great. If the glider is already banked, it may be rolled right over and 100 feet or more may be lost recovering to level flight. Near the ground, recovery from a steep bank in a glider is abnormally poor because the lower wing may be as much as 40 feet below the other wingtip. The lower wing is then in a much lighter wind than the other and has, therefore, a much lower airspeed and less lift. This difference helps to steepen the bank and reduces the effectiveness of the ailerons when they are used to attempt to bring the wings level. (See Fig. 58.)

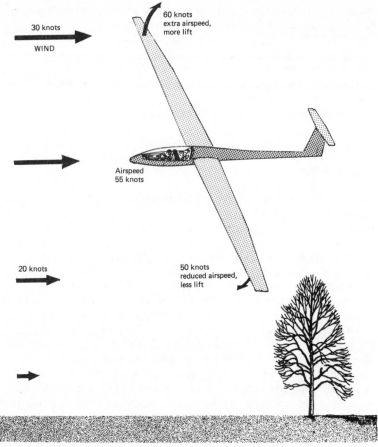

58. The effects of the wind gradient when turning close to the ground. The rolling effect may overpower the effectiveness of the ailerons.

The wise glider pilot will always approach from a much greater height in windy conditions; he avoids obviously turbulent areas whenever possible and approaches with plenty of speed to combat the effects of the 'wind gradient'. This does not entail excessive retrieves because in any case the glider makes little progress against a strong wind.

The approach may be upset by strong sinking air and extra height should be allowed for this possibility. At times the rate of descent may reach 15 – 20 feet per second in these down-draughts so that 200 or 300 feet may be lost in the time it takes to turn and make towards the nearest landing area into wind. In such conditions, it is always necessary to fly in a position from which a safe landing can be made even if 200 or 300 feet are lost without warning.

Special precautions

The effect of the wind on the track and ground speed of the glider is very much more marked in strong winds, and can lead the unwary into difficult situations. Flying downwind, the ground speed is often doubled and this necessitates commencing a turn across wind long before it is normally necessary if the glider is not to be taken beyond the downwind boundary during the turn with little hope of regaining the airfield. (See Fig. 38 on page 94.)

The inexperienced pilot may also be tempted to try and reduce the ground speed by raising the nose, and this will result in flying too slowly and even stalling. This is particularly easy to do in heavy rain, when the noise of the airflow and rain may give the impression of normal flying speed when in fact the glider is almost stalled. The gliding angle in relation to the ground will be much flatter flying downwind and this may upset the judgement on the circuit. Across the wind the glider will drift at a considerable angle and once again the inexperienced pilot may try to eliminate this sideways movement by applying rudder. This misuse of the rudder by skidding the glider will result in additional drag, loss of speed and hence possibly the conditions for a spin. The effect of the wind makes it particularly dangerous to make a 360° turn anywhere near the downwind boundary as it results in the glider being drifted over the boundary.

Penetration

Into wind, the glider will make little progress at normal flying speeds so that, if the approach is started from behind the boundary, it may easily end by a landing on the fence. A sound rule is not to go behind the boundary when the wind is very strong and this is almost universal practice. Unfortunately, an error of judgement or a moment of carelessness can easily result in finding oneself too far back and in a difficult situation. What glider pilot sooner or later does not find himself in this predicament? You must try to avoid it and know exactly what is the best action to take if it does occur.

The instinctive reaction to undershooting is to try to stretch the glide by raising the nose. This is the wrong thing to do at any time but is fatal in windy conditions because a reduction in speed reduces the ground speed still further and so results in losing height without so much forward progress. Also, of course, this will give the 'wind gradient' the opportunity it is waiting for to stall the glider.

If there appears any chance of undershooting, the nose should be lowered well below the normal attitude to gain speed as rapidly as possible. Although this will result in a rapid loss of height, the glider will then penetrate against the head wind. A further advantage is that the glider arrives close to the ground at high speed where the wind is lighter and considerable distance will be covered floating with the excess speed. It is interesting to consider the speeds and angles of glide against strong winds in order to decide upon a sound policy for situations like this.

The examples given in Fig. 59 show diagrammatically the effects of flying at various speeds into a head wind of 20 knots. These distances are seldom achieved in practice because of the height and speed losses caused by gliding down through the 'wind gradient'.

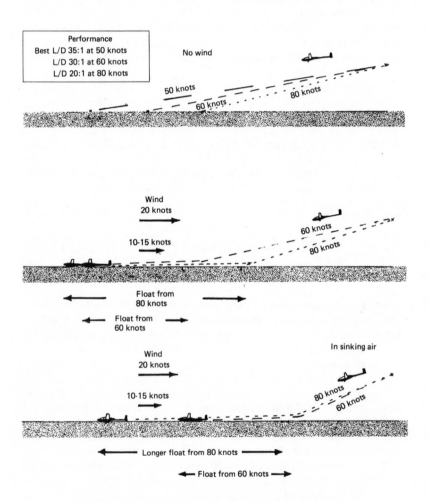

59. Penetrating against a strong wind. Extra speed is vital.

It will be noted that the penetration against a strong wind improves with an increase in speed and remains good up to speeds which are at first sight impracticably high. At low speed, penetration is very poor, besides there being little or no excess speed with which to float during the hold-off period.

The best speed for penetration can be found by the simple rule-of-thumb method of adding one-third wind speed to the speed for best gliding angle in still air. This simple method gives reasonably accurate results for most types of gliders, and is a suitable minimum speed for normal approaches in windy conditions. If the glider has been allowed to get into a critical situation, there must be no mistake. It is better to fly even faster than the theoretical speed for penetration. This will result in very little loss and will minimise the effects of any turbulence or down-draughts encountered. This example shows that the penetration is virtually the same at speeds between 60 and 80 knots. The moral is clear: if in doubt fly faster.

There will be no second chance if the speed is too low because an undershoot is then inevitable.

The speed for best penetration should also be used in flight at any time when it is essential to make progress against the wind in spite of losing height. For example, on some sites the ridge is well upwind of the launching point and it is necessary to penetrate against the wind to reach the ridge. Here the best speed will be that for best penetration, or slightly above that if it is considered likely that the glider will be flying in the down-current or turbulence behind the hill-top.

Conclusions and points to remember

1. Special care must be taken all the time when handling the glider on the ground in high winds. Allow six people for each glider and ensure that they are well briefed and under the control of one person.
2. If the conditions are deteriorating, stop flying long before handling on the ground becomes dangerous. Gliding in very turbulent high winds is risky.
3. Do not fly far beyond the downwind boundary in windy conditions.
4. Be prepared for the effects of 'wind gradient' near the ground. The initial climb must be gradual and immediate action taken to regain speed for the approach if the cable breaks. The approach speed must be adequate—if in doubt, approach too fast rather than too slow. Avoid turns near the ground.
5. Avoid approaching over obstructions or landing in the turbulent area in the lee of them.

6 . Always initiate the turn from the downwind leg of the circuit onto the base leg much earlier than normally to ensure that the glider does not get blown downwind of obstructions in the turn.

7 . Flying downwind ignore the high ground speed and ensure that a safe *airspeed* is maintained. In rain, hail or snow beware of the apparent speed caused by the appearance and noise of it. (Rain may make the airspeed indicator read incorrectly. It spoils the performance and usually increases the stalling speed by 5 – 8 knots.)

8 . If the glider is allowed to drift too far downwind in windy conditions lower the nose and gain extra speed for penetrating. Too much speed is better than too little. Land short of the landing area rather than stalling onto the boundary.

Above all, fly within easy reach of a safe landing area allowing for a possible loss of height of several hundred feet at any time.

15 Sideslipping

Straight sideslips—Slipping turns

After the first few hours' solo flying, you will be taught how to sideslip. This manoeuvre is particularly important if you are flying a glider which has ineffective airbrakes, as it can make it possible to make a landing in a restricted space with less risk of damage to the glider.

A sideslip is a useful way of losing height without increasing speed. You will find that at first it is difficult not to co-ordinate with the rudder as you apply the bank.

There are several slight variations of the normal straight sideslip.

Straight sideslips

The glider is put into the sideslip by applying a little bank and then sufficient opposite rudder to keep it from turning. The normal approach speed should be maintained by a slight backward pressure on the stick to keep the nose from falling.

The rate of descent can be adjusted by varying the angle of bank. The maximum angle of bank in a straight sideslip is limited by the power of the rudder, which depends upon the design of the particular glider. In modern gliders, only a small angle of bank can be held straight and this considerably restricts the value of the sideslip as a means of losing height.

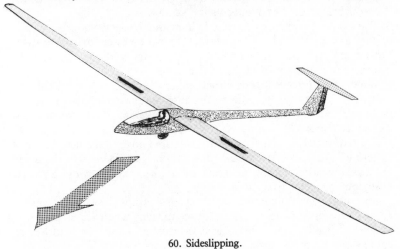

60. Sideslipping.

Care must be taken when recovering from a sideslip to relax the backward pressure on the stick or an unintentional stall may occur.

One easy way of entering a sideslip is to freeze your feet on the rudder to stop any movement of it and to apply the bank with the ailerons only. Then, as the aileron drag swings the nose to the side, the rudder can be smoothly applied to hold it in position and prevent the glider turning.

Most gliders are fitted with a pot pitot in the nose and suffer from very large airspeed indicator errors during sideslips. The speed must, therefore, be assessed by the attitude, sound and response to the controls. The noise, however, may be misleading because the turbulence caused by the large angle of yaw may increase the noise round the cockpit. Always check the airspeed immediately after recovery.

First attempts at sideslipping on an approach must be made in a two-seater under the guidance of an instructor.

Slipping turns

The slipping turn is sometimes useful because steeper angles of bank are possible, with a higher rate of descent. However, if the pilot realises that he is far too high on the base leg, it is better to open full airbrake and to drop back a little to lengthen the approach, rather than make a slipping turn with the airbrakes open. It is only too easy to attempt a slipping turn and then find difficulty in getting properly aligned for the landing.

The glider is put into a slipping turn by banking it to start the turn and then by using opposite rudder. The angle of bank and the amount of opposite rudder are regulated to control the rate of the turn and the rate of descent. A slipping turn enables height to be lost very rapidly indeed if the airbrakes are being used at the same time.

The maximum angle of sideslip is increased because with full rudder applied a steeper bank can be used since it is not necessary to keep straight. Once again, care must be taken to check the actual reading of the airspeed indicator immediately after recovering from the sideslip.

Where the glider is a type which cannot be held in a steep sideslip because of the relatively ineffective rudder, alternate sideslips to left and right can be used, changing over as the nose begins to fall through lack of rudder control.

A variation of this, the flat sideslip, or fishtailing, is an emergency way of getting rid of excess speed near the ground. The glider is yawed quickly from side to side with alternate full rudder, keeping the wings level. (It is seldom very effective.)

Care must be taken not to continue steep sideslips close to the ground, particularly in turbulent and windy conditions when slight errors in handling, together with unexpected turbulence, could result in loss of control and an incipient spin during the recovery.

The decision to sideslip should be taken as soon as it becomes certain that the approach is going to continue to need full airbrake and there is a possibility of an overshoot. Otherwise the glider may eventually arrive in a position so high that only the most violent sideslips would be of any help.

Flying from an airfield or gliding site where a landing a few hundred yards downfield is not serious, the need for sideslipping should not normally occur and should be considered as a sign of poor judgement on the part of the pilot.

Some gliders have relatively ineffective airbrakes, so that sideslipping has to be used. On these, any approach which requires the continuous use of full airbrake is unacceptable since starting too high, or the effect of flying through rising air, would result in overshooting.

Sideslipping is a greatly neglected manoeuvre although it is both pleasing and exacting as a test of handling skill. Every pilot who flies across country should be able to sideslip effectively.

It is vital to practise some very high approaches starting with full airbrake and then using a sideslip to lose the excess height. The recovery should be at a safe height and in the position where the approach can once again be controlled accurately with the airbrakes.

Many pilots have difficulty getting into the slip quickly and holding the direction of the approach. The most critical moment is just after the recovery. The actual airspeed *must* be checked and if low must be corrected ready for the round-out and landing. If necessary the airbrake setting must be reduced to allow a normal landing.

16 Local soaring and efficient cruising

Things to do—Small triangles—Efficient cruising—Trimming—Aerobatics

No gliding club can afford to have its gliders damaged or even hazarded by careless or irresponsible flying. For this reason, an unauthorised cross-country flight or a landing away from the site is treated as a serious misdemeanour and disciplinary action is usually taken against the pilot even though there is no damage to the glider.

Unfortunately, many glider pilots become anxious to start cross-country flying as soon as they have made one or two soaring flights. Often they do not appreciate the subtleties of thermal soaring and fail to realise that their soaring flights were probably only made because of the exceptionally easy conditions at the time. Most pilots do not have the necessary background of experience needed for safe cross-country flying in this country until they have completed at least one season of local soaring. This period of gaining experience can be used to prepare for the future or, as often happens, it may be wasted so that the pilot is still not proficient by the following season. Only a few pilots make any real attempt to develop their skill and technique at thermal soaring systematically at this stage. It is those few who are most likely to become the outstanding pilots of the future.

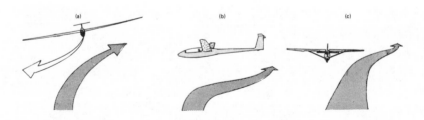

61. Collision avoidance. (a) Head-on: both turn right. (b) Converging courses: give way to a glider on your right. (c) Overtaking: the overtaking aircraft must keep clear of the other.

Things to do

A map should always be carried and used when it is possible to soar a few miles from the site. Map reading is not difficult, but it does require practice. Unless there is a head wind, most gliders will cover at least four miles for every 1,000 feet of height lost. (Gliding angle 20 : 1.) This means that on a good soaring day, a glider at 4,000 feet can safely explore the countryside within a radius of 10 miles of the gliding site and still be within easy reach of the field at any time. At first the pilot should learn to recognise the nearest landmarks to the site. Then gradually he should extend his range until eventually he is able to find his way back by estimating and then flying the compass course which will bring him back to the field, even when it is out of sight or concealed by cloud shadows. It is essential to gain experience at steering a compass course and turning on to course quickly, as the compass is a particularly difficult and obstinate instrument to use.

Local soaring means keeping within easy gliding distance of the site at all times. There must be no question of landing 'away' because of an error of judgement or becoming lost. However, the pilot should practise selecting suitable fields for a landing, and should try to identify the various types of crops and the surface and size of the fields. These can often be verified by going to have a look at some of the fields on foot. In particular, the pilot should train himself to notice any slope in the ground or bad features of a particular field at a glance.

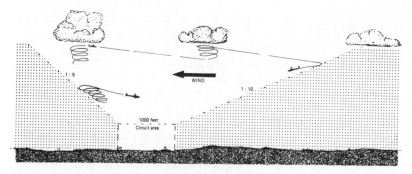

62. Safe local soaring. To be absolutely safe, keep within an angle of 1 : 10 when upwind and 1 : 5 when downwind of the field. Or in light winds allow about 2 miles per 1,000 feet with 1,000-feet margin for the circuit.

On a really good soaring day, the pilot may find that it is so easy to stay up that there seems little to be gained by carrying on. These are occasions when it is interesting to see exactly how long it takes to climb to a certain height, for example, 3,000 feet, and descend quickly to 1,500 feet again to look for another thermal. A pilot who can descend to this height and be reasonably confident of finding another themal should have a fair chance of staying up when the time comes for him to fly across country. Trials of this kind are exciting and of far greater instructional value than many hours of thermal soaring at 3,000 or 4,000 feet where the thermals extend over a very wide area.

Many of my most exhilarating flights have been of this nature and I recall one flight in particular, early in the spring. This flight was made with the intention of flying the glider to the hangar, as many club members apparently considered that the soaring conditions were beginning to fade out. I was launched by tow car at about 5.30 and was soon climbing rapidly in a strong thermal. At just over 5,000 feet I flew into the small wispy cumulus cloud which seemed to be capping the haze layer which marked the inversion level. After a few moments' practice flying on the turn and slip indicator in the cloud, I decided to practise aerobatics on the way down. A series of almost continuous loops, chandelles and spins followed by a circuit with the airbrakes open concluded the flight, which had lasted just twenty minutes from take-off to touchdown.

During this stage of a pilot's career, it is a good idea to make every approach without the use of the altimeter. Eventually, the pilot should be able to make a good landing in a chosen position on every flight.

Small triangles

On a day with a light wind, it is possible to fly 30 or 40 miles without being out of gliding range of the take-off point. If the turning points for a triangular flight are selected carefully so that all three are about seven miles from the site, a height of 4,000 feet will be sufficient to keep within gliding range thoughout the flight. This is an excellent opportunity to practise photographing turning points and selecting good clouds along a definite route instead of just trying to stay up.

If, through a bad error of judgement, it becomes doubtful whether it is possible to reach the gliding site, the safety of the glider must be the main consideration. A suitable field should be selected in plenty of time in order to ensure a safe landing. Never risk a landing on the fence or just short of the site by hoping that there will be lift to help the glide. The slightest risk of damage to the glider is far worse than an unauthorised landing in a field.

There are numerous electronic systems available which can tell the pilot at what speed he should be flying for the conditions at that moment. However, they all require a judgement by the pilot about the distance and strength of the thermals ahead. This will seldom be accurate as it is largely a matter of experience and judgement.

Club gliders very rarely have such expensive and sophisticated instruments and it is therefore necessary for every pilot to have a basic knowledge of 'speed to fly theory'. This will also be needed to detect a fault in the instruments, whether it is caused by an instrument failure or by the pilot setting it up wrongly.

Efficient cruising

A pilot should know a sufficient amount about the performance of his machine to make the most of varying conditions.

The gliding angle is measured as a ratio of the distance travelled for the height lost, e.g. 40 : 1. It varies considerably at different flying speeds and depends upon the ratio of the lift and drag. The best gliding angle occurs when the lift/drag ratio (L/D) is at a maximum. This is usually about 15 knots above the stalling speed. The best gliding angle for a particular type of glider can only be increased by improving the lift or by reducing its drag.

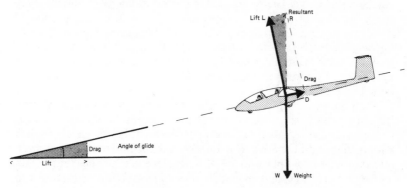

63. The angle of glide and the lift/drag ratio.

The rate of descent depends on the gliding angle and the flying speed.

A low rate of descent can be obtained by building a light glider with a large wing area, but a flat gliding angle is only possible by careful design and construction for low drag. A strutted glider such as the old Tutor or Grunau Baby with a gliding angle of 16 : 1 at 30 knots has the same rate of descent as a machine with a gliding angle of 27 : 1 at 50 knots. The latter has almost twice the chance of finding a thermal but costs much more.

Many pilots are puzzled by the fact that the best gliding angle is unaffected by an increase in weight. The extra weight requires a higher flying speed to obtain more lift, but as both lift and drag are proportional to the square of the velocity, the ratio between the lift and drag remains

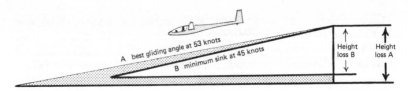

64. The minimum rate of sink occurs at a lower speed than the speed for the best gliding angle. (See also Fig. 110.)

the same. The rate of descent will have increased although the glider will still fly the same distance from a given height. The increase in flying speed is an advantage when flying against a strong wind, whereas a low rate of descent is valuable when the thermals are very weak. Gliders of advanced design carry water ballast tanks so that the load can be varied according to conditions. When the tanks are full, the increase in sinking speed is insignificant while the thermals are strong and the raised cruising speed is an advantage. When the strength of the thermals decreases, the water can be released and the lowered sinking speed will help the glider to keep up.

At first while still learning to soar it is best to limit the cruising speed between thermals in order to have more time to react if an area of lift is found. Until you are fairly experienced, flying the theoretical 'optimum' speeds usually results in a rapid descent back to the airfield, or worse still, into a farmer's field.

The principles behind cruising efficiently are explained later in chapter 19 and the basic rules are important to every pilot.

It is important to realise that, except for the final glide down to a landing, the cruising speeds should NOT be increased when flying into the wind. At other times the optimum speed to fly depends only on the strength of the lift being used and on whether the glider is flying through an area of rising or sinking air.

Flying faster than the optimum, which for weak conditions will be only slightly above the best gliding angle speed, will only result in more height loss and more time spent climbing. This lowers the average speed through the air mass.

Unless the glider is flying through rising air it is almost always flying through sink and therefore it should be flown faster than the best L/D speed when searching for thermals. A common error with inexperienced pilots is to fly at minimum speed in the belief that they are conserving height. They would do better to consider the best L/D speed (about 50 knots for most machines) as a minimum cruising speed. Unless the sink is very strong, avoid flying at very high speeds. It is far easier to find and get into thermals if the cruising speed is kept down to about 50–55 knots. The exact speeds to fly are relatively unimportant but the principle of flying faster through sink and slower in rising air applies at all times.

On a final glide back to the airfield, we are no longer concerned with the average speed or with climbing back up. The aim is then to go the furthest distance for the loss of height against the prevailing wind. In this case it is vital to fly faster against a strong wind. The best speed can be found by using a calculator or by adding about one-third of the wind speed to the speed for best gliding angle in still air, e.g. maximum L/D 53 knots, headwind 20 knots, best speed 53 + 7 = 60 knots.

Trimming

Unless the elevator forces are extremely light it will be a distinct advantage to retrim the glider for any prolonged thermalling. This makes it much easier to keep a steady speed so that you can spend more time looking round for signs of better conditions, watching for other nearby machines and, on a cross-country flight, snatching a few moments to look at the map. The trimmer should be reset after leaving the thermal and at any time that a constant pressure is required on the stick.

Aerobatics

Most modern gliders are permitted to carry out simple aerobatics such as loops and chandelles but are not designed for rolling or inverted flight. The limitations of the particular type of glider are clearly stated on the cockpit placard. Aerobatics should not be carried out in turbulent conditions and care must always be taken not to exceed the maximum permitted speed for the type of glider. The controls should be moved smoothly but firmly.

If at any time during aerobatics a very steep stall or a tailslide seems imminent, the pilot should hold the controls firmly against the stops to prevent them flapping violently and damaging the hinges. The glider will fall into a steep dive from which a normal recovery can be made.

Stall turns are not recommended for gliders because there is a serious risk of the glider tail sliding. The chandelle or wing over is a much safer manoeuvre which is just as spectacular to the onlooker and requires skilful piloting.

Glider aerobatics require very different control forces and movements from most powered aircraft. It is therefore prudent for power pilots to have at least one dual flight with an instructor experienced at glider aerobatics before attempting them solo.

The special problems are explained in detail in my book *Understanding Gliding*.

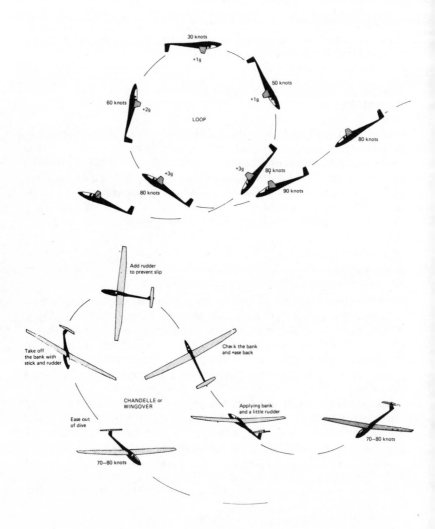

65. Simple glider aerobatics.

SECTION III

Exploring the skies

Having mastered the elementary principles of gliding, you can now begin to enjoy the rewarding pleasures of soaring flight.

At most of the larger clubs, there are schemes for advanced instruction to prepare you for cross-country flying and you are advised to take advantage of them, particularly if you intend to buy a glider or a share in one.

The majority of modern high-performance gliders are easy to fly and safe enough for even inexperienced solo pilots. However, they can be very expensive and even dangerous unless you are prepared to limit your activities to local flying until you have done at least 20 hours of solo flying and have been systematically trained to deal with the problems of field landings.

17 The instruments and their limitations

The airspeed indicator (A.S.I.)—The altimeter—The variometer—Total energy compensation—The turn and slip indicator—The compass—Special glider compasses—The artificial horizon—The barograph

The instruments generally fitted to gliders are the airspeed indicator, the altimeter, the variometer, the turn and slip indicator and the compass. Every pilot should know how they work and their principal limitations.

The airspeed indicator (A.S.I.)

The A.S.I. is an air pressure gauge designed to measure the pressure developed by the forward movement of the aircraft.

This instrument really makes a comparison between the pressure built up in a forward-facing pitot tube or pressure head mounted out in the airstream at some convenient place on the aircraft, and the atmospheric or static pressure at the time. Both the pitot tube and static vents must be situated in positions where the influence of the shape of the fuselage or other parts of the aircraft is at a minimum, or large errors will occur. The pressure head may be an open tube facing forward on the nose or wing, or a hole in the centre of the nose.

Compared with a pitot tube, the 'pot' pitot in the extreme nose of the fuselage has the great advantage that it does not ice up.

In some open-cockpit gliders, the air pressure in the cockpit is near enough to the true atmospheric pressure to use it as the static for the airspeed indicator. On most other gliders, the shape of the cockpit causes changes in the pressure at different speeds which would cause large errors in the instrument. It is, therefore, necessary to provide an accurate static pressure and this is usually done by connecting the instrument to two small holes, one either side of the nose or just behind the wing where the air pressure in flight is unaffected by varying speeds. These are known as static vents.

Never blow down the pitot tube in an attempt to test the airspeed indicator. This causes serious damage to the expanding capsule in the instrument so that either it is rendered completely useless, or reads 40 – 50 knots too high all the time. The 'pot pitot' is difficult to blow down and almost 'boy' proof.

152

When the glider is being stalled in order to check the A.S.I., the speed should be reduced at a rate of about 1 knot per second.

For the reader's benefit, speeds are given in this book in knots, but 1 knot is slightly more than 1 m.p.h. (66 kn = 76 m.p.h) and conveniently 1 knot is almost exactly 100 feet per minute.

The airspeed indicator suffers various errors with variations in height and temperature and in the position and type of pitot head and static vents.

Height and temperature errors are the result of calibrating the instrument on the assumption that the atmosphere has standard properties at all heights, instead of allowing for variations of temperature and pressure with height.

These errors are of no importance to glider pilots during local flying but are of general interest to the pilot flying above about 8,000 feet. The A.S.I. under-reads at high altitudes because of the reduction in the density of the air with an increase in height. However, the indicated stalling speed and, therefore, the best indicated cruising speed remain the same although the true speed is higher. This increase is approximately 1.75 per cent of the indicated speed per 1,000 feet of height. The glider cruising at 10,000 feet has the advantage of an increase in cruising speed of 17.5 per cent and this is a very welcome help on long flights. (This increase also results in an increase in the normal rate of sink of an equivalent amount since the gliding angle remains the same.)

Above 10,000 feet it is important to limit the indicated speed so that the true airspeed is kept below the 'placard' speed (Vne). Otherwise there may be a serious risk of flutter and structural failure.

Changes in temperature can also cause errors as they affect the density of the air, but these can be ignored except for test flying purposes or for special high altitude cross-countries.

It is important to realise that large errors can occur with a pot pitot when the glider is yawing. For example, in spins and side slips the indicator needle usually moves back through the zero position to read a fictitious speed until the glider resumes normal flight.

Position errors are nearly all caused by errors in measuring the static pressure. Typically there may be an error of one or two knots at low speeds increasing to up to ten knots at Vne. If the error is small it can be ignored altogether.

The position errors should be taken into account when calculating the optimum cruising speeds for a 'speed to fly' ring. If the performance curve used for these calculations is in 'equivalent' airspeed, the corrections for position errors can be applied to give the corresponding 'indicated' airspeed for use in flight. A graph of the position errors will be found in the glider handbook.

If a change is made in the position or type of pitot or static heads, it is important to check whether the position errors have changed. Otherwise it is conceivable that the glider might be flown at a true speed above the maximum for which it has been designed although the indicated speed may not exceed the 'Placard' speed in the cockpit.

The position error on a towing aircraft may be as much as 8 or 10 knots at low speeds because of the nose-up attitude of the tug. It is this position error which often accounts for the large difference in indicated speeds between the tug and glider and sometimes accounts for the rather fast tows some tug pilots give.

Airspeed 'lag'. If the airspeed indicator is serviceable, it has little lag in recording changes in speed. However, the 'lag' in the airspeed is frequently referred to in gliding, and this really refers to the time taken for the glider or aircraft to change its speed following a change in attitude. When the attitude of the glider is changed, e.g. if the nose is lowered, the inertia of the glider makes it continue at the original speed for a short time before gradually gaining speed. Eventually, a steady speed is reached depending on the steepness of the attitude.

A further source of error may be leakage in the tubing and connections between the pitot head and the instrument. These should be checked over periodically, and the tubing replaced if it shows signs of deterioration. A useful test for the system and instrument is to seal off the open end of the pressure head with a finger and rub the tube hard. The frictional heating expands the air inside the tube and operates the A.S.I. over the range normally used when gliding. On no account should blowing directly down the pitot tube be resorted to as this will cause damage.

The altimeter

The altimeter is a sensitive type of aneroid barometer calibrated to read heights in feet or metres. On the modern altimeter, the indication is given by clock-like hands. The large hand reads in hundreds of feet, one rotation indicating 1,000 feet; the hour hand indicates thousands of feet and a very small pointer indicates tens of thousands of feet. This type of calibration enables the instrument to be read quickly and apparently down to the nearest 10 feet. However, a glider in flight does not provide enough vibration for the instrument to read absolutely accurately because of the friction in the lever system, etc. This friction can be overcome by gently tapping the instrument panel (NOT the instrument itself) but, since an exact indication of height is seldom necessary, it is better practice to allow for the instrument error of 50 – 100 feet during descents and to judge the height above the ground by eye for the approach and landing.

The altimeter can be set before take-off to read either the height of the airfield above sea level for cross-country flights, or to zero feet for local flying. A setting of 1013 mb is standard in airways.

Quite serious errors can be caused during the course of a flight by changes in atmospheric pressure. These are particularly important if the flight is over a long distance as the pressure may change by 10 or 20 millibars making a difference in reading of hundreds of feet. If the altimeter is set before take-off, it will not read correctly over ground of different height and it is, therefore, worse than useless for making approaches into strange fields. In fact, it is unwise to get into the habit of using it below a height of about 500 feet where the pilot's judgement is more dependable at all times.

Like the A.S.I., errors are caused by both changes in temperature and static pressure errors. However, static pressure errors are so small that it is not unusual to leave the altimeter open to the cockpit pressure. This avoids any possibility of it becoming iced up or blocked in flight.

Most altimeters are calibrated on the assumption that the atmosphere has a regular reduction in temperature with height.

In practice the temperature varies considerably, causing errors in the altimeter readings at height. These are seldom of importance or interest to the glider pilot except in the case of height record attempts.

The variometer

The most important instrument carried in the glider on soaring flights is the variometer. This is a very sensitive rate-of-climb-and-descent indicator which enables the pilot to detect rising air and to find the position of the best 'lift'.

The operation of the variometer, like the altimeter, is dependent on the change of atmospheric pressure with height. The variometer, however, measures the rate of change of pressure as the glider gains or loses height. Most glider instruments consist of a flow meter which is connected to a thermos flask acting as a capacity.

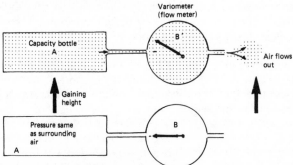

66. The variometer. When climbing, the atmospheric pressure drops so that air flows out of the capacity. In level flight the pressure in the capacity equals that in the surrounding air. No air flows so the variometer reads zero.

As height is gained, air flows from the thermos through the instrument which measures the rate of flow and indicates it as a rate of climb. When height is lost the pressure inside the flask is less than the outside atmosphere and air flows through the instrument and into the flask. Obviously for low rates of climb and descent the amount of air involved is minute and it is surprising that it can be detected by mechanical means.

One of the best types of mechanical instruments is the vane type. It consists of a cylindrical chamber with a very close-fitting vane mounted on jewelled bearings and centralised by means of a hair spring. The air flowing to or from the thermos is directed in a jet against the vane, deflecting it round and moving the indicator needle. Carefully shaped slots below the vane provide an escape for the air so that the position of the vane regulates the size of the outlet. The whole instrument is a masterpiece of precision and it is sensitive and has very little time lag. The circular dial and regular calibration makes it particularly suitable for determining the best speeds to fly between thermals, since a movable 'speed to fly' ring can be mounted round the face of the instrument as in Fig. 109 on page 283.

Many of the earlier mechanical variometers have been superseded by electrically operated ones because of their quicker response and better sensitivity. In some of these instruments the flow of air is detected by its cooling effect on thermistors. Changes in their resistance are amplified and shown on a sensitive meter. The time lag and inconsistencies associated with overcoming the friction of the vane are avoided and both very small and large rates of flow can be accurately measured.

The range of the instrument can be varied electrically to suit the strength of the lift by means of a switch changing the amplification. Furthermore, a simple attachment can be fitted to give audible indications of lift from a small loudspeaker. This is particularly valuable in difficult conditions near the ground or in a crowded thermal when it might be dangerous to concentrate on watching the instruments.

Another advantage of the electric variometers is that they can be incorporated into a much more sophisticated electronic system. For example, with some the average rate of climb can be continuously computed so that the pilot can see how efficiently he is climbing. At the touch of a switch he can select either the normal variometer readings or an indication of what the air mass itself is doing, and often the best speed to fly is presented by a simple indicator telling him to increase or decrease speed through the sinking or rising air.

Electric variometers are very reliable and will operate for many days' flying on a small torch battery. However, because of the faster response the installation is more critical and a poor one may cause excessive fluctuations which can be very confusing. For example, these instruments should not be coupled direct with the same static source as the A.S.I. or changes in speed may cause false readings on the variometer as the capsule of the A.S.I. expands and contracts sending small pulses of air along the tube.

It is difficult to achieve accurate results in all conditions and, for this reason, most pilots use two variometers: usually a vane type with a 'speed to fly ring' for using in cruising flight between thermals and an electric instrument with audio for centring in the lift. This is a good insurance against the possibility of instrument failure, besides giving the pilot the reassurance that the systems are working accurately.

Variometers may be calibrated in knots, feet or metres per second according to personal preference. However, if the A.S.I. is also in knots, the gliding angle can be assessed by dividing the estimated ground speed by the rate of descent (e.g. headwind 10 knots, speed 60 knots, rate of sink 2 knots . . . gliding angle is $60 - 10 \div 2 = 25 : 1$). Conveniently 1 knot equals almost exactly 100 feet per minute so that if the height gained is timed for 30 seconds or a minute the rate of climb can be found without calculation (e.g. 550 feet gained in 1 minute is 5.5 knots).

Inaccuracies in either the variometer or the A.S.I. will lead to flying at inefficient speeds and even to making wrong decisions. To fly with confidence, these instruments should be recalibrated every year so that any errors are known and can be taken into account.

Since no two installations are identical, it is a great advantage to practise regularly with the same aircraft and instruments.

Total energy compensation

A variometer should enable the pilot to fly the glider into the strongest part of the lift. Inaccuracies in flight caused by the turbulent air or by poor piloting result in a change of airspeed and affect the readings on an ordinary variometer. If the nose of the glider is raised for a moment, the glider will tend to gain height as the speed decreases. This will be indicated as a reduced rate of sink or a gain of height and will be registered on the variometer. Similarly, if the nose of the glider is lowered the variometer will show an increase in the rate of descent. These indications of climb and descent can very easily be mistaken for a sign that the glider has flown into rising or sinking air. The false indication of climbing which is caused by a backward movement on the stick is known as 'stick lift'. (See Fig. 69(a) on page 160.)

The total energy variometer is a variometer which is compensated to eliminate any apparent lift or sink caused by changes of airspeed.

Since it is usual to fly faster between thermals and to slow down as the lift is encountered, the normal variometer gives very misleading indications of strong lift as the speed is reduced. These can easily result in the pilot wasting time on non-existent or poor lift.

Any type of instrument can be converted to total energy by fitting a

Brunswick tube or venturi. These produce an exact amount of suction
and are connected to the static side of the variometer. (Fig. 67.)

In flight at a steady speed, the suction produced by the venturi is
constant and the variometer is unaffected and reads the normal rate of
descent.

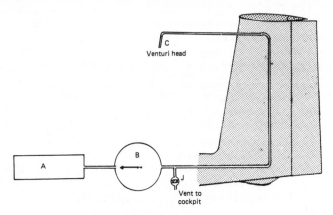

67. Total energy compensation.

If the speed is increasing at any particular moment, the nose of the glider
is lower than the normal position for steady flight at that speed. This results
in the glider having a higher rate of descent than would normally occur
at that speed in a steady glide. However, with the total energy variometer,
the increase in speed also increases the suction at the venturi and this
exactly compensates for the increased rate of descent caused by the
changing speed. It follows that at any given moment while the speed is
changing, the variometer reads as though the glider were flying steadily
at the speed indicated at that moment.

It is, therefore, possible to assess the position of the lift even though
the glider is being flown inaccurately or while slowing down after flying
at speed through a down-draught.

The ordinary variometer indicates a rate of change of height, i.e. the
change in potential energy of the glider. The venturi corrects for changes
in speed or kinetic energy of the glider. The total energy variometer
indicates the combination of changes in potential and kinetic energy.

Unfortunately, the airflow in a thermal has horizontal gradients or gusts,
and the total energy variometer responds to any increase in speed by
indicating a higher rate of climb or less sink as if the nose has dropped.
In this way horizontal gusts give misleading indications of lift or sink and
these are often as much as 4 or 5 knots. This can be overcome by fitting
a restriction or gust filter in the tube between the instrument and the total
energy device. A time lag of several seconds will eliminate most of the

effects of horizontal gusts without effecting the total energy correction for normal speed changes.

In principle it is most efficient to slow down in lift and to speed up in sinking air. The amount depends on the strength of the lift and sink, and can be determined by using a MacCready speed to fly ring on the variometer (see Fig. 109, page 283). However, with an ordinary total energy variometer the correct speeds to fly have to be found by a series of approximations. For example, if the MacCready ring shows that the cruising speed should be 65 knots, as the speed is increased to that figure, the rate of descent of the glider increases, calling for an even faster cruising speed. After several corrections the two will eventually coincide, but the process of adjustment must start again as soon as any lift or sink occurs. This problem can be avoided if the variometer shows the movements of the air instead of the climb and descent of the glider. The ring will then indicate the correct speed immediately. This is then known as an AIRMASS or NETTO variometer.

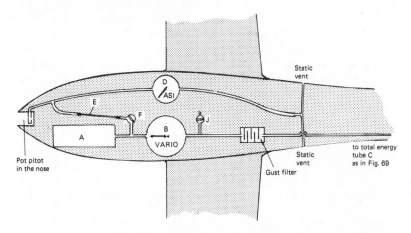

68. The air mass or Netto variometer. The normal total energy system is coupled to the airspeed pressure head or pot pitot in the nose. E is a fine capillary tube leaking air into the variometer system. F is a pneumatic switch to cut off the leak to allow the pilot to select either air mass or a normal reading. A gust filter is incorporated to smooth out the effects of gusts.

In addition, while flying at high speed between thermals, this makes it much easier to tell if the glider is flying through lift. With an airmass or Netto variometer, immediately the variometer needle moves up above the zero, the pilot knows that he is in rising air and can start to slow down. With a normal total energy variometer the pilot must guess what the normal rate of descent would be at that particular speed and deduce the strength of the lift, a tedious and often inaccurate procedure.

Being able to recognise even weak areas of rising air while flying at high speed enables the pilot to slow down and conserve height. Height is also saved by recognising the sinking air immediately and speeding up through it. In this way the gliding range between thermals can be greatly increased, making Dolphin techniques worthwhile in quite low-performance machines.

A simple and inexpensive method of making the variometer read air mass is the MacCready leak. Air is leaked from the airspeed pitot head through a fine valve or capillary tube to the capacity side of a normal total energy variometer. The leak is arranged so that *in still air* at any airspeed the variometer reads zero instead of the normal rate of descent of the glider. As the speed is increased, more air flows through the capillary, maintaining the zero reading in spite of the greater rate of descent of the glider.

The only problem with using airmass or Netto is that it is too easy for the pilot to make the mistake of starting to circle when the variometer reads 1 or 2 knots up. This would probably result in a gradual descent instead of the hoped-for climb because, of course, the glider's rate of sink while circling will probably be more than that amount. To avoid this confusion it is normal to have a switch to enable the pilot to change from airmass back to a normal reading for the climbs and to use the airmass setting only for straight cruising. With a flapped machine this switch can be coupled to the flap lever so that when the flaps are lowered for circling flight the variometer is switched automatically to the normal thermalling mode.

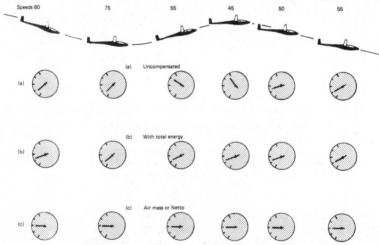

69. The effects of diving and zooming in normal air. (a) On a normal variometer. The variometer indicates very high rates of climb and descent known as 'stick' lift. (b) With total energy compensation. Stick lift is eliminated and the vario indicates what it would if flying steadily. (c) With air mass or NETTO. The vario reads zero at all times unless the air mass is moving up or down.

A further small modification with an electric variometer turns it into a *flight director* to indicate what the pilot should do to fly at the correct speed from moment to moment. The pilot has to set his estimate of the rate of climb (like setting the 'speed to fly' ring) and the instrument needle then indicates whether more or less speed is required to reach the optimum cruising speed for the conditions. In sinking air the needle will move down telling the pilot to go faster and as the correct speed is reached the needle will read zero. Combined with an audio device, this enables the pilot to vary the speed accurately without reference to the instruments, flying faster through the sink and slowing down in the lift.

Some directors are arranged so that at low speeds they switch automatically to indicate the rate of climb that can be expected if the pilot decides to circle and use the lift. This makes it even easier to decide whether to circle or carry straight on at low speed to a better area of lift.

Electronic systems measuring the speed and height changes by pressure-measuring transducers have revolutionised competitive gliding. These provide accurate total energy and other information such as the average rates of climb, the distance already covered and the height required to glide to a destination.

All this exotic variometry can be very expensive and beyond the means of many pilots. However, it costs very little to have really good total energy compensation and this together with airmass or Netto must be considered an essential minimum if the pilot is to get the best out of any glider.

The turn and slip indicator

The turn and slip indicator is the most important instrument for blind flying. It is fitted to aircraft as a standby to use when the limitations of pitch or roll for the artificial horizon have been exceeded. The turn and slip indicator is exceptionally reliable and does not become unusable even if its limitations are exceeded in flight, since it recovers immediately.

It consists of two instruments mounted in a single case: the rate of turn indicator, which is a gyroscopically operated indicator showing the direction and rate of turn, and the slip indicator, which is a simple ball bearing in a liquid-filled glass tube.

a. The rate of turn indicator
This is operated by an electrically driven gyroscope mounted so that it can only tilt in the rolling plane, and having the axis of the rotor parallel to the lateral axis of the aircraft. Rolling movements of the gyro are controlled by a spring and damping system. When the aircraft changes direction, the yawing movement causes the gyro to precess and tilt against the tension in the spring, so that the angle of movement is proportional to the rate of turn. The indicating needle connected to the gyro gimbal

registers against the scale showing the actual rate of turn. Adjustments can be made to the spring to calibrate the instrument so that a rate 1 turn is a turn of 450° per minute. Ordinary powered aircraft instruments are calibrated to indicate a rate 1 turn as a turn of 180° per minute and are unsuitable for gliding unless they are readjusted to reduce their sensitivity or are run at lower rotor speeds.

Turn indicators for gliders are driven by a battery-operated electric motor forming the rotor, and these are regulated to maintain a constant speed for a large variation in voltage of the battery. Ordinary dry batteries are sufficient power for many hours' operation but care must be taken to check them on the ground to ensure that there is no possibility of the battery failing in use. Immediately after changing the batteries a test should be made to ensure that they have been connected correctly, since reversed connections result in reversed indications. When the instrument is switched on, swinging the glider to the left should make the needle show a movement to the left. The batteries should preferably be of a type fitted with terminals since there must be no chance of a poor connection at any time.

Earlier types of instruments are operated by a gyro rotated by jets of air. The air is drawn into the instrument by suction from a venturi tube mounted in the airflow. This type of instrument has several disadvantages on gliders although it is used in many powered aircraft where the suction can be provided by an engine-driven pump. Unless the venturi tube is large enough, the necessary airflow cannot be obtained at the low normal flying speeds of the glider. Furthermore, because of its size, the venturi causes high drag and may easily become iced up, rendering it useless just at the time when the turn indicator is absolutely vital.

Most faults occurring in the electrically operated turn indicator are caused by poor connections, unsatisfactory switches and flat batteries. However, after a great deal of running the carbon brushes in the instrument may fail to make good contact on the commutator and cause inconsistent starting and running. Since the instrument must be completely dust-free it should not be opened and tampered with except in dust-free conditions.

b. The slip or balance indicator

The slip or balance indicator consists of a steel ball in a liquid-filled tube. When the aircraft is standing on the ground with the wings level, the ball should come to rest in the central position. Whenever the flight is unbalanced, the needle or ball of the slip indicator shows a deviation from the central position, caused by the offset loading on the ball. In a correctly balanced turn the ball is held in position by the centrifugal force produced by the turn.

The ball in the tube is an exceptionally simple and foolproof device which does not stick or give trouble. The liquid, together with a slight bow in the tube, damps out any tendency for the ball to oscillate excessively in turbulent conditions.

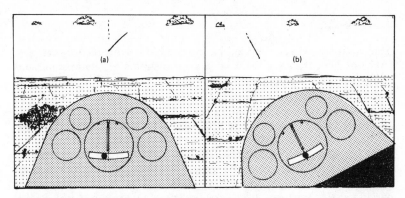

70. The slip indicator and yaw string. (a) In skidding flight, with the ball out to the left and the yaw string to the right, more left rudder (or less left rudder) is required to swing the fuselage into line with the airflow. (b) In accurate turns, both ball and yaw string are exactly central.

The turn and slip indicator is seldom used in a glider except for flying in cloud or very poor visibility. A 'yaw string', consisting of a few inches of flexible wool taped at one end to the canopy, gives a far more accurate and reliable indication of slip and skid at glider speeds.

It should be exactly in the middle in straight flight or in any turn. At any time that it is off to the left-hand side, a little more right rudder is needed to re-centralise it.

The position of the wool tuft can be significant and the best position can be found by putting two or three separate yaw strings along the centre line of the canopy and selecting the best one by trial. In a poor position the string will be slow to return to the middle position after recovering from a slight yaw.

Errors in the indications of the turn and slip indicator
An incorrect rate of turn will be indicated by the instrument if, for some reason, the speed of the gyro rotor is too low, although the indications will remain in the correct sense. If the battery driving the instrument is running down, the sound of the rotor revolving is noticeably different and the instrument will under-read the rate of turn. When this happens the pilot should use only a small rate of turn to prevent the true rate of turn becoming excessive, and he should seek clear air before the battery fails altogether. A second, standby battery eliminates this worrying possibility.

During the recovery from 'dives' or 'spirals' any slight rate of turn is greatly exaggerated by the change of direction in the pull out from the dive. In this way, even a slight turn during a recovery from a dive will be indicated as a high rate of turn. As soon as the loading is reduced again, the correct rate of turn will be shown.

The compass

The compass is an essential instrument for flying across country. Unfortunately, the normal aircraft type of compass has many limitations and errors which make it difficult to maintain an accurate course. Most inexperienced pilots greatly underestimate the difficulty of flying on a compass course.

The normal type of compass used in gliders is of the 'wall' type and is fitted on to the instrument panel. It consists of one or more small bar magnets suspended in a liquid-filled container. Attached to the magnet system is a small drum engraved with the cardinal points of the compass and in divisions of 5 or 10 degrees. These can be read through a glass window so that the reading of the scale against a line on the window gives an accurate indication of the magnetic heading of the aircraft. The liquid, which is usually alcohol, helps to damp out the oscillations of the compass.

Magnetic and true north

Magnetic north is some distance from the geographical North Pole about which the earth rotates, so that the compass magnet does not point towards true north. A correction known as variation must be applied to any 'true' heading measured on a map, to give the equivalent 'magnetic' heading. Lines joining places with equal variation are marked on most maps so that the correct average variation for a particular flight can be ascertained. Owing to the continuously changing location of the earth's magnetic field, the variation marked on the map is subject to a slight yearly change but this can be ignored.

The method of applying the correction can be easily remembered by the rhyme:

1 . 7   Variation West—Magnetic Best (i.e. greater than True)
       Variation East—Magnetic Least.

For example, the variation for the London area is 6° west (1986) and is subject to a change of about 8″ per year. Since it is impractical to fly to that degree of accuracy, 6° west would be a quite satisfactory correction for the next few years.

Deviation

Deviation, another source of error in the aircraft compass, is caused by the magnetic influence of metal components in the aircraft itself or the electro-magnetic field set up by some electrical instruments. The compass should not be mounted close to these instruments or it may not maintain the correct reading when they are switched on.

Deviation varies according to the direction in which the aircraft is heading and can be reduced to less than 5° on any heading by a process known as swinging the compass. This is done by taking careful readings on the compass every 45° and comparing them with the reading of a hand-held bearing compass outside the aircraft, so that the errors can be measured. The compass can then be adjusted by means of the corrector magnets in the instrument to reduce the overall error to a minimum. A card of compass deviations can then be made out listing the corrections to be applied to the magnetic readings in order to obtain the correct course to steer on the compass.

Deviation cards are, however, seldom used in gliders although it is highly desirable to swing the compass and reduce the deviation to a minimum if cross-country flying is contemplated since, otherwise, errors of 15° or more may occur.

The process of arriving at the required course to steer on the compass can be summarised as follows:

1. Measure the angle of the track relative to the nearest meridian of longitude or other line running true north and south on the map (example 000° (T)).
2. Apply the variation (000° + 6° = 006° (M)).
3. Apply the deviation if a deviation card is fitted to get the required course compass. (006° (M)) + 4° = 010° (C), where + 4° is the correction for the deviation.)

Although the glider pilot is unlikely to go to this trouble to find the compass course for a certain heading, it should now be clear that the readings of the compass can be considerably different from those intended. Whenever the compass is used, every opportunity should be taken to confirm that the glider is actually heading where the pilot wants to go.

The problem becomes even more complex when an attempt is made to use the compass in flight since it suffers several temporary errors during turns and accelerations, and only reads correctly in steady straight flight.

Acceleration and turning errors
Owing to the type of suspension of the magnet system in the normal type of aircraft compass, any change of speed or bank causes temporary error in the reading of the compass so that until steady, straight flight at a constant speed is resumed, the readings of the compass are of little use.

Summarising these errors, the effects of lowering and raising the nose (gaining or losing speed) are shown in the table.

Magnetic heading	Nose-down effect	Nose-up effect
N	Nil	Nil
S	Nil	Nil
E	Indicates an apparent turn to left	Indicates an apparent turn to right
W	Indicates an apparent turn to right	Indicates an apparent turn to left

(These effects are at a maximum on east and west and decrease to a minimum on north and south.)

Turning errors

If a steady continuous turn is made watching the compass it will be noted that on some headings the movement of the compass is slower and on others much faster than the rate of turn. This makes it difficult to turn onto a definite heading by observing the compass reading. After the turn is stopped the compass may take time to settle to the actual heading which will not, in all probability, be the one required.

These turning errors are at a maximum on northerly and southerly headings and together with acceleration errors make it extraordinarily difficult to come out of a turn on the required course when watching the compass. If before attempting to straighten up on a definite heading the turn is reduced to a gentler one (rate ½ – 1 on gliders) the turning error can be more easily appreciated and allowed for, so that approximately the correct heading can be assumed without delay.

The turning errors are such that the pilot should stop the turn at least 30° before the desired heading if it is in the northern quadrant or about 30° late if it is in the southern quadrant. On easterly or westerly directions there is no turning error, but it takes at least 10° to straighten out from even a gentle turn in a glider and this must be allowed for.

These turning and acceleration errors make it vital to settle down in straight flight for some time before attempting to read the compass. A correction can then be made by turning for a judged length of time. A further check of the compass reading can then be made after allowing it to settle down again. In this way, the glider can be turned onto the desired heading in cloud.

In visual conditions, the errors and fluctuations of the compass are of less consequence as the approximate direction can usually be judged by the position of the sun or landmarks on the ground. However, it is still necessary to be flying straight at a constant speed before reading the instrument.

Special glider compasses

The Cook compass was specially designed for gliding and has few of the errors which make the normal type of compass so difficult to use.

The magnet system is mounted between two bearings so that it is able to rotate but not tilt. This type of suspension eliminates acceleration errors, leaving only the turning errors caused by the angle of 'dip'.

However, when the instrument is mounted so that it can be tilted to be horizontal in relation to the earth's surface in a turn, it is not affected by either acceleration or turning errors. It is then possible to straighten up onto a definite heading after prolonged turning. The pilot must adjust the tilt of the compass during and after each turn, but this is a small inconvenience compared with the advantages gained.

The BOHLI compass has the magnet mounted in the centre of a tiny gimbal so that acceleration errors are completely eliminated.

Like the Cook compass it is necessary to tilt the instrument manually to keep it parallel to the horizon. In that position it indicates the heading very accurately in the turn with virtually no lag. Indication of the heading is given by a tiny bead on the end of a pointer.

During a turn the bead rotates in a circle giving the pilot a very good idea of the angle of bank as well as the heading. These compasses are particularly valuable for cloud flying when it is essential to stop circling on the correct heading.

The artificial horizon

The instruments so far described, the airspeed indicator, altimeter, turn and slip indicator, variometer and compass are sometimes known to powered aircraft pilots as the primary instruments or limited panel. Most powered aircraft are fitted with an artificial horizon and directional indicator which make it much easier to fly accurately by instruments. However, these instruments may often have limitations of pitch and roll which render them useless for recovery from steep attitudes such as spins. If these limitations are exceeded the horizon bar oscillates wildly and it is quite useless until it can be caged and set up again in level flight. The primary instruments are much less likely to fail and, except for their inherent errors, can be relied upon when the artificial horizon and directional indicator have 'toppled' through exceeding their limits.

The artificial horizon shows both the position of the nose and the angle of bank instantaneously so that safe and accurate instrument flight can be maintained by this one instrument alone, in the same way as in visual conditions the glider can be flown by direct reference to the real horizon. Changes in attitude are indicated, and can be corrected before the glider has had time to change speed. This prevents most of the difficulties arising from gusty conditions which may result in loss of control on primary instruments.

Similarly the directional indicator shows a change in direction immediately, and suffers from none of the errors of the compass since it is not magnetic. It requires resetting fairly frequently to indicate the compass heading because it gradually wanders from the correct readings.

Both of these instruments are expensive and when electrically operated require sizeable batteries and a D.C. to A.C. converter in the glider. In spite of these disadvantages many glider pilots use them and consider the weight well worth while because of the ease and the high standard of instrument flying possible when they are fitted.

Air-driven artificial horizon and directional indicators are available but are not recommended because of the drag and risk of icing of the venturi producing the suction to drive them.

Since the artificial horizon can be toppled by allowing the glider to dive or bank very steeply, or may fail through weak batteries, it is essential that glider pilots should be able to fly on the primary instruments alone if they are going to attempt flying in clouds.

The barograph

The barograph is a recording altimeter which is carried in the glider in order to provide a permanent and definite record of the height of the glider throughout the flight. It is compulsory for all the tests for the International Gliding Awards (Silver, Gold and Diamond 'C') and for National and International records.

A barograph is an important part of normal equipment for a modern glider and not just an instrument to be carried on special flights. There is no way of telling when unusual soaring conditions may occur and it is a pity to miss any opportunity for an interesting and perhaps record-breaking flight. For official flights, the instrument must be sealed by an official observer before the flight and remain sealed until it is handed back to an observer after the flight. The trace can then be compared with the calibration chart and the gain of height measured with a pair of dividers. (Club officials and instructors are almost always official observers.)

The instrument consists of an aneroid barometer (or altimeter) recording with a pen onto a revolving drum. A clock mechanism drives the drum at a set rate, usually one revolution every five or ten hours, so that the recording pen traces the height from moment to moment on paper round the drum.

Countless experiences of the unreliability of recording in ink have led to the almost universal use of a pen or stylo tracing on smoked paper or aluminium foil. Ordinary smooth paper smoked over a sooty flame can be used and there is no possibility of the pen failing to leave a clear trace. The barograph chart can be made permanent by dipping the paper into a weak solution of shellac and methylated spirits, or by spraying it with hair lacquer.

Recording on smoked paper has many advantages over the use of a pen and ink. It cannot freeze at high altitudes, or dry up if the instrument is not used for some time. Furthermore, the stylo can give a good trace with only the minimum of pressure (and therefore friction) on the paper. Any barograph can be used with smoked paper without changing the ink pen although a better trace is usually obtained with a specially made stylo.

After smoking the drum, the instrument should be switched on so that the pen is in contact with the paper, and then a base or datum line should be made by turning the drum through a complete revolution. This marks a line from which any measurements of heights can be made. It eliminates

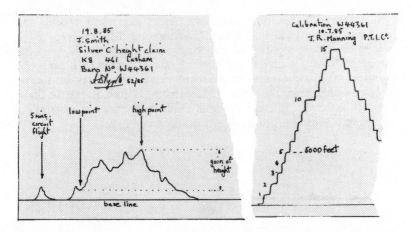

71. Barogram and calibration chart. This barogram shows a typical trace after being certified. A calibration chart enables the Official Observer to check the gain of height accurately.

errors caused by not having the edge of the paper straight or lined up with the edge of the drum. It is not necessary for the base line to be made on the day of the flight as it is only a datum and need not coincide with the trace made on take-off.

For badge and record attempts an Official Observer (usually a club official or instructor) checks and seals the barograph before the flight and unseals and certifies the trace before it is 'fixed' and made permanent.

The barograph is an expensive instrument but it is important to buy one which will be absolutely reliable and will record any height which you are likely to reach in the future. The clockwork mechanism is vital, as a barograph which stops occasionally is worse than useless. Ideally it should run continuously for at least twelve hours, rotating once every five or ten hours, so that it can be started in the morning before the glider leaves the hangar and be left on all day. There is then no possibility of forgetting to switch it on before a flight.

It should record up to about 22,000 feet for normal use and up to 35,000 or 40,000 feet if the glider is likely to be fitted with oxygen equipment. These heights may seem excessive but there have been many cases in the past of the pen going off the top of the drum so that the actual height reached could not be verified after the flight.

Barographs can be seriously damaged by dropping them or by careless handling.

The barograph should be calibrated by taking it to an aircraft instrument testing department and asking them to put it in an altimeter testing chamber. The ideal calibration chart should show a climb and descent from normal sea level pressure in steps of 1,000 feet over the range of the instrument.

All barographs should be recalibrated every year when possible and immediately after Gold or Diamond 'C' heights or height records as the calibration will be needed for checking. Most pilots like to keep the barograph records of their best flights and mount them in their log books together with a few notes about the flight. Barograph charts can also be analysed to determine the actual achieved rates of climb during the flight and it is interesting to compare these results with those of other pilots who were attempting similar flights on the same day.

18 Thermals

Thermals and cumulus clouds—Where to find a thermal—Surface
heating—The contours of the ground—The type of soil and surface—The
wind—Coastal effects—Visible indications of thermals—Stubble fires—
Isolated thermal bubbles

Thermals and cumulus clouds

A thermal is a mass of air which ascends because it contains water vapour
or is warmer and therefore less dense than the air around it.

As the thermal rises, it mixes with the surrounding air and grows larger.
Usually it seems to break away from the ground as a bubble and then
it develops into a doughnut or vortex ring shape which gradually grows
in size as it gains height. In hot climates the thermals may take the form
of long columns, but in British conditions there is ample evidence to
suggest that many of the thermals are of bubble form. (Fig. 76 on page
183.)

The reduction in the atmospheric pressure with height causes both the
thermal and the surrounding air to cool down with height. Unless the
air is very dry, the moisture in the thermal will eventually condense out
to form a cumulus cloud. As this happens, the latent heat absorbed when
the moisture was evaporated on the ground is released. This extra heat
helps to strengthen the lift in the cloud while the cloud is developing.

The life of a cumulus cloud is of particular importance to the glider
pilot. The first sign of the cloud is a patch of milky haze; then wisps of
cloud form which rapidly develop into a firm-looking cloud with a flat
base and rounded top; after about ten minutes, the edges and bottom of
the cloud become ragged and the cloud quickly erodes and disappears.

Sometimes this process is prevented by a fresh thermal revitalising the
cloud or, if the cloud is a large one, it may develop on one side and dissolve
on the other. Large cumulus clouds have a number of cells at different
stages.

(a)   (b)   (c)   (d)

72. The life of a cumulus cloud. (a) Patch of haze. (b) Cloud begins to form. (c) Cloud
fully developed. (d) Cloud evaporating and breaking up.

171

When the air in the cloud starts to descend, the cloud begins to evaporate and this will absorb large quantities of heat. The cooling of the air because of this evaporation will cause strong down-currents. Elsewhere there is a gradual subsidence of the air which compensates for the rising air in the thermals.

The glider pilot must, therefore, learn to distinguish which clouds are still developing, and must try to avoid flying near any which have started to decay.

The stability of the air varies from day to day and governs the strength and height to which the thermals will go. Unstable air produces good thermals with showers or thunderstorms if there is sufficient moisture for their development. Stable air prevents the thermals from penetrating very high.

Cumulus-type clouds occur when the upward movement of the air is rapid and the air is unstable; whereas stratus or layer-type clouds are formed when the air is stable and rises more gradually. For example, layer cloud will form when the air is lifted over rising ground or over a very shallow wedge of colder air, as with the approach of a warm front.

The general characteristics of a thermal vary considerably in different conditions. Some thermals are large and smooth, and others narrow and turbulent. In good conditions the rate of ascent of the air may be as high as 20 feet per second, giving the glider a rate of climb of over 900 feet per minute. (This compares favourably with the rate of climb of a light aircraft.) In thunderstorm conditions rates of climb of 2,000 feet per minute are quite normal.

The size of the thermal is important from the glider pilot's point of view since, to make effective use of it, the glider must be able to keep inside its bounds. Below about 500 – 600 feet most thermals are either too weak or too narrow for the average glider to use effectively. The thermal is drifted downwind as it rises, so that any cumulus cloud formed will be downwind of the thermal source. For example, in a 15 knot wind, with a thermal giving 4 knots rate of climb in the core, the whole bubble may be ascending at less than 3 knots or an angle of only 1 : 5 from the source. However, in the early stages it often rises much more steeply for the first thousand feet or so.

Where to find a thermal

If cumulus-type clouds are forming, clearly the best method of finding a thermal is to search underneath or close to the cloud for the thermal which is producing it. However, on many occasions there are no clouds, and the pilot is forced to transfer his attention to the ground in order to try to determine the most likely place for the production of thermals.

Since the thermal is produced by the air in one area becoming warmer than that surrounding it, it should be possible to decide on the most likely places for this to occur. Unfortunately, there are so many interdependent factors involved that it is impossible to give any rules. However, the pilot who knows the area over which he is gliding has a distinct advantage, since good thermal-producing areas give off thermals at fairly regular intervals on most soarable days.

The factors generally accepted as affecting the source of thermal production are:

The intensity of the heating by the sun and other sources of local heating.
The contours of the ground.
The type of soil, crops, or surface of the ground and the effect of colour contrast of them.
The wind strength and direction.
Coastal effects.

Surface heating

The essential condition for the production of a thermal is that one mass of air should become warmer than the air surrounding it. The actual temperature of the main air mass is unimportant and, in fact, thermals can be found in both tropical and arctic conditions.

When the heat and light waves from the sun strike the ground, some are absorbed and raise the temperature of the surface, but the rest are reflected back into the atmosphere and dissipated. The increase in temperature of the ground will vary with different surfaces and with the intensity of the radiation.

If the heat waves have to pass through a layer of cloud or dust before reaching the earth, a large proportion of them are absorbed and do not reach the ground. A thin layer of cloud or the smoky haze downwind of an industrial town can prevent or seriously limit thermal activity, and these conditions may often act as a barrier preventing progress on a cross-country flight.

During the course of a good soaring day with the development of cumulus clouds, there are often several periods when the cloud develops to such an extent that it completely cuts off the direct sunlight. This results in a period of poor conditions as the cloud disperses and is followed by a gradual improvement to another peak of activity. This 'cycling', or 'over-development' as it is known in gliding circles, spoils many otherwise promising days. It generally occurs when the air is very moist and when the forming cumulus is prevented from developing vertically by a stable layer. Where the cloud forms just below a layer of stable air, the cloud cannot develop upwards and it spreads out rapidly, often forming a complete cover in less than twenty minutes. Usually, on a day when the cumulus cloud develops quickly early in the morning (apparently promising a perfect day for soaring), there is more likelihood of the cloud over-developing, so that by midday conditions will have deteriorated. Only the approach of a drier air mass will prevent this happening.

The shape and form of thermals is very complex and variable and there seem to be no hard and fast rules for their development. However, on a particular day, the position of the best lift will usually be found to be consistent in relation to the clouds and cloud shadows. Even isolated cloud shadows have a significant influence on thermals. The pilot should try to analyse the position of the best lift relative to the cloud on the first few thermals used and see if all the thermals conform to that pattern. If they do, it will save time to go directly to that position under each cloud.

In clear air, very little of the sun's radiation is absorbed before it reaches the ground and the surface heating will be strong. Unfortunately, in anticyclonic conditions, although often the sky is clear and the sun's heat intense, the air may be very stable and the thermals poor or non-existent.

The amount of radiation absorbed by the earth also depends upon the angle at which the sun's rays strike the ground. In winter, the days are very short and by the time that the ground has become warm enough to set off the thermal activity, the sun is beginning to go down again. It is most unusual to get good thermal activity for cross-country flying in Great Britain during the winter months.

In hilly country the surface heating will be much greater on slopes facing south, where the sunlight strikes the ground almost at right angles. This, together with the prevailing south-westerly winds in this country, make a slope facing south or south-west ideal for hill and thermal soaring sites.

Factories, towns and heath fires are reliable thermal sources used by gliders, although compared with the enormous heat output of the sun, the heat from factory chimneys, etc., is small and is seldom sufficient alone to produce continuous thermals either strong or wide enough to be of use to a glider. Even without their artificial means of heating, factories and towns are in themselves good sources of thermals when warmed by the sun, so that in doubtful circumstances it is always worth trying the area just downwind of such places, where the sun's heating is boosted by artificial heat.

If the air is stable, even the hottest factory chimney or sun-scorched area will not provide a useful thermal. It is, therefore, well worth while consulting the nearest meteorological station before announcing a record-breaking cross-country attempt. However, the forecaster, who is used to dealing with powered aircraft, may refer to the conditions as being stable when a thin layer of dry unstable air to 3,000 or 4,000 feet is lying below very stable upper conditions. Such a day might, in fact, give excellent soaring up to that height. (This would happen if the stability of the upper air kept the sky clear of cloud and allowed uninterrupted sunshine.)

The contours of the ground

Usually, high ground or hilly ground is good for producing thermals, and thermals starting from hill-tops are likely to be stronger than those originating from the adjacent valleys. There are several reasons for this. High ground is usually better drained than low-lying land and, therefore, warms up more rapidly. Also, although the sun's radiation will raise the temperature of similar ground in the valley and on the hill-top by the same amount, a thermal leaving the valley will have lost part of its heat by the time it has risen some way above hill-top height. It will therefore be cooler and weaker above that height than a thermal starting from the hill-top.

If warmed air is blown up the slope, it is given the initial upward movement necessary to start it breaking away from the ground. This makes it possible to soar above a suitable hill in very light winds.

Air which has been gradually warmed up may often remain on the ground for some time unless it reaches a high temperature or is disturbed. In windy weather, the layers of air in contact with the ground are constantly being disturbed so that it is difficult for large areas of air to accumulate and warm up sufficiently to produce a good thermal. Where the country is hilly, the warm air is often able to lie undisturbed in the lee of a hill or in any small valleys, and these areas become good thermal sources in windy conditions. These are generally known as 'wind shadow' thermals.

Wind

73. A wind shadow thermal on a south-facing slope sheltered from the wind.

Where a thermal forms and is blown over the top of a ridge of hills, it may be broken up by the strong turbulence or 'curl over' effect just behind the crest of the hill. If the thermal is large, it will reform as soon as it has passed the turbulent area, but in many cases it is broken up so much that it becomes useless for soaring. This phenomenon gives the impression that the thermal has been lost but, if height permits a few minutes' continued circling, the lift may reappear when the glider and thermal have drifted farther downwind.

The increase in surface heating on a south-facing slope has already been mentioned and this effect will become very marked when combined with a 'wind shadow', i.e. when there is a light northerly wind so that the south face of the hill is also in the 'wind shadow'.

The type of soil and surface

The type of soil, the surface and the crops all have a very marked influence on whether a particular area will be a good thermal source. It is difficult to assess this from the air unless the area has much concrete or metal, which always heats up rapidly and is a reliable source of thermals in sunshine.

Sand and chalk soils are good thermal producers whereas clay is generally poor. A study of a geological map is often valuable when planning a long-distance flight. It may indicate the ranges of hills and high ground and will show the changes in subsoil and rock.

Drainage is often the most significant factor of all and even a slight shower will cool the ground sufficiently to prevent thermals forming for some time afterwards.

A dark surface will absorb more heat than a light one, but the effect of this may be offset by the ground being damp or covered by various types of crops which all affect the rate at which the ground will heat up.

Woods are very slow to warm up, and usually are much cooler than any surrounding fields until late in the afternoon. Once they have warmed up, they give off their heat slowly and remain much warmer than their surroundings later on in the day. This is because the trees trap large quantities of air which take a long time to warm up. It is difficult for this air to escape as it is protected from the wind. Thermals from wooded sources generally seem to be large areas of very weak lift which are often best used by cruising without circling. If the woods are extensive, a slight diversion to fly over them may enable the flight to be carried on for many miles at a time late in the day when all other thermal activity has died out.

Long corn and similar crops can trap large quantitites of air and prevent it from breaking away from the ground until it has reached a high temperature, giving good thermals.

A rather interesting example of thermal production is the formation of 'dust devils' on hot summer days. When the surface heating is very intense, and the wind is very light, the surface of the ground reaches extremely high temperatures. If the air is very unstable, a small dust devil may develop in size until it becomes a freak storm or whirlwind capable of damaging buildings or overturning gliders. Special care must be taken to picket gliders securely on hot, calm, thermic days as the surface wind may change without warning and blow over an unattended glider. This is a frequent cause of damage to gliders in the tropics.

The wind

The wind strength and direction is, as already stated, an important factor in determining where thermals will be produced in hilly country.

In open fields, the effect of the wind blowing over a row of trees or other obstructions often disturbs the warm layer of air close to the ground. This is a most noticeable feature on aerodrome sites. Aerodromes are well drained and provide an almost continuous stream of warmed air, which is swept by the wind over the obstructions on the downwind boundary giving a stream of weak lift. This is met on nearly every approach and causes much frustration, as although it comes when the glider is too low to soar it upsets the approach.

High winds make it difficult for large thermals to exist near the ground, although even on the windiest days there may be strong lift just below the cumulus clouds. Since the rising air drifts with the wind as it gains height, it is often dfficult to know the source of a particular thermal. On calm days, the upper wind is frequently quite different from that on the ground so that the path of the thermal may be quite irregular. Searching for thermals above 1,000 feet is, therefore, mostly a matter of trial and error unless there are cumulus clouds developing.

Frequently there will be a large-scale wave motion set up by hills or mountains nearby or even hundreds of miles away. While not strong enough to produce usable lift, the areas where the air is subsiding gradually inhibit the thermal activity and even promising and well-developed cumulus clouds do not 'work' well.

If the wave motion is a little more organised it will sometimes be seen that the lines of cloud are forming across the prevailing wind and not up-and downwind as is normal. In this case it is worth climbing as high as possible under a cloud before moving forward into wind. Quite often it is possible to climb up the face of the cloud in the wave lift and gain many thousands of feet. In these conditions and at any time that there is a distinct shear with height, the thermals are often badly distorted and difficult to stay in. It may be necessary to make a centring move upwind or in a particular direction on almost every turn. Once this has been noticed, the same movement should be tried in every thermal on that day as it will save time and frustration. In normal conditions no such correction is needed as both the glider and the thermal drift together as they gain height.

Coastal effects

The coastline has a pronounced influence on the formation of thermals. The sea temperature is not greatly affected by the sun's heating during the day and remains at an almost constant temperature. In summer the land soon becomes warmer than the sea, but cools down again at night so that it becomes cooler than the sea once the sun has gone down. This causes the sea and land breezes. The cool air from the sea takes some time to warm up enough to produce thermals so that, with an onshore wind, few thermals are formed within about five to fifteen miles of the coast. If the wind is blowing offshore good thermals are possible near the coast and the contrast between the ground and sea temperature produces a band of thermal lift just over the sea. Although sometimes only just strong enough to support a glider, this lift can be used by flying along it without circling, which enables long distances to be covered very quickly. Where the sea breeze meets the normal air mass, the cool air from the sea forms a wedge which forces up the warmer unstable air and produces exceptional soaring conditions along a belt parallel with the coastline. This area of rising air is often marked by a line of larger cumulus cloud or by a line of wispy cumulus cloud forming well below the normal cloud base. Little or no thermal activity is to be found beyond the front. On hot days with light offshore winds, the sea breeze front may penetrate 30 – 40 miles inland during the daytime. It moves inland more rapidly if the coastline is parallel with the prevailing wind and the frontal effect is less marked.

The influence of the coastline is important on long cross-country flights in England, because the coastline usually limits their distance. Gliding sites near the sea are generally poor for thermals unless the wind is blowing offshore, and this restricts cross-country flights.

In winter the sea is often warmer than the land and thermals can and do form out over the sea.

Visible indications of thermals

Often the problem in soaring is to make contact with a thermal from the limited height of the launch. Visible indications of the whereabouts of a thermal will enable the glider pilot to find one more easily, and once a height of 2,000 or 3,000 feet has been reached there is every chance of finding another.

The formation and development of cumulus cloud indicates that a

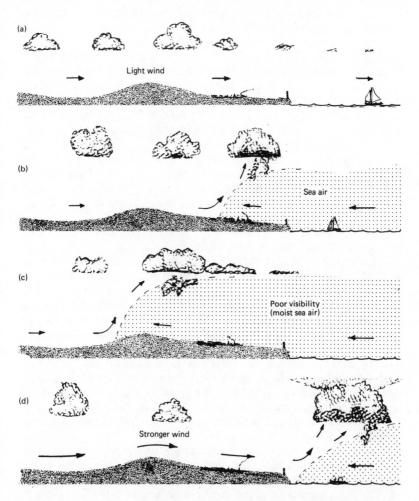

74. The sea breeze front. (a) Light offshore wind in the morning. (b) Slight drop in pressure inland causes sea breeze to move inland. (c) Front continues to move inland with distinctive 'curtain' cloud below the normal cloud base. (d) Stronger offshore wind produces front over the sea.

thermal has recently left the ground. In some conditions cloud does not form but a milky patch of haze may be noticeable if there is not quite enough water vapour to produce a proper cloud. Wearing sunglasses will help to make these haze patches more visible. In conditions when very thin clouds are forming the pilot must aim for the haze patch before it becomes distinct wisps of cloud. By the time that the cloud has formed the lift may be finished and only sinking air will be found. These clouds should therefore be avoided.

Birds are keen on thermal soaring and have an uncanny instinct for finding thermals. Circling birds are a sure sign of rising air although quite often the area of the lift is too small to be of much use. Swallows flying high indicate lift and, in fact, few birds take the trouble to climb high except by using thermals.

The observant glider pilot can gain a great deal from watching the birds and sharing their thermals. It is always worth while to move into their part of the lift even if you are climbing rapidly. If, by chance, you happen to be going up faster than they are, they will be quick to join you. If there are a large number of birds, or several groups, they will all join those in the best area of lift. This is noticeable abroad where there are more soaring birds, and Philip Wills has referred to the habits of the vultures who fly for miles to join other birds in a good thermal.

If the thermal is strong, dust and pieces of paper may be carried up giving a clear indication of its position.

Perhaps one of the most noticeable indications of thermals leaving the ground on a comparatively calm day is the variation in surface wind. The occasional cool breeze felt on a summer day is the air moving in to take the place of that rising in a thermal. Since it blows in towards the thermal, it is possible for a glider, taking off within a short time, to fly over to the area and find the lift. The indications of two or three wind socks placed round the field will also show changes when a thermal leaves the ground near by, and in a similar way smoke gives an excellent indication.

If the crops are long, the passage of a thermal as it leaves the ground can be seen by the disturbance of the crop, or if the heating is strong enough, by the formation of a dust devil or whirlwind. And, of course, the sight of smoke rising from a freshly lit stubble fire is a clear invitation to divert to it and use the lift there.

Various methods of marking a thermal with strips of paper, smoke puffs, confetti, etc., have been tried, but since the variometer gives ample evidence of the presence of the thermal, there seems little point in marking it. The main need is for some means of finding it in the first place.

Even on days with no cloud, the lift and sink will tend to lie in 'streets' lying up- and downwind. Using this fact you can greatly increase your prospects of finding lift by noting the position of other gliders circling in the neighbourhood. Often there are gliders climbing in several separate areas of lift giving a subtle clue that there is a thermal street running up- and downwind between them. Although these gliders will be out of range from you, it will be worth while flying across the line between them rather than making a random search elsewhere. Usually lift will be found, and then after a brief climb it may be possible to fly up or down the 'street' to join one of the other gliders if they are still climbing well.

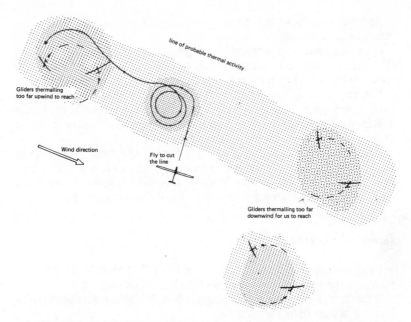

Gliders thermalling
too far upwind to reach

line of probable thermal activity

Wind direction

Fly to cut
the line

Gliders thermalling too far
downwind for us to reach

75. Using lift 'streets'. In blue conditions, use other gliders to indicate possible lift streets.

Stubble fires

Although the farmers are discouraged from burning off unwanted straw and stubble, stubble fires do produce incredibly strong thermals. Usually the initial blaze draws all the warmed up air from the surrounding fields and for about five minutes the lift is terrific. Then the fire dies down again and the smoke ceases to rise much and any lift is weak and broken. This cycle may be repeated a number of times until all the field has burnt.

Always double-check that you, and everything else in the glider, are securely tied down. The turbulence can be frightening! Experience shows that it is most unwise to enter the smoke from a stubble fire at low altitude. Even flying with extra speed it is quite common to be thrown completely out of control and speed fluctuations of up to 20 knots can result in the glider becoming completely stalled without warning.

Always check that there is a suitable field for a landing close at hand before entering the smoke plume. If it proves difficult to get into the lift properly, the nearby sink is so strong that after one or two circles attempting to centre you may find yourself on an approach to land.

Rates of climb of over 2,000 feet per minute are possible and the extremes of lift and sink and the narrowness of the lift make it dangerous to circle anywhere close to other machines.

At times the smoke may be very thick and eventually it usually turns into a dense cumulus cloud.

Quite large pieces of soot and burning straw are often carried up several thousand feet and collect along the leading edge of the wing and tail. These spoil the laminar flow and ruin the performance just like rain or insects.

Flying in stubble fires is not for the faint-hearted and it is good advice to try to get some experience dual before attempting it solo. You can have a really wild and frightening ride with the airframe creaking and groaning as it is heaved about by the violent turbulence.

It is comforting to know that if you keep well below 75 knots, the turbulence, however strong, will not cause damage. Several times I have been in a glider flying at over 50 knots and had it suddenly stop flying and fall several hundred feet because of a sudden loss of speed.

Isolated thermal bubbles

Most of our thermals seem to break away from the ground as bubbles and probably develop an internal motion like a vortex ring. (Fig. 76.)

If that is so, it certainly helps to explain some of the curious things which seem to occur when thermalling.

One of the problems is that the effects of any horizontal gusts causing a change in the airspeed can so easily be misinterpreted as rising or sinking air. For example, it is difficult to tell the difference between meeting a sudden gust which increases the airspeed and being lifted by rising air. The pilot feels them both as a surge of lift. Since the gusts cause changes in airspeed, the total energy compensator picks them up and makes the variometer register extra lift unless the gusts are filtered out. Without a gust filter the variometer will show very high fluctuating readings.

In fact the effects of flying into a gust will be an increase in speed and this increases the wing lift, checking the descent or increasing the rate of climb for a few seconds. Even an experienced pilot is likely to think he has flown into lift.

Since most thermals have both horizontal gusts and areas of strong-up draughts, centring in thermals is still very much a matter of trial and error.

Unless the bubble is rising very slowly, gliders entering the thermal are carried up rapidly in the strong, central core to the 'cap', where they collect, climbing slowly together. In this way gliders may soar for long periods without falling out of a thermal, even if it is only 500 to 1,000 feet deep.

In the base region, the inflow helps to centre the glider and improves the climb when the bank is steep. Bad centring results in false variometer readings and misleading sensations as the glider meets the inflow and gains speed and height. These tell the pilot that there are two areas of lift, the centre of the thermal, and the place where the inflow is met head-on.

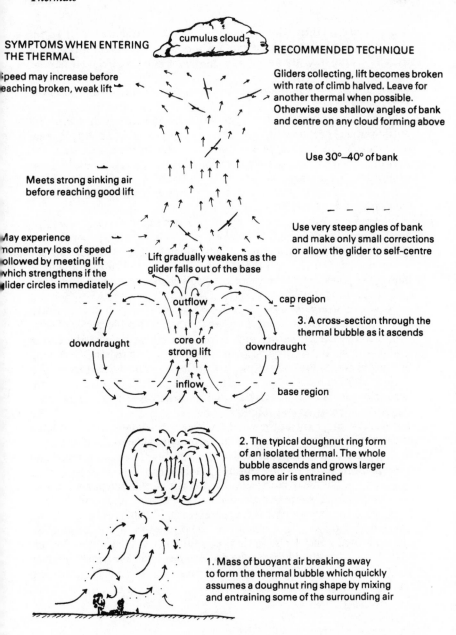

SYMPTOMS WHEN ENTERING
THE THERMAL

cumulus cloud

RECOMMENDED TECHNIQUE

Speed may increase before
reaching broken, weak lift

Gliders collecting, lift becomes broken
with rate of climb halved. Leave for
another thermal when possible.
Otherwise use shallow angles of bank
and centre on any cloud forming above

Use 30°–40° of bank

Meets strong sinking air
before reaching good lift

May experience
momentary loss of speed
followed by meeting lift
which strengthens if the
glider circles immediately

Use very steep angles of bank
and make only small corrections
or allow the glider to self-centre

Lift gradually weakens as the
glider falls out of the base

outflow   cap region

3. A cross-section through the
thermal bubble as it ascends

downdraught   core of   downdraught
               strong lift

inflow   base region

2. The typical doughnut ring form
of an isolated thermal. The whole
bubble ascends and grows larger
as more air is entrained

1. Mass of buoyant air breaking away
to form the thermal bubble which quickly
assumes a doughnut ring shape by mixing
and entraining some of the surrounding air

76. Isolated thermal bubbles.

When entering a thermal, the base can sometimes be identified by a drop in airspeed just before the lift is found. Unless a turn is started immediately, the misleading indications of better lift ahead will take the pilot beyond the real centre.

Notice that in these thermals the best lift is usually to be found near to the stronger sink.

In the cap region, the turbulent mixing of the air together with the outflow makes centring difficult and the rate of climb is, at best, the rate of ascent of the bubble, or less than half that in the core. Again the horizontal gradients can cause problems. Entering this region, the increase in speed caused by meeting the outflow gives an impression of lift before the real lift has been reached. A turn at this moment just results in a frustrating loss of height.

Whenever possible, the cap should be left without delay in search of another core. In good conditions, several gliders bunched together circling mark a cap, and usually at that level it would only be worth while slowing down and passing through the thermal. However, when the bunching gliders are above your level there is a good chance of finding their core and of climbing quickly to their level.

These characteristics also occur in cloud. The easiest climbs are made by entering the cloud in strong lift when the thermal is self-centring. Then, after a while, the lift becomes more broken and weaker and the glider is often thrown out of the side of the cloud as the cap region is reached. Starting in poor lift usually results in a difficult and unsatisfactory climb.

Since all gliders in a thermal tend to collect in the cap within a few minutes, there is a serious risk of collision when even two gliders enter the same cloud at several minutes' interval.

If the rate of ascent of the whole bubble is less than the rate of sink of the circling glider, a gain of height is only possible in the core of the thermal. Even then the glider is, in fact, gradually sinking down through the bubble instead of rising through it to the cap.

Where the bubble is rising rapidly, the glider will not remain in the core for very long before being carried up to the other gliders in the cap. However, a number of short and apparently rapid climbs seldom achieve a very high average rate of climb because of the time spent looking for lift and centring each time. In these conditions it will pay to come lower so that fewer, longer climbs can be made. These will give a much higher average rate of climb but an increased risk of landing if the expected thermal is weak or non-existent.

19 Thermal soaring

Searching for thermals—Centring methods—Tightening on the surge—
Moving away from the sink—Straightening up on the surge—Blue days—
Safety in thermals—Hints for beginners

Searching for thermals

If the glider is launched by aerotow to several thousand feet on an unstable
day, on most occasions it will meet a thermal during its descent. In the
same way, where ridge soaring is possible, the glider is able to keep flying
until contact is made with a thermal.

However, when launching by winch or autotow from a flat site, there
is very little time to search for a thermal and a sensible search can greatly
improve the chances of finding one. It is clear that there is an element
of luck in finding a thermal on any particular flight. The luck element
is, however, greatly overrated, and it is usual to find that in good conditions
a skilled pilot will find and be able to make use of a thermal at least on
every other launch, whereas the unskilled pilot may try all day without
success.

The situation is much the same on a cross-country flight once the glider
is down to about a thousand feet or so. A thermal must be found and used
efficiently or a field landing will be inevitable.

Since at least 500 feet of height is needed to use thermals safely, it is
obvious that the height gained on the launch is of great importance. A
glider launched to 1,500 feet instead of 1,000 feet will have double the
chance of finding a thermal.

On many occasions, strong turbulence and an abnormally high rate of
climb at the top of a winch or car launch may indicate that the glider has
been launched into a thermal. In this case it is always worth while circling
immediately after release in the hope of flying back into the area of lift.
It is not advisable to release before the full launch height has been gained
as the extra height increases the chance of the thermal being large enough
to be used easily.

It should be obvious that the glider with a flat gliding angle will be
able to search a larger area for a given launch height. Although even an
open primary glider can use thermals, the chances of it finding them are
poor, and only a strong thermal will result in a climb.

A comparatively inefficient glider with a low normal flying speed can
often outclimb the high-performance sailplanes with their higher speed
and consequent larger turning radius. This is because the slower glider

185

is able to fly in the narrow core of very strong lift without using excessive angles of bank. However, the high-performance craft has a greater gliding range and, therefore, has a greater chance of finding a thermal in the first place and needs fewer thermals to cover a certain distance.

Thermals are often produced at fairly regular intervals from a definite source on the ground, and when this occurs it is possible to gain height in one thermal and then fly upwind to pick up the next of the series. In windy weather it may be necessary to do this several times before sufficient height is gained to glide to the next good thermal source. In these conditions the clouds may form into definite cloud streets so that once height has been gained, rapid progress can be made along the line of clouds without losing height for many miles. Good progress can be made across wind on days with parallel cloud streets by gaining height along one street before hopping across to the next one. The air between the cloud streets is usually descending and should be crossed as quickly as possible.

If no thermal is found during the flight, the glider must be in a position to make a normal approach and landing. If one is found, the glider should be able to climb as high as possible before drifting downwind of the field. Ideally, then, the search should be made upwind of the launch point so that the wind will gradually drift the glider down the field as it gains height. At any time, the circuit may be joined without the necessity for a complicated approach and the need for S-turns.

The pilot must be able to fly the glider smoothly at a steady speed and be able to enter turns quickly and accurately. He must also cultivate the ability to read the variometer at a glance so that he can fly accurately, keep a sharp lookout for other aircraft, and at the same time keep a constant picture of the variometer readings.

The reading of the variometer just after release should be ignored. The variometer will often show a climb which can easily be mistaken for a thermal. If no lift is encountered at the top of the launch and no particular area is favoured as a likely thermal source, a systematic search should be made upwind of the airfield.

At low altitudes or whenever the conditions look poor, the glider should be flown at the speed for best gliding angle so that the maximum amount of air is covered. If the rate of sink of the glider is abnormally high, indicating that the glider is flying through sinking air, height will be conserved by flying a little faster for a few moments to reach better conditions. If rising air is encountered, even if it is too weak to result in anything but a reduced rate of sink, speed should be reduced to that which gives minimum sinking speed (about 8 – 10 knots above stalling speed in most gliders).

The search should consist of a cruise over the area considered most likely to produce a thermal, preferably returning to a position off to one side of the field at about 600 feet so that a normal circuit and landing is possible. The aim should be to cover as much air as possible and no circling should be carried out unless lift or delayed sink is found. Circling flight outside a thermal is a quick way of losing height without searching any new area.

During the search, it is important to fly the glider in straight lines and not to let it turn. Otherwise, it will wander or turn away slightly as it is affected by the outskirts of the thermals. Inexperienced pilots often unconsciously let the glider influence them into commencing a turn when it is banked almost imperceptibly by lift. In this way the glider will find its way between the thermals.

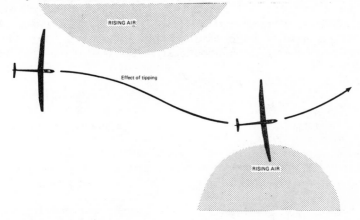

77. Fly in straight lines and watch for signs of tipping when searching for thermals.

The height obtained on a car or winch launch gives a good chance of finding one thermal on each flight. If rising air is found and is discarded without gaining height, there is usually very little hope of finding another thermal before having to land. It is important, therefore, to work any lift encountered and not to assume that something else will be found by further searching during that circuit. Higher up, the pilot can be more selective and use only those thermals which give a good rate of climb, but low down it pays to work each thermal as though it were the only hope.

Reduced sink may indicate that the glider is on the edge of a thermal, or that a thermal is just forming or has just petered out. A turn should be made *immediately* to explore the surrounding area for stronger lift. Since the variometer has a slight time lag before the true indication is shown, it is important to apply the bank quickly. Unless this is done, the glider may be some distance from the thermal by the time a smooth and accurate turn has been obtained. Many pilots wait until the variometer actually shows a rate of climb before starting to turn and they ignore a reduced rate of descent. Any reductions in the normal rate of descent of the glider, which is about 1½ – 2 knots at cruising speed, indicates rising air which may be the edge of a strong thermal. Unless the glider is turned immediately it may fly out of the edge of the thermal and have little chance of finding it again. Experience shows that nine times out of ten the glider flies across the edge of the thermal in this way so that the chances of soaring are greatly reduced if the pilot waits hopefully for the variometer to show a good rate of climb before circling. (See Fig. 78.) Generally, slight turbulence and then a sensation of rising will be felt as the lift is encountered. This warns the experienced pilot to prepare to make a turn. If the glider happens to fly through the extreme edge of the lift it may be tipped away from the thermal and a turn should immediately be started *towards* the wing which was raised. (Fig. 79.) If there are no indications which side the lift is, the direction of the turn is immaterial. The essential thing is to make the turn without delay so that contact with the lift is not lost.

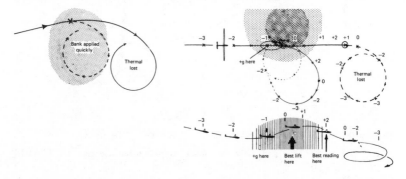

78. (a) The advantages of turning promptly and applying the bank quickly. (b) Do not wait for the best variometer reading.

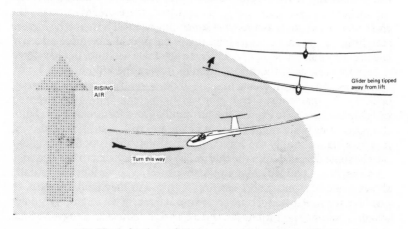

79. Watch for signs of tipping and turn towards the lift.

Within a few seconds of starting the turn, the variometer shows whether it has been made into or away from the lift. If the turn has been made the wrong way, it is best not to try to change the direction of turn but to keep a steady turn with a constant speed and angle of bank. This will ensure that the glider will come back to the lift again and that there is no chance of losing all contact with it. The most common fault amongst beginners is to start a turn in lift and then to give up and search elsewhere the moment the glider starts to sink. It is wrong to assume that the thermal has been lost or that you were mistaken because the variometer changes to read sink as the turn is initiated. This merely confirms that the lift is on the other side of the circle and that the turn must be opened out away from the sinking air to find it. The problem is then to centre the aircraft in the lift so as to obtain the maximum rate of climb possible.

Centring methods

One of the simplest methods of centring in a thermal is first to assess the readings of the variometer to find where the best lift lies and then to move the glider over until it is circling in the strongest part of the thermal. As the thermal is normally invisible and of a small area compared with the amount of air flown through in the course of a few minutes' flight, the problem requires quick thinking and accurate and sensitive piloting.

The beginner should remember that if the lift is of any practical value it will remain useful for long enough to allow time for the glider to be centred stage by stage without any large corrections. Below about 1,500 feet, once the thermal is lost it is most unlikely that it will be picked up again. Therefore, the beginner is well advised to concentrate on careful, accurate circling as this is the key to staying with the thermal.

The radius of turn can be affected by a change in angle of bank, variation in airspeed and by inaccuracies such as slipping or skidding in the turn. Unless the bank is held constant and the speed is steady, the turn will be uneven, and this may result in the glider flying out of the thermal altogether. (See Fig. 80.) Since the air is generally turbulent in and near the thermal, constant care is required to keep a steady turn. Unless the variometer is fully compensated for changes in airspeed, any variation of nose position and speed will cause the variometer to show climb and descent not related to the position of the area of lift. Fortunately, it is a simple and inexpensive matter to adapt any variometer to read total energy and this eliminates these effects, which are known as 'stick lift'.

Fig. 82 shows the most cautious method of centring the thermal. The first indication of the thermal is a decrease in the rate of descent together with a slight feeling of buoyancy. In this example the decision was made to turn to the right, and by the time zero sink was indicated a smooth turn had been initiated with about 30° of bank and at a speed just above

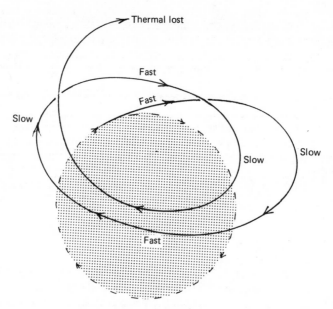

80. The effects of varying the bank and speed in a turn. The thermal will be lost.

normal cruising. Unfortunately, the turn was away from the lift but as the turn was held, the glider came back into the lift as it completed the orbit.

Since the area of lift is generally small, no attempt should be made to correct an error like this by changing the direction of turn. The poor rate of roll and the difficulty in determining the exact moment to change the turn generally result in the lift being lost altogether as in Fig. 81. Note that a tighter turn, if you can do it accurately, will keep you closer to the lift.

A second orbit can be made, checking the variometer readings approximately every 90° so that the position of the lift can be estimated. This time, as the glider is approaching the area of lift, the bank should be *reduced for one or two seconds* and then, regardless of results, the turn should be resumed as before. This should move the circle nearer to the lift, but even if an error has been made, it is unlikely that contact with it will be lost. Further circles, alternately checking the position and strength of the lift and making corrections, should result in the glider eventually circling with an almost constant rate of ascent all the time. This indicates that either the glider is centred in the thermal or that the area of lift is so large that the whole turn is well inside the lift.

Depending on the particular thermal, it may pay to adjust the angle of bank to see if a higher rate of climb can be obtained.

It is an advantage to use a steep angle of bank in order to fly in the more powerful core of the thermal. Since the core may have twice the rate of

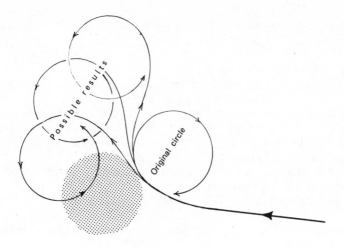

81. Never reverse the turn.

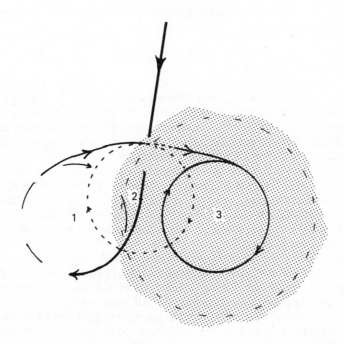

82. Simple centring. Move a little way towards the better area on each circle.

ascent of the rest of the thermal, the slight decrease in efficiency caused by the steep turn is well worth the advantage gained by being able to stay in the stronger lift. If the pilot is unable to maintain an accurate steep turn to stay in the core, it is better to adjust the angle of bank to one which is well within his capabilities.

But if no core of strong lift can be found, try gradually opening out the turn as this will result in a bigger difference in variometer readings on opposite sides of the turn, which may make it possible to re-centre more accurately than before. If the area of lift is very wide, opening out the turn will reveal this fact and possibly bring to light a strong area of lift on one side which, otherwise, might be undiscovered.

Since the thermal becomes wider with an increase in height, the angle of bank can be reduced to advantage above about 1,500 feet.

The position of the best lift in a thermal may change constantly, so that the expert will want to adjust his circles all the time in order to achieve the best rate of climb. Obtaining the best rate of climb is an art requiring constant practice, and is the key to successful soaring.

Rapid centring and the highest possible average rate of climb must be the aim of the more experienced pilot. He must not be content with just climbing but must keep exploring the air around to make sure that he is in the strongest part of the thermal. If it is weak he must leave it and search elsewhere.

Tightening on the surge

A useful method of doing this is shown in Fig. 83. The turn is gradually opened out to cover a wide area in search of a stronger core of lift. The moment that good lift is felt, the turn is tightened into a very steep turn in order to centre on that spot. If the variometer confirms a high rate of climb this turn can be continued and the bank reduced slightly to improve the efficiency of the turn and re-centre. However, if the rate of climb is not satisfactory, the turn is again opened out gradually to search again.

The advantage of this method is that it is based on a certainty. At the moment of tightening the turn, the lift is known to be stronger. The only question is whether the glider can be made to circle in it and also whether the rate of climb is the highest possible.

Either flying too fast or too slow will reduce the rate of climb.

It is definitely detrimental to fly too slowly when soaring. It increases the sinking speed and makes the handling more difficult, so that any turbulence may leave the glider stalled and losing height rapidly. Also the area of lift may be lost altogether during the subsequent recovery.

Flying too fast results in a higher rate of descent and a larger radius of turn, both of which are undesirable when soaring.

The best speed is usually just above the minimum at which no difficulty

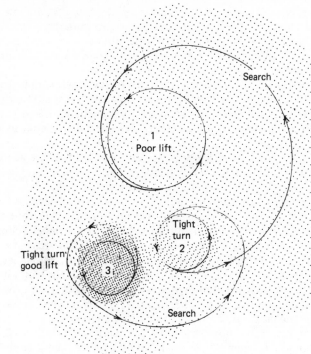

83. Tightening up on the surge.

is experienced in handling and at which no pre-stall buffeting occurs.

Thermal soaring is largely a matter of good orientation. The pilot must maintain a mental picture of the distribution of the lift in relation to his circles. This is made easier by bearing in mind the position of the gliding site, the sun or a cloud. He must also allow for the lag in the variometer and the time taken to manoeuvre when making corrections to the turn and when interpreting his instruments.

An experienced pilot can detect changes in the lift by the sensations of acceleration up or down. These feelings are instantaneous and have no lag like a variometer. The quicker response of the electric variometers, together with audio attachments, has reduced the need for a good sense of feel which used to be essential for efficient centring.

The variometer is the heart of the glider and no pilot can soar efficiently without at least one good variometer. No two systems will give identical indications and the pilot must fly the same machine regularly if he is to learn to interpret the instruments to the best advantage.

Unfortunately, the sense of feel cannot detect very gradual changes in acceleration, and variometer readings have to be used to confirm feelings of lift and sink.

Of course, with a good system, the variometer will always show an improvement just after the glider is straightened up from the turn. This is because the glider is more efficient in straight flight and has a definite increase in sinking speed as the turn is steepened. Ignore the vario readings during and immediately after any centring move.

Power pilots are usually inhibited from turning steeply enough to make good use of the core of a thermal. 'Surely,' they say, 'it cannot be right or efficient to turn like that.' But, of course, the advantage of being able to circle inside the stronger lift far outweighs the loss of efficiency in the turn.

They are also sometimes deceived into believing that they are already turning tightly because of the very high rate of turn (a normal rate 1 turn used in power flying takes 2 minutes to complete a circle, whereas an average thermalling turn may take only 15 to 20 seconds). Thermals drift down wind from the ground so that at low levels other thermals from the same source will usually be found upwind of the cloud. During the climb, the glider and the thermal drift downwind together so that a constant turn will normally keep the glider in the lift. However, if the cloud is large, it may often be fed by several thermals, which may enter the cloud base at various points or may combine to produce a large area of lift with several strong cores. Sometimes, the lift will peter out just below cloud. A search round below the cloud may result in contacting another thermal which is still feeding into it, but otherwise this is normally a sign that the cloud is fully grown and is beginning to decay, and the glider should be flown on to a more promising area where the clouds are still forming.

The visibility just below cloud base is often poor as the moisture is beginning to condense and it is wise to stop circling and head away while still several hundred feet below cloud. A decision should be made whether to enter cloud long before the cloud is reached. In most countries cloud flying is prohibited by civil flying regulations, but, in any case, no inexperienced pilot should venture into cloud without a good knowledge of the problems of instrument flight.

After even a few moments in cloud, it is easy to come out heading downwind and some way from the airfield and by the time the airfield is found, the glider may be too far downwind to be sure of getting back. Often the base of the cloud is concave, so that an attempt to fly out of the lift may be difficult without having to fly through the cloud. At cloud base, if the air is unstable the lift will become stronger, and even diving or with airbrakes out, it may be difficult to keep out of the cloud. If cloud is entered, it must always be remembered that during the course of only a few minutes the cloud can grow to many times its original size. It is not unusual to enter a small patch of cloud expecting to fly through it in a few moments and to fly on for ten minutes or more without sight of the ground, gaining several thousand feet in the meantime.

Although thermals do peter out sometimes after only a few hundred

feet and at other times just below cloud base, the majority of thermals
are lost through inaccurate flying. An admission of this fact will help to
develop better thermal soaring technique and to prevent that 'oh well,
it wasn't really worth trying for' attitude which marks the poor soaring
pilot. The excuse seems convincing because the thermal is seldom found
again once contact has been lost. Remember that the chances of finding
a lost thermal, particularly low down, are very remote even if the
approximate location is known.

There are definite advantages in making the first circle really small.
Since we only know for certain that there was worthwhile lift at the position
it was felt and that it was confirmed a few seconds later by the vario
readings, a tight turn is obviously much more likely to keep our glider
close to that area. Furthermore, if, as so often happens, the vario
immediately changes to down, indicating that we have flown out of the
lift or perhaps turned the wrong way, a tight steeply banked turn will bring
us round much more quickly to a position where a centring movement
can be made.

If we look at Fig. 84 it shows that turning in either direction a correction
is certain to be required if the glider is to be centred on the position where
the lift was first encountered.

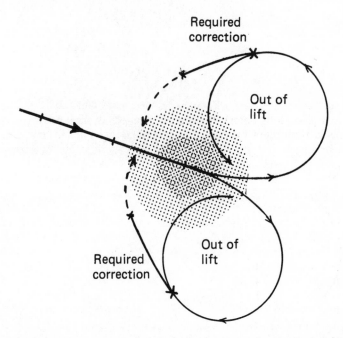

84. Why the first turn nearly always requires a correction to get back to the original position.

This suggests that on finding lift we should generally start to turn immediately, applying the bank as quickly as possible to establish a steep turn at low speed and that we should expect to have to make that correction on many occasions.

If we have made a mental note of our original heading, we should be ready to straighten up for a few seconds after turning a little less than 270° before continuing to circle. If, during the initial circle, the variometer continues to show lift, no correction is needed, but this is less likely to happen.

This, of course, is in contrast to the tactics to be used at higher altitudes, where the loss of one thermal is seldom important. In this case the glider is slowed down as it flies into any lift but is not circled unless the lift is worth while. Amongst the wider areas of lift at height there are usually a few narrow cores of stronger thermal and the same technique of applying the bank quickly and turning tightly can be used to get into them.

Whereas it is a definite advantage in cruising flight to speed up in sinking air and to slow down in lift, this does not apply while circling in and out

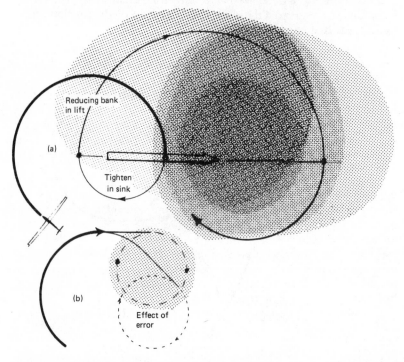

85. (a) The Reichmann method of centring. Open out when the lift is improving and tighten to get round and out of the sink quickly. (b) The effect of a few seconds' error while turning tightly in the sink.

of lift in a thermal. Increasing the speed in sink will increase the radius of turn and take the glider further out into the sink, costing even more height before it comes round into a position to move towards the better lift.

Ideally it would be best to slow down and tighten the turn in the sink to get round and out of it quickly, and this is a method advocated by some experts, including Helmut Reichmann, twice World Champion. His method of opening out towards the better lift is obviously good, but tightening up the turn to avoid the sink makes the timing of the next move towards the lift very critical. In a tight turn an error of even a few seconds, which is almost inevitable, results in a large error in positioning and in many cases results in losing the thermal altogether. I would suggest that it is unwise to use this method at low altitudes as it is gambling with your chances.

Certainly it is good policy not to get caught flying into strong sink in a gentle turn, and this adds weight to the suggestion that tight turns are a good thing and that the first turn should always be tight.

Do not get over-concerned about the efficiency of the glider, which obviously deteriorates with steeper-banked turns. What really matters is getting into and staying in the best area of lift and this is often only possible with a very tight turn.

It is an important principle that the glider should never be flown through any bad area twice. Continuous circling half in and half out of an area of lift without making any attempt to move is obviously bad. Circling in normal air or in sink is also a sheer waste of time and height. The same height could be used to cover a large area with a better chance of flying into a thermal.

Moving away from the sink (Fig. 86)

Glider pilots all soon learn to recognise the upward surge as the glider flies into lift. But perhaps it is even more important to train yourself to recognise the feeling when the glider mushes down as it flies out of lift or into some sink.

If, as the glider circles, a bad area is felt, the effect can be confirmed a few seconds later by the readings on the vario and the turn can be opened up almost immediately to move the circle a little further away from the bad area.

This is quicker than noting the stronger surge and having to fly almost a complete circle before being in a position to move the circle.

In making this kind of correction, if the complete circle is to be moved in the desired direction, the straightening up movement has to be started far earlier than one might at first think. With the higher speeds of many of the later designs and particularly when carrying water ballast, the corrections need to be very quick and very small, using all the available

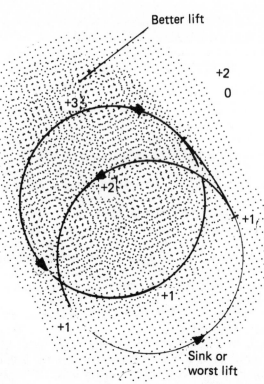

Better lift

+2
0

+3½
+2
+1
+1
+1
+1

Sink or
worst lift

86. Moving away from the sink. Never fly through the same area of sink twice.

aileron power with a large amount of rudder for a few seconds. In most cases, straightening up and going back into the turn immediately will have moved the circle a significant distance.

When using the method of moving away from the poor area, it is usually best to straighten up for the briefest moment before continuing the turn. Since the variometer will be giving misleading indications anyway as the glider is straightened up, the effect of the correction is best assessed by whether an improvement has been made on the *bad side* of the circle. Usually if the readings are up on one side and down on the other, the net result is a gradual loss of height. A small movement away from the sink will turn this into a positive gain.

Straightening up on the surge

Another method of centring on thermals is to straighten up quickly when a surge is felt. Although this is sometimes better than nothing, on most occasions it moves the circle in the wrong direction.

However, it is easy to make a correction on the next circle to compensate for the wrong displacement, and this is worth doing. On the next turn the glider is straightened up quickly about 90° before the previous correction and this should result in getting back into the best lift.

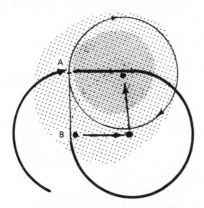

87. Straightening up on the surge (at A). Note that the circle is moved the wrong way. This can be corrected on the next circle as shown. (Straighten at B.)

Alternatively, on the second circle the turn can be opened up just before the position in which the surge was felt and the turn tightened up as it is struck the second time.

A somewhat similar system can be used to increase the chances of getting into the best lift quickly. If the glider is already in lift but not well centred, it can be straightened up deliberately early to cater for the chance that the position of the best lift is not where it was thought to be. After bringing the wings level for the briefest moment, the turn is resumed. If there is an obvious improvement felt, the turn is continued. However, if as would be expected nothing is felt, the turn is opened out a second time after about 90° and the tight turn continued. This turn should be in the better lift. The advantage of this system is that it guarantees that the move will be early rather than it being a possibility of being either early or late. If a correction is made late, another complete turn must be made in poor lift before getting to a position to make a further correction.

It is this kind of thought process which can speed up the process of centring in a thermal. In competition flying it is often the case that the day is won by precious seconds gained during the climbs. However, for the beginner it is always 'safety first' and the main thing is to get turning quickly and keep a steady turn.

It is a distinct advantage to retrim the glider for any prolonged thermalling.

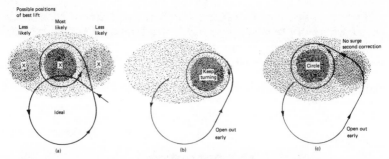

88. Quicker centring. The exact position of the lift is seldom known after one turn. It may be to one side or the other of the estimated position. If the turn is opened out deliberately early, the opportunity for centring quickly is doubled. If a surge is felt, keep turning as in (b). If no surge is felt, straighten again after about 90° and then turn as in (c). This gives two good chances instead of one.

Blue days

Just because there are no clouds in the sky it does not necessarily mean there are no thermals. But it does make finding them much more difficult. Either the air is too dry to allow cloud to form, or the air is so stable that the thermals cannot rise very far before meeting an inversion.

This often happens if a large area of high pressure becomes established over the country. With a 'high', the air becomes more stable each day so that the thermals become fewer and fewer and eventually only penetrate to a thousand feet or less. This is fine weather for sun-bathing but not for soaring.

One advantage of having no cloud is that the heating from the sun is more intense. Unless the air is too stable it is likely that there will be plenty of good thermals if only you can find them.

If there is more than a very light surface wind, it is likely that there will be some 'streeting' of the lift. Do not glide directly up- or downwind unless you are actually in lift. If you fly for more than a minute or two without finding anything, always turn off across wind. You may have been flying directly up a street of sink and turning off will give you a far better chance of cutting across a street of lift. If any turbulence is felt, turn back into or downwind to contact a usable area of lift.

Flying along a cross-wind track, it pays to imagine the streets and fly along them, jumping across nearly at right angles to the next street.

On a blue day, the towns, factories and high ground will usually give good thermals so that a cross-country flight may well consist mainly of hopping from town to town.

The thermals are often stronger and more frequent on these days than on a cloudy one where so much of the heating is cut off by the clouds obscuring the sun. Therefore do not be over-cautious if you find good conditions. With a modern machine you have a very good chance of finding lift in spite of the lack of obvious clues and once above two thousand feet or so there is no point in creeping along at very low speeds.

Safety in thermals

The risk of collision during thermalling is a very real one, and therefore each pilot must know the positions of nearby gliders at all times and all *must* turn in the same direction.

When joining other gliders in a thermal, it is dangerous to fly straight into the centre even when the other machines are well below. The difference of height will disappear very quickly as you fly through the sinking air near the thermal and as the other gliders continue to climb. Instead, start in a wide turn outside the other gliders and only move in when you are opposite to the nearest one. This gives the other pilot a reasonable chance to see you.

Never pass close under or over another glider. It may dive or pull up without realising you are close by.

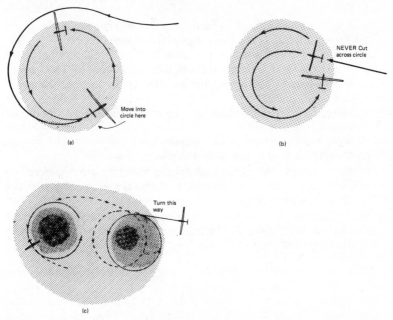

89. Joining other gliders in thermals. (a) Always join outside their circle and only move in when on the opposite side. (b) Never join by cutting across another pilot's thermal. (c) Always circle in the same direction as any nearby glider to make joining each other safe and simple.

When two gliders are climbing in nearby cores, both pilots should take care to prevent their circles from intermeshing. Any need for sudden avoiding action is a sign of danger.

Never assume that the other glider has seen you or will take avoiding action. Always leave the thermal if you lose sight of a nearby glider for more than a few seconds.

It is generally easy to see why inexperienced pilots are failing to soar. Often they fritter away their height without making any effort to search under the clouds. They ignore other gliders using thermals when they could move over to join them and in almost every case it is either that they are delaying far too long before starting to turn or that they are not using enough bank to keep inside the lift.

Until you have a considerable amount of experience, turn immediately you feel the lift and the vario needle is moving up towards zero. Apply the bank quickly and use at least 30° of bank, keeping the airspeed down to the minimum for good handling without any pre-stall buffeting.

Hints for beginners

1. Search below the best-looking cumulus within easy reach.
2. Turn immediately the vario confirms that the acceleration you felt was lift. Do not wait for it to show a climb.
3. Apply the bank quickly, use a well-banked turn (40°) and circle at low speed. (Just above the pre-stall buffet but sufficient for adequate control.)
4. Never wait for the highest reading on the vario. You will always be past the best lift.
5. Keep the bank and speed constant.
6. Do not increase speed in sink while turning.
7. Never reverse the turn except to conform with other gliders.
8. Move away from any poor part of the circle, making a small correction each circle.
9. Tighten up the turn if the lift feels good or on any surge of lift.
10. Keep a sharp lookout, especially when you are climbing well. Everyone will come and join you.

GOOD LUCK!

20 Hill soaring

Hill lift—Top and bottom sites—Special rules—Technique—Using thermals—Landings—Downwind landings

Hill lift

When wind blows over a hill or similar obstruction, the air above it is deflected upwards and can be used by a glider. If the hill is small or the wind is light, this lift may only be sufficient to delay the descent. In better conditions the lift may be sufficient to support the glider up to two or three times the height of the hill. Provided that the wind keeps blowing in the right direction, there is almost no limit to the duration of soaring flight in this kind of lift. Naturally, the height, shape and length of the hill have a great influence on the strength and area of the lift. (Fig. 90.)

The wind meeting the hill will try to avoid flowing directly over it and will spill round the ends of the hill, so that the lift there will be poor. A long ridge of hills is, therefore, much better for soaring than a short

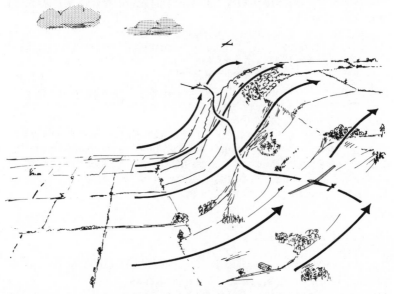

90. Hill Soaring. Gliders are flown to and fro along the face of the hill using the effect of the wind blowing up and over the hill.

or isolated hill of the same height. The lift may also be spoiled if the ridge is in the lee of other hills. An isolated hill allows the wind to flow around it so that the lift may even be strongest behind the hill where the diverted airflow meets again. This is an example of the rather unexpected things which have been found on gliding flights.

Provided that the shape of the hill is reasonably smooth, the best lift will be found over or in front of the steepest slope. A cliff will give good lift but there is often an area of turbulent air close to the face where the air piles against the steep obstruction. This results in the main area of the lift near the ground being well in front of the cliff face as the false hill of air close to the cliff acts as the slope with the main airstream flowing over it. Also the surface of the hill can seriously affect the strength of the lift, particularly at low altitudes. If the slope and foot of the hill are wooded or broken ground, the lower layers of air will be retarded and made turbulent so that, although the lift may be strong at height, the lift near the hill-side may be poor and patchy, resulting in a forced landing if the glider gets low.

The lift is stronger and extends higher on days when the air is unstable. Also, in some circumstances the hill may produce or reinforce standing waves, which make it possible to climb many times higher than in normal hill lift. It seems to be very difficult to predict the strength of the lift for a particular day since the hill lift is usually helped by a certain amount of thermal activity, and is affected considerably by the exact direction and strength of the wind above the hill, and this cannot easily be measured from the ground.

The direction and strength of the wind are the greatest factors affecting the soaring conditions. Good soaring is usually only possible when there is adequate wind blowing within about $20° - 30°$ of a direction perpendicular to the line of the ridge. However, if the hill has spurs and indentations, it is often possible to soar a very limited part of the hill, wherever there is a long enough face more or less into wind, or to fly to and fro from one spur to the next.

Most of the recognised soaring sites in Great Britain have ridges which face the prevailing westerly winds and can be used on many days of the year. A ridge which does not face a suitable direction may appear to be a perfect hill soaring site, but is of little use if the wind only blows in the right direction once or twice a year.

Top and bottom sites

The take-off and landing area may be either at the top or the bottom of the hill. Ideally, suitable fields should be available in both positions, so that launches can be made from the top and emergency landings at the bottom without risk of damage. (See Fig. 92.)

The greatest disadvantage of the site on top of the ridge is that when the wind is strong and, therefore, ideal for soaring, there is likely to be an area of strong turbulence and very high rates of sink on the approach and landing. This makes it less suitable for training.

In marginal conditions, the site at the bottom has a distinct advantage, as soaring can continue below the top of the hill and still end with a normal landing on the site. Provided that the wind is on the hill, there will be no extra turbulence during landing and take-off, although if the field is very close to the hill-side, it may be difficult to lose height for the approach.

Special rules

Good hill soaring conditions encourage overcrowding and there is always a risk of collision if a good lookout is not maintained by all the pilots all the time. As many as twenty gliders may be using a comparatively shallow layer of rising air in front of the hill, and it is essential that good flying discipline is maintained. Certain special rules for hill soaring help to reduce the chance of an accident and these must be rigidly adhered to. Most club rules state that:

All turns on the ridge must be started by turning out *away* from the hill-side and a glider must not circle in the vicinity of other machines near the hill. Some dictate a height below which circling is prohibited.

When overtaking along the ridge, the glider *overtaking* must pass *between* the other glider and the hill so that if the other starts a turn there is no danger of a collision. Unfortunately this rule is not international. If you are flying in another country you must make sure you understand their regulations.

Gliders overtaking or meeting at or near the same height must avoid passing directly over each other.

Technique

The glider is flown into a position in front of the brow of the hill and is moved along the ridge by turning slightly out of wind so that a gradual movement along the ridge is obtained without being blown beyond the top of the hill-side. In good conditions it is generally possible to maintain a height of one or two times the height of the hill. The rate of climb at hill-top height will be good but will gradually fall off with extra height until only level flight is possible.

The position of best lift in relation to the hill-side varies considerably. Only constant experiment will show whether it is better to keep almost vertically above the hill-top or fly well forward. Similarly, the strength of the lift varies considerably along the ridge, particularly if the hill-side is broken and has spurs or gullies in it. The wind direction will largely determine the places to expect the best lift. If the wind is not at right angles to the main line of the ridge, the side of a spur facing directly into the wind will often provide the best lift.

It is difficult to determine if good soaring conditions are the result of good hill lift or whether they are a combination of thermal and hill lift. Even on the coldest day thermals may form. If the conditions are thermic, lift will be strong in the thermals but often very weak at other times. In these conditions it is common to soar for long periods well above normal ridge soaring heights for the strength of wind, and then shortly afterwards to find insufficient lift to soar at all.

Except in very high winds, true ridge lift remains comparatively consistent in relation to the contours of the hill and does not provide high rates of ascent unless the glider is close to the hill-side. Thermal lift encountered when ridge soaring is generally strong, inconsistent, and remains active for a short time but extends to greater heights.

After a pilot has gained some experience of ridge soaring the limitations of ridge flying should be realised. Since the hill lift reaches only a very limited height, it is not much use except for extended flights such as the five-hour duration leg required for the Silver 'C' badge. Therefore, the hill lift should be considered solely as a means of extending the search for thermals or waves. Once a strong thermal has been found, a climb can usually be made to several times the height of gliders hill soaring. Even if it is intended to carry out local flying it is an obvious advantage to be able to fly from cloud to cloud instead of up and down the hill-side amongst other gliders, where a slight change of wind may result in a landing at the bottom of the hill.

Even an experienced soaring pilot should always seek advice from the local instructors or club members before flying from a strange site, and no club of repute would allow a stranger to the site to fly their aircraft without at least a familiarisation flight to indicate emergency landing fields, etc. Certainly an inexperienced pilot would be ill advised to fly from a

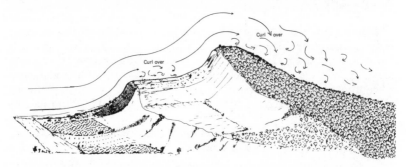

91. Curl over effects. A double ridge like this is particularly dangerous.

strange hill site without at least obtaining a careful briefing. It costs nothing to ask for advice and most people appreciate being asked for it, but it is too late to ask after an accident, when the damage is done.

Using thermals

Generally speaking, it is unwise to attempt to circle in thermal lift on the hill when closer than 500 feet to the hill-side. If there are other gliders on the ridge, circling upsets the normal routine and increases the risk of collision. Any soaring near the hill-side should, therefore, be in the form of 'beats' along the hill, with turns outwards away from the hill. When strong lift of either hill or thermal source is encountered, a turn should be made into wind. The speed should be reduced to that for minimum rate of sink, or to the speed necessary to maintain position without being blown backwards by the wind. In this way the glider can be kept in the strong area of lift until no more height can be gained, before turning again and proceeding to another part of the ridge. If the wind is not strong enough to allow the glider to remain stationary while it is at its best speed for minimum sink, a very short beat or S-turn can be made from side to side in order to centre on the best lift. Often, the feature on the ground creating the lift can be seen and the glider can be manoeuvred accordingly. The lift from a small spur can be soared effectively in this way.

If the lift is thermic, close to the hill-side the same technique of flying to and fro in it can be used. As height is gained, it is wise to work forward away from the hill so that once a safe height is reached, normal thermal soaring turns can be made without risk of turning too close to the hill-side or upsetting the traffic patterns. The thermals can sometimes be traced to particular villages, factories or other sources of heating, and these often act as continuous thermal sources throughout the day, giving an almost constant boost to the hill lift. If these sources are well upwind, local variations in wind direction cause the position of the lift to move to and fro. When the source is smoking, these changes may be seen by the change in the smoke. If a series of strong thermals are found at approximately the same place on the ridge but only last for a few moments, they may be from a fixed source but be moving along the ridge because of wind changes. The problem is then to tell to which side the lift has moved. If the glider is flown so that it creeps slowly along the hill across the thermal instead of directly into wind, when the lift decreases it is reasonable to assume that the area has been passed through, and a turn can be made with a very good chance of running into the lift again in its new position farther along the ridge. In this way there is a better chance of staying in the thermal lift than by steering straight into wind and guessing which direction to look when the lift disappears. On unstable, thermic days there are areas of turbulence and rapidly sinking air reaching 10 – 20 feet per second, and these often completely obliterate the hill lift for short periods in spite of a reasonable wind. It is, therefore, necessary to be very alert all the time to get out of such areas before too much height is lost. Ten seconds of flight in sinking air can lose up to 200 feet of height, and a turn or even delay in taking action may result in so much height being lost that a landing at the bottom of the hill may be necessary. If an abnormally high rate of sink is encountered, it is best to lower the nose of the glider *immediately* to gain speed, even apparently at the expense of height, so that the area of sink is flown through as quickly as possible. At the same time the glider should be turned so that the beat along the ridge is continued. Never attempt to change the direction of 'beat' while in a high rate of sink near the ground as it takes time to turn and considerable height can be lost by staying in the sinking air. When conditions are very marginal, be prepared to reverse the 'beat' whenever any lift is found and the glider is nearing the end of the 'beat'. This will decrease the chance of having to make the turn in sink at the extreme end of the hill while losing height.

As height is lost, it is necessary to fly closer to the hill-side to find the best lift. The lift near the ground is often turbulent, and within about 300 feet of the hill-side care must be taken to fly at a speed which gives safe handling in these conditions and not normal gliding speed for the minimum rate of sink. Failure to observe this precaution is a common cause of loss of control when soaring in marginal conditions. It is particularly tempting for an inexperienced pilot to try to keep the glider up by raising the nose as the ground gets uncomfortably close, and this error will result in stalling without height for recovery. If the glider is in the correct position in relation to the hill-side, and is being flown at the correct speed, a further loss of height shows that the conditions are unsoarable and a landing should be made. A planned forced landing in a field at the bottom need never damage the glider, whereas a hill-side arrival or unpremeditated landing at the last moment may easily result in serious damage.

Landings

Once the glider sinks down to the level of the hill-top, the possibility of a landing at the bottom must always be considered. There is bound to be a certain amount of lift from the hill even if it is only sufficient to delay the sink of the glider. It is, therefore, possible to cruise for some distance along the face of the hill to the most suitable forced landing field or to a part of the ridge where there are suitable fields below. The flight can then be continued in the hope of the lift improving, with the intention of carrying out a landing in the selected field if any more height is lost.

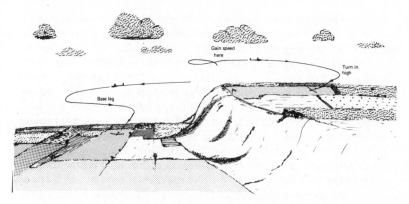

Gain speed here

Turn in high

Base leg

92. Landing at top and bottom landing areas.

Landing in a field of suitable size below the hill presents few difficulties. Like any landing away from base, the altimeter should be ignored so that any difference in height from take-off point cannot possibly cause confusion. At the bottom of the hill it is usual to find that the wind is much lighter and, if this is allowed for, a landing into or across wind will be straightforward, provided that the decision to land is made in plenty of time. If a landing becomes necessary it is usually best to start by moving out well away from the hill-side and beyond the chosen field. The circuit and in particular the base leg will then be well clear of any weak lift near the hill.

The majority of our hill sites are, unfortunately, at the top of the hill. There is nearly always an area of extreme turbulence downwind of the hill-top and this necessitates care when approaching to land. The airflow is unable to follow the sharp change in curvature of the ground and breaks away into turbulent vortices in the same way as the airflow over a stalled aerofoil. This turbulence may extend for more than a mile behind the hill but is particularly violent close behind the crest. Here the air may even be travelling against the prevailing wind and have large changes in speed and direction within a short distance. It is, therefore, necessary to approach very high and with a good margin of flying speed so that there is no possibility of the glider being stalled, or control being lost, near the ground.

The minimum height at which to leave the hill lift to return to the site for landing depends on the nearness of the field to the hill-top, but it is generally most unwise to leave at less than 300 feet above the height of the hill unless the conditions are known to be smooth. Even then, if unexpected sink is encountered it will be necessary to turn in to land without delay or there may not be sufficient height to complete the final turn safely.

Nearly every well-known site has particular areas to be avoided and it is wise to take advice from the 'locals' on how and where to approach and land. When a ridge wind is blowing, it is usually not safe to fly beyond the downwind boundary of the field even if surplus height is in hand. This ensures that even if sinking and turbulent air is met, there can be no possibility of falling short onto some obstructions on the boundary. This 'clutching hand' effect behind a hill in windy conditions has to be experienced to be believed and most clubs have very rigid rules to prevent undershoot accidents through going beyond the boundary.

A landing at the top of the hill away from the launching site is inadvisable unless it is planned in plenty of time. As soon as the glider is flown behind the top of the hill, the 'curl over' effect may result in very rapid loss of height, leaving very little time for the choice of a suitable landing area, and the turbulence may make a low turn dangerous. Since it is necessary to leave the hill lift at several hundred feet above hill-top level when landing at the top, the conditions have to be much better to allow soaring to continue than when the landing area is below the hill. It is still essential to have suitable fields in which to land in an emergency because it is possible for conditions to change so quickly that it may be impractical to land at the site.

It is possible to have high winds blowing but for the hill to be unsoarable. This is generally caused by the normal hill lift being deadened by the down-current of a lee wave or by turbulence from another hill upwind of the site. A slight undetectable change in wind speed will shift the position of the wave, and normal hill lift may return immediately. While the wave interferes with the hill lift, it is probable that the normal lift becomes restricted to a very shallow layer close to the hill-side, which is too thin to soar in safety.

Where the hill is high, the wind in the valley may be very light so that although the wind on the hill-top appears strong enough there may be very little lift, particularly below the level of the hill-top. The first flight on any particular day is usually rather unpredictable, and the pilot should try to keep within easy gliding distance of the field and to explore the ridge gradually to see where the lift is dependable.

The technique of hill soaring can be summarised in the following points.

The best lift is found in front of the crest of the hill, the exact position depending on the slope and the conditions at the time of the flight.

The glider should be flown in long 'beats' along the ridge making all turns outwards, away from the hill. When flying in rising air, speed should be that for minimum rate of sink or as necessary to prevent drifting with the wind; in sinking air, speed should be increased to progress along the ridge in search of better conditions. If high rates of descent are encountered, increase speed immediately for a few moments and turn along the hill.

Within 500 feet of the hill-side (or the height laid down by the local regulations) no thermal turns should be made. Any thermal turns should commence with a turn away from the ridge during which a good look-out must be kept for other gliders. If good lift is encountered, speed should be reduced and a turn made into wind away from the hill. In sinking air, turn so as to drift closer to the hill-side back into the hill lift.

At low altitudes it is necessary to fly close to the hill-side to stay in lift.

Select suitable fields for emergency landings immediately after being launched or arriving over the ridge.

If the landing area is on the top of the hill, return to a position close to a safe landing area if conditions become at all uncertain.

Do not go behind the leeward boundary and use plenty of speed on the approach.

Decide on a minimum height for turning in to land at the top, and prepare to go to the bottom and land in a field if you get below that height. Select the most suitable field within easy reach, remembering that a safe landing is far more important than an easy retrieve.

If height cannot be maintained below the hill-top when flying at a speed above that for minimum sink, the decision should be made to land by 500 or 600 feet above valley level.

Throughout soaring flight watch the wind and weather and try to anticipate changes in conditions. The passing of a large cumulus cloud or shower will change the wind velocity and upset the hill lift.

Always fly in a position from which, if height is lost rapidly, a landing at the bottom is possible. It is easy to reach the hill from too far out in front but not from too far back.

It is seldom worth working hard to gain an extra 100 feet in hill lift unless there is any possibility of wave activity.

Safety in flight on a crowded ridge depends on every individual pilot keeping a careful lookout all the time and obeying the rules of the air. Particular vigilance is necessary when there are only a few other aircraft flying and a lookout seems less important.

Be prepared for a landing away by knowing the most suitable fields for landing at the bottom of the hill. If conditions deteriorate and it is impossible to get back to the landing ground, don't be too proud to make the decision early to land at the bottom.

When thermalling on a ridge it is only too easy to continue circling until the glider has drifted back too far behind the hill. If the upper wind is strong, it will be a struggle to penetrate forward against the wind.

Since the wind speed is much stronger at circuit height than at ground level, the glider will make very little progress at normal flying speeds. It should be flown back at considerably more than the normal best speed for the wind strength because of the likelihood of meeting turbulence and the violent curl-over behind the hill-top.

Keep this speed until you either regain the hill lift or decide to abandon trying to reach it.

Don't assume that you will make it. Pick possible landing places and fly from one to another so that at all times you are in a position where, if you fly into very strong sinking air, you can make a safe landing.

Remember that if you do get low in the lee of the hill-top, the 'clutching hand' effect will almost certainly get you! If it looks marginal, select a landable area ahead and get down into it quickly.

Never attempt a low circuit in the lee of the hill. Most unsuccessful attempts to reach the lift are caused by not flying fast enough; or slowing down or changing speed several times on the way.

Downwind landings

On a site some distance behind the hill-top, it is sometimes possible to reach the landing ground by making a downwind landing when there is not enough height for a normal circuit.

It is always very tempting to take a risk in order to avoid the embarrassment of a landing in a field, but this consideration should never be allowed to influence the decision. Even very slight damage to a glider will put it out of action for much longer than the time taken to retrieve it from a field and even a minor incident may result in costly repairs.

Compare a landing into wind with that of a downwind landing when the wind strength is 15 knots. (Fig. 93.) The touchdown speed of a glider would be about 20 knots into wind and 50 knots downwind (assuming an airspeed of 35 knots at touchdown in each case). The glide path relative to the ground will be very flat when gliding downwind, which will make a landing in a small field bounded by a hedge or trees impossible. (With full airbrake in this case the angle of the glide path would be over 10 : 1.)

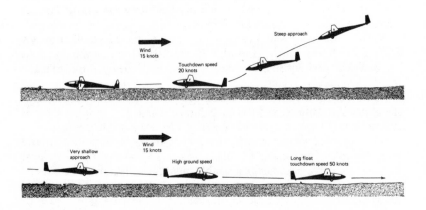

93. Downwind and into-wind landings.

Furthermore, not only is the landing speed increased, but it will not be possible to maintain control all the time after the touchdown. As the glider slows down after landing, at a ground speed of 20 knots, there will be no airflow over the controls because of the following wind, and the pilot will be powerless to prevent a wingtip from touching the ground. This may swing the glider round so violently that the main wheel or skid is ripped off and both the bottom of the fuselage and the wingtip are damaged. If a downwind landing is inevitable, therefore, care should be taken to keep the wings exactly level and when possible the approach and landing should be made exactly downwind. It is vital to cross the boundary of the field as low as possible without any excess airspeed.

When the risks of a downwind landing in a strong wind are compared with the inconvenience of retrieving the glider from a field outside the site, there is seldom any doubt as to the correct decision to make. However, in light winds landing downwind has no particular problems apart from the risk of floating on too far and overshooting the landing area.

21   Wave soaring

Lee waves—Lenticular clouds—Using wave lift—Rotor flow—Other wave systems

Lee waves

In certain atmospheric conditions the airflow over hills or mountains forms into wave-shaped disturbances which continue up to great heights and can be propagated for long distances to the lee of the original source.

A standing wave can be considered as an example of hill lift in which the deflection of the airflow over the hill is transmitted from layer to layer of the air, to heights of eighteen to twenty times the hill height and sometimes possibly more. If the wind speed is sufficient, the lift will enable the glider to climb to great heights, provided it is flown in the correct position in front of the crest of the wave. In high winds, rates of climb of 600 feet per minute are common, together with similar or higher rates of descent in the corresponding downward part of the wave. The airstream behind the hill will be affected, and a series of 'lee' waves will form, continuing for great distances downwind of the original obstruction and gradually diminishing in strength. (See Fig. 94.) The distance between the wave crests (i.e. the wave length) depends on the wind speed, and the size of the obstruction, and the atmospheric conditions at the time. In light winds, the wave length may be so short that the formation of the wave is easily upset by any slight thermal activity or disturbance caused by another hill or obstruction. It is possible for thermal activity to exist amongst a wave formation provided that the thermal is small in comparison with the size of the wave. If the air is generally unstable, however, no wave is likely to occur.

Lenticular clouds

Visible evidence that wave conditions exist is very limited unless the air is moist enough to form cloud. The clouds generally associated with wave formations are in the form of long strips or bars of cloud of more or less an elliptical or cigar shape, lying approximately at right angles to the wind, parallel with the hill, and remaining nearly stationary in spite of high winds. These clouds are known as lenticulars and may be low, medium or high cloud and are often notable for their smooth, silky outline. They mark the crests of the wave forms at the particular level at which cloud

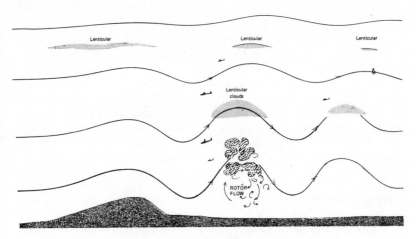

94. Lee waves and the rotor.

is forming, but the wave lift does not cease at the cloud level and often there are several sets of lenticulars at different levels.

If the air mass is very moist, the cloud will take up the wave pattern without any gaps between each crest. It is often difficult to realise that the lenticular clouds at low altitudes are, in fact, standing in a constant position, since the individual particles of cloud continuously condensing at the front edge are swept back at high speed. However, the edges of the cloud remain stationary relative to the ground. The cloud sweeping back from the crest of the wave reaches the rear edge and then dissolves instantly. Although the whole cloud remains stationary, the air passing through it may be moving at 40 – 50 m.p.h. and resemble the torrents of a waterfall.

Changes in wind speed result in a change in wave length, or the collapse of the system altogether. Several ranges of hills may help the formation of a wave pattern if they are suitably spaced. However, unless the wind strength is such that the wave length will fit the position of the hills, they may destroy the wave formation or result in unusual local soaring conditions on those hills.

In 1951 there was an interesting example of this at the Derby and Lancs Club site at Great Hucklow, where the National Gliding Contests were being held. Normal hill soaring was in progress and seven or eight sailplanes were soaring at about 700 feet above the hill. Soaring conditions were satisfactory with a wind of about 15 m.p.h. on the hill-top. Suddenly, without any warning, the hill lift was almost completely squashed by what must have been the down-current of a wave. Four of the sailplanes were forced to land in fields at the bottom while the others were just able to reach the normal landing area on top of the hill. Although there had been no detectable change in wind speed or direction, and the wind sock had remained straight out all the time, the cause was almost certainly a change of wave length in a wave pattern formed by hills some miles upwind, which resulted in this marked change in soaring conditions. About fifteen minutes later, normal soaring returned and wave conditions were found by a few of the competitors.

The discovery of lee waves has opened up great new possibilities for long-distance cross-country flights. The high wind speeds generally associated with good wave soaring conditions result in very high ground speeds, and since heights of 15,000 feet have been reached in the vicinity of 1,000-feet hills, this opens up the fields of high-altitude flights during the winter months when there is little chance of thermal soaring.

Using wave lift

The lift associated with wave conditions is in the form of comparatively large areas of rising air lying more or less parallel with the hill range causing it. The lift in the wave is generally abnormally smooth because of the stable and laminar type of airflow. The smooth airflow is a distinctive characteristic of wave conditions and has a marked effect on the handling of the glider. The normal slipstream noise during flight is considerably reduced—probably by the elimination of some of the turbulent airflow over the aircraft as a whole. Often the air is so smooth that no control movements are needed for minutes on end.

Lenticular clouds or thin patches of cloud in amongst the waves give a good indication of the position of the peaks and troughs of the waves. If the glider is flown to a position just upwind of the edge of the cloud, it is easy to keep station with it and climb using it as a marker. If the cloud base is low, it is unwise to climb above cloud unless it is well broken as, if the wave conditions fail, the gaps in the cloud may quickly close in leaving no alternative but a blind descent through cloud.

Another excellent way of plotting the area of lift is to fly in company with one or two other gliders. If one glider drifts back too far, the other continues to mark the area of lift and then there can be no doubt which way to go to get back into the lift.

If a wave is formed by one hill or ridge of hills on a particular day, other waves will be formed by other hills elsewhere. It is possible to climb up in one wave and fly downwind through successive lee waves, finally perhaps contacting a new series of waves from another hill to continue the flight for some hundreds of miles. If the flight is made at 10,000 feet or more a very high cruising speed can be obtained once the initial climb has been made.

Flying at high altitudes, because of the reduction in the density of the air, the glider will have to fly faster to develop normal lift. However, the indicated airspeed (I.A.S.) and the indicated stalling speed remain the same at all heights. The increase in true airspeed is about 1.75 per cent per thousand feet of height and results in an increase of about 35 per cent at 20,000 feet. So the true airspeed (T.A.S.) would be 81 knots when the I.A.S. is only 60 knots. However, the rate of sink would also be 35 per cent more than normal.

This effect plus the very strong winds at these heights can mean ground speeds of 150 knots or more and the potential for travelling long distances downwind at high altitudes is unlimited.

It is important to realise that the maximum diving speed will be exceeded, with a serious risk of flutter unless the indicated speeds are limited. Most modern machines have restricted diving speeds above 15,000 feet because of this effect. Typically, a glider with a placarded Vne of 135 knots should be kept below an indicated airspeed of 85 knots at 20,000 feet and down to under 65 knots at 30,000 feet. This is because the onset of possible flutter depends on the true airspeed and not the speed indicated by the instrument. (The indicated stalling speed remains the same at all heights.)

The flight downwind through the down-current of one wave into the next wave will involve considerable loss of height unless the correct speed is flown. It is reasonable to expect rates of sink much greater than the rate of climb obtained during the climb.

As soon as the rate of descent falls, a turn into wind can be made and the glider allowed to drift back into the next area of lift for another climb. It is usual to find that after two or three waves the system begins to deteriorate until finally, as each crest is reached, it is only worth while to reduce speed in order to get the farthest distance possible.

Very often it is possible to get into a wave system from hill lift. If there are obvious signs of wave activity, such as lenticulars or cumulus clouds with rather silky smooth tops, it is well worth climbing as high as possible in the hill lift and then moving out upwind.

The first signs will probably be that it becomes possible to get much higher than before and that the air has become very smooth.

With wave lift it pays to be very patient and to work every bit of lift carefully to get as high as possible. Once in wave it is important to try to hold your position over the ground and to keep checking it to see that you are not drifting slowly backwards. Try to select a convenient landmark on either side of the aircraft and keep station in relation to them.

Like hill soaring, you may have to beat to and fro to avoid moving forward but do not make a long beat at first. Explore along the wave very carefully, holding position in any areas which seem stronger. The waves are normally lying parallel to the ridges forming them and not necessarily at right angles to the wind. This can often be seen by the position and lie of the lenticular clouds. However, very often there is strong wave lift with no cloud forming.

On no account circle or you will fall back into the sink, which will cost you hundreds if not thousands of feet.

It may be necessary to fly faster to stay in position as you gain height and reach the stronger winds. Good wave conditions require a strengthening wind speed with height, and winds of 60 or 70 knots are quite usual.

Try to avoid climbing up through the actual cloud as it may give you sufficient icing to ruin the performance of the glider.

It is vital to make contingency plans against the possibility of a cloud sheet forming below. Make sure that you know which way and how far you can safely fly downwind to get over open country where there are no hills or mountains.

There will be very little warning that the gaps in the clouds below are closing in. Air that is more moist will cause the cloud to form or thicken without warning and you should be watching below and ready to open the airbrakes and descend quickly if there is any risk of being cut off above solid cloud cover.

Cross-country flights along and across the wave systems can be fascinating. It pays to work along the wave lift to a point where it is weak before attempting to move forward against the wind. Where the wave is weak the sink will also be weaker and this will save you height penetrating forward against the strong wind.

Remember that if the wave is giving you lift of 6 knots (600 feet per minute) the sink will give you a rate of descent of nearly 10 knots (1000 feet per minute). Moving forward a few miles to the next wave will often cost four or five thousand feet!

The primary wave is usually the strongest and this is generally about 2 to 4 miles downwind of the hill or mountain producing it. Just downwind of this lift is a zone where there may be 'rotor flow'.

Rotor flow

Waves are more likely to form when there is a strong wind blowing more or less at right angles to a ridge, when the wind direction remains more or less constant and when the wind speed increases with height. Ideally there should also be a rather unstable shallow layer near the surface, a stable layer above it and a slightly more unstable layer above that. This allows the wave to resonate.

In some conditions the air just below the primary wave forms a rotor, which upsets the stable air so that it becomes violently unstable. This is the destructive turbulence which can sometimes be so severe that it will break up almost any kind of aircraft including gliders.

Whenever possible rotor flow should be avoided. Usually it is possible to miss the worst of it by towing out to the side of the wave where it will be weaker.

Before take off, it should always be assumed that rotor may be encountered. *Nothing* must be left insecure in the cockpit, least of all the pilot. It is not unusual to experience plus and minus 2 or 3 'g' in rapid succession and just keeping control of the glider can be a problem. Both the down of the wave and the rotor can come right down onto the ground. This could make a landing very dangerous because of the turbulence and the rapid changes in wind speed and direction.

If rotor is known to be bad and directly over the field it will usually be safer to land elsewhere a few miles away.

On some occasions there is thermal activity mixed up with the rotor flow and it is possible to thermal soar using tight turns to stay in the very broken lift. Then, once a reasonable height has been gained, a move forward can be made into the primary wave. Suddenly the turbulence ceases and the silky smooth wave lift is yours.

Like all wave lift, the rotor may be marked by cloud or be invisible.

Rotor cloud usually looks like very ragged cumulus but the swirling motion can be clearly seen. The line of the cloud is parallel to the hills and does not move in spite of the strong wind. On a classic day the rotor cloud may be capped with layer upon layer of lenticulars.

It seems fairly certain that now wave flying is receiving more attention from glider and power pilots than ever before, cross-country flights of great distance will be made.

Already flights of 1,000 miles have been planned in the United States and heights of 45,000 feet have been obtained, using standard gliders equipped with oxygen. However, these flights rely on the wave formations set up by mountain ranges much higher than any we have in this country.

Other wave systems

So far, the glider has proved to be the best means of investigating both waves and thermals, and nearly all the significant factual data about these movements in the atmosphere have been recorded by amateur glider pilots.

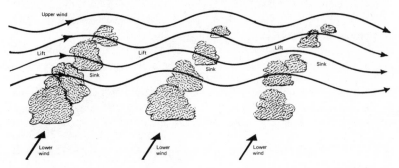

95. Wave formation above cumulus 'streets'. Note the difference in wind direction above the clouds.

Wave systems may also be caused by a change in wind direction and strength just above an unstable layer of air in which the lift or cloud is forming into organised streets. These streets act as if they were ridges of high ground causing a train of lee waves above them. This kind of wave system can be entered by climbing as high as possible in the cloud and then flying upwind into the up-current area just ahead of the cloud.

An interesting discovery is that there can be travelling waves moving downwind instead of remaining stationary as with standing and lee waves. Waves of this kind can occur in 'jet streams', the high-speed streams of air which are encountered by high-altitude aircraft. The possibility of being able to soar in the jet streams with wind speeds of 100 – 200 m.p.h. opens up a complete new field for distance flying. Whether the glider pilot will learn to use these moving waves remains to be seen, but their existence opens up tremendous possibilities of flights of thousands of miles at great heights.

The existence and strength of wave lift enabling flights to be made to 45,000 feet above a 12,000-feet range of mountains seems remarkable, but the real potentialities can be realised when these flights are compared with flights to 25,000 feet above mere hills of less than 1,000 feet. Given the equipment, much greater heights would appear to be obtainable when the soaring conditions are right.

22 Landing in strange fields

Choosing a field—The wind direction—Location—Size—Surface—Slope—
The approach and landing

Inexperienced pilots often have little idea of the problems which they may
have to meet if they are forced to land in difficult country. It is not sufficient
that the pilot can soar. He should have a minimum of new problems and
experiences to face on his first solo cross-country flight and he must have
enough flying background to be able to extricate himself from any difficulty
which might arise when landing in a strange field.

A good soaring flight can easily be spoilt by damaging the glider on
landing. Every year several high-performance sailplanes are badly damaged
during landing in strange fields, for the sole reason that the pilots had
left their choice of landing ground much too late. These accidents result
in a great financial loss, which could easily be saved by observing a few
simple rules. Even slight damage to a glider takes many hours of skilled
work to repair and may prevent further flying for several days. A safe
landing should be the foremost aim in mind for every flight. This can
only be ensured if the landing area is carefully selected while still at
sufficient height and if a definite decision to land is made in plenty of
time. The exact height at which this decision must be made depends upon
the type of country over which the flight is being made and on the
experience of the pilot. Inability to find a really suitable field for a safe
landing is proof that the decision has been left too late. There are only
three main causes of accidents to gliders landing in fields:

1. Those caused by selecting an inadequate field because of lack of
   time or height.
2. Those caused by poor piloting or judgement in failing to make a
   satisfactory approach and landing.
3. Minor accidents caused by running over hidden obstructions, such
   as rabbit holes, etc., after landing.

Choosing a field

In many accidents caused by poor flying technique or misjudgement, the
selection of too small a landing area is a contributory factor. For if a
reasonably large field is selected, the permissible margin of error in under-
or over-shooting is much greater, and only a very serious error would result
in an accident. Until the pilot has considerable experience at landing in

fields, the largest good field should always be selected.

The mere fact that the choice of field has been left too late may tend to make an inexperienced pilot panic, with the result that he may make a hasty and misjudged decision. Once this has happened, the pilot will often fail to regain control of the situation, and then only luck can prevent a serious accident. The best insurance against panic is to see that the situation is never allowed to develop into an emergency. This needs a clear understanding of all the factors involved in landing in fields, and the use of a methodical plan to ensure a good approach. It also means basically sound training to develop a true sense of self-confidence and a sensible realisation of the limitations of personal skill and judgement. This must be based on true standards; for example, the ability to land in a marked area on the gliding site, even without the use of an altimeter, may give the impression that a safe landing could be carried out in a similar-sized field, which is not necessarily so. This type of test seldom has any element of surprise or hazard and the direction of approach is invariably one which is used during normal flying.

If the altimeter is used all the time during training and subsequent flying, there is a tendency to rely on it for indicating the height for the final turn before landing. This is a bad practice because it discourages the pilot from relying implicitly upon his own judgement, with the result that he may even doubt it when faced with a landing in a difficult field. Furthermore the instrument is always liable to error, and never reads correctly for a landing away from the take-off point.

Although it is not suggested that the altimeter should be deleted entirely, more confidence in self-judgement is developed when the instrument is partially blanked off so that heights below 300 – 400 feet cannot be read. Every approach must then be judged and errors in the instrument caused by sticking, differences in the height of the ground, and incorrect setting cause no difficulty. Quite often the pilot may subconsciously develop a tendency to compromise between relying on his own judgement and on the altimeter reading, with the result that he develops little confidence in either.

Before embarking on cross-country flights, the pilot must find out how far he can trust his own judgement by making landings in strange landing areas, e.g. in odd corners of the gliding site or suitable fields. These landings must be made without the help of the altimeter.

The ideal approach is one using about half airbrake to land on the desired spot. An approach so high that full airbrake is required all the way may end as a disastrous overshoot should the surface wind prove a little lighter than was estimated, or in the event of flying through any lift.

In many parts of Great Britain, the average size of fields is too small to allow much error of judgement on landing. Over open country, the choice of field should be made by about 1,000 feet so that there is no possibility of being caught low without a good field in mind. A landing in bad country should be avoided whenever possible by keeping high enough to glide to a better area or by diverting round it.

The wind direction

Wind direction and strength are vital factors to take into account when choosing a landing area and, for this reason, the pilot must be aware of the direction of the surface wind at all times. This may change completely during the course of a flight so that the pilot should take notice of any indications of wind which he may see as the flight progresses, to avoid the need for a frantic search for them at the last moment. Near the coast the sea breeze effect may cause a complete change of wind direction.

Smoke is the best wind indicator, as both direction and strength can be accurately assessed at a glance. (Smoke from moving trains or ships must not, of course, be used.) Flags, ripples on trees, corn, or large areas of water are also useful in windy weather and, when the glider is below 1,000 feet or so, it may be possible to check the wind by noticing the amount of drift when flying across wind.

Although the upper wind is seldom exactly the same direction as that on the surface, the direction of movement of the shadows of the clouds on the ground may give a general indication of the wind.

If the wind is strong, the search for a good field should be made by flying downwind since this enables the glider to cover the greatest distance and, therefore, gives the best choice of fields. Upwind, the choice of field will be limited to those almost below, and an isolated field must not be selected upwind unless there is ample height to reach it with height to spare, even allowing for the most adverse down-currents on the way. This is important, because until the pilot has had considerable experience of selecting fields from the air, it is probable that a closer look at the field may show some unexpected obstruction which will make a further choice necessary. There must be sufficient height and time to allow another field to be found and reached.

The landing should be made as near into wind as possible in the direction giving the best approach and landing run. This has the advantage of giving a steeper approach, lower landing speed and shorter landing, all most useful in a strange field. The difference in touchdown speed alone should discourage downwind landings, which are out of the question except for landing up sloping ground. The surrounding countryside will also affect the local wind strength and probable up- and down-draughts must be taken into account. For example, if the field chosen lies in the lee of high trees or a hill, strong turbulence and wind gradient effect are likely near the ground in windy weather, but the surface wind may be quite light. Great care is needed to guard against these effects, particularly in windy weather.

Location

In England the choice of field should *never* be influenced by the convenience of retrieving, since the inconvenience and expense of even slight damage by far exceeds that of carrying the glider across a few fields after landing. In this country, there are few areas of farm land from which a glider cannot be readily retrieved and the best choice is always the largest good landing area within easy gliding range.

Fields alongside main roads almost always have power or telephone wires along them which can be invisible from the air and greatly reduce the effective run of the field if they have to be crossed during the approach.

Fields adjoining rivers, lakes or flooded areas slope down towards the water and should be avoided when possible. Any slope which can be seen from over 500 – 1,000 feet is much too steep for a safe landing, and flat-bottomed valleys often have irrigation ditches which are difficult to see from the air. Any area in the lee of hills should be avoided in anything but very light winds because of the turbulent conditions often prevailing there.

Size

The effective size of the field depends on its direction in relation to the wind and on the heights of any obstructions on the approach.

Whenever possible, a path should be selected which avoids the need to approach over high trees or buildings, since this will give the longest effective run over the field. In most cases a slightly smaller field with a low fence gives a longer effective run than a large field which has tall obstructions on the approach. Besides this, an undershoot on the approach is disastrous if the boundary of the field has large solid obstructions.

On a calm day, the landing area is effectively shortened by about eight times the height of any obstruction. This reduces a 400-yard long field to only 275 yards if there are 50-feet high trees on the boundary.

The direction and the strength of the wind must also greatly influence the choice of landing run, and particularly in light winds a long landing run across wind is usually preferable to a shorter one directly into wind.

Any slope in the field has a most marked effect on the landing run and the landing must always be made up or across the slope regardless of wind direction.

With few exceptions, the best field is always one with a good flat surface and the largest effective landing run.

Surface

The surface of the field is important, since even a good landing in rough ground or tall crops will cause serious damage to a glider. The glider pilot must, therefore, be able to recognise the appearance of different crops and types of farm land from the air to avoid such major blunders as selecting deep unripe corn by mistake for grassland. At different times of the year, the appearance of the ground changes considerably and an elementary knowledge of farming is most useful in reaching a sound decision.

Every pilot should practise selecting suitable fields quickly from the air on local soaring flights, and then try to criticise the decision and find a better choice nearby. This is of even greater value if there is time to visit the field afterwards to see the size and surface of the field and to reconsider the approach selected from the air.

Although in England grassland is often ideal for a landing, this is certainly not true in all countries. Often the ground is badly rutted by the cattle in the winter time when the ground is very soft and wet. It may be very rough and stony ground which cannot easily be cultivated for other crops. It is always better to land in ground which has obviously been cultivated at some time than to go into a grass field. If it has been cultivated it must be smooth enough for the machinery and it is unlikely to have large holes or rough areas.

On one occasion during a competition I landed in grass which looked fine from a height but which turned out to be more than 3 feet deep. If it had been windy it would have been easy to realise that it was deep by the ripples in the grass.

You certainly will be unpopular with the farmer if you happen to land in grass which is being grown for the seed, as it is a very valuable crop which can easily be damaged.

It is easy to recognise a field which has just been cut for silage or hay as it is a distinctive bright yellowy-green colour for a few days afterwards. It will not have any electric fences as it won't be any good for cattle until the grass has had time to grow again.

The hay is usually left lying in lines and although they may make the field look very rough, a landing can be made along or across the lines with little harm. The surface must be reasonably smooth or it could not have been cut by the machine.

At other times of the year, grass can be identified by looking for fields with sheep or cattle grazing in them and picking similar-looking fields nearby. Usually a farm will have several pastures and will use them in turn. Do not land in fields with stock in them unless there is no really safe alternative. Cattle are very inquisitive and can cause damage to the glider.

Grass fields must be inspected for any signs of a colour change which might indicate an electric cattle fence. Never land across a colour change, a path or obvious mark running across a field. It may be caused by a fence or a deep rut which could damage the glider.

A newly erected electric fence may not be detectable until it is seen during the final stages of the approach or landing and this is a hazard in any grass field. So landing in grass is always just a little bit risky and there is no time to relax until the glider has come to rest.

If the ground is under regular cultivation, it is unlikely to be too rough for a safe landing, since otherwise it would be difficult to use mechanised ploughing, etc. However, it is important to land along the lines of the furrows or crops even if it means a crosswind landing.

Most farmers use a system we call 'tram lines' for sowing, spraying fertiliser and spraying pesticides. The same tracks are used over and over again by the tractors so that only a minimum of the crop is damaged by wheel marks. However, if the ground is at all soft at any time, the wheel marks become very deep ruts which would certainly cause damage to any glider landing across them.

Tram lines are almost undetectable except from immediately above the field or when looking along the lines. Tram lining is not normally used on grass fields and should be taken to indicate some kind of crop. *Never* land across tram lines.

Young corn and other similar crops are scarcely damaged by a glider landing but no sympathy can be expected from the farmer if the crops are almost ripe. Although the landing itself may not cause much damage to the crop, considerable damage can be caused while derigging and moving the glider out, particularly by spectators who trample the field without a thought of the damage they do.

The glider is usually severely damaged by the drag of long corn on the wings and tail. The low position of the tailplane on many sailplanes results in it breaking away and, sometimes, snapping the rear of the fuselage. If one wing is low, it may catch the corn and wrench the wing badly. This is one of the main advantages of a Tee tail: it is well clear of the crops.

After the harvest there are plenty of stubble fields and these make ideal landing areas. Look carefully for the tram lines and land parallel to them.

If there are no tram lines, from a height it is sometimes difficult to tell if the field is a ripe crop or has already been cut and harvested. Look at the edges and for signs that some of the crop has been flattened by the wind.

A cut field will usually show light-coloured wheel marks across it where the farmer has driven to collect the bales of straw. There may be the odd bale or even a straw stack left in the field. If the straw has not yet been baled, land along the direction of the straw lines, taking care to keep the wings level.

A freshly burnt-off stubble field is easy to identify and ideal for landing. In many parts of the country it is possible to fly from airfield to airfield so that a premature descent does not involve landing in a field. Abandoned airfields are, usually, good forced-landing grounds, although the runways must be carefully examined before landing as they may be obstructed or broken up in places.

Golf links and race courses sometimes have usable landing areas and large playing fields can be guaranteed to be safe landing areas provided that they are deserted at the time. A single cricket or football field is too small for a safe landing in calm conditions.

Slope

One of the major factors which must be considered when choosing a field from the air is the slope of the ground.

A landing on sloping ground must always be up or across the slope, *never downhill*.

If the slope can be clearly seen from directly above, it is too steep for a safe landing and a further choice of field should be made. It is easiest to see any slope by moving out and viewing the fields and the surrounding country from several sides. Look at the lie of the land nearby in order to see the general trend of the hills and valleys in the surrounding country.

Fields near rivers and lakes slope towards the water. Fields with darker green areas indicate waterlogged or low-lying ground and are usually sloping towards the darkened areas.

Although it is not recommended, gliders can be landed up fairly steep slopes without damage provided that they do not slide down after landing. If this happens, the tailplane and rear of the fuselage may be seriously damaged by any obstruction unless the pilot is quick enough to get out and prevent the glider from running away.

Most gliders are fitted with a wheel brake but it is seldom very effective. However, it will shorten the landing run and also prevent the glider moving after landing.

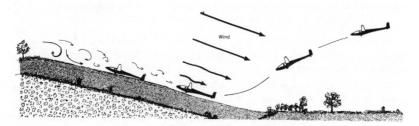

96. Landing on uphill slopes. More speed is essential to allow for the extra wind gradient, down-draught and turbulence.

Even a slight downhill slope will make it almost impossible to make the glider touch down, and the glider will tend to roll on without losing speed. The pilot will almost certainly have to put one wingtip on to the ground to prevent the glider running into the far boundary of the field. It is almost impossible to make a successful downhill landing, and even if a downwind landing is necessary, it is vital that the landing should be made up, or across any slope.

Often on the circuit a subtle cross-slope becomes apparent and it may be useful to change the approach to take advantage of it by landing uphill.

Extra speed is vital when landing up a slope since the change in attitude is more pronounced and a heavy landing will result if the glider flies into the slope.

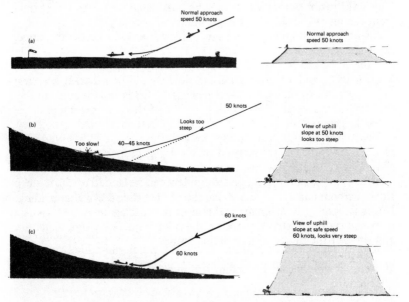

97. (a) View at a normal approach speed to a flat field. (b) A similar approach on an uphill slope looks far too steep. More speed and careful monitoring of the airspeed are essential. (c) View at a safe speed of 60 knots looks very steep but is safe.

It is particularly important to monitor the approach speed carefully during an uphill landing. Extra speed is essential but remember that the approach will appear to be far too steep and this frequently results in the pilot allowing the approach to become less steep, so losing speed and making a very heavy landing unavoidable. Even a slight uphill slope will result in a very short landing run so it is seldom necessary to make a very low approach over the boundary of the field. Furthermore, there will almost certainly be more turbulence and wind gradient effects in the lee of any slope.

If the wind direction is up the slope, the landing can be made across wind. This is not difficult, as an approach with the 'into wind' wing down counters the crosswind effect and gives more clearance for the wingtip.

It is wise to avoid choosing fields at the top of hills. If the ground does slope, the glider may slide to the bottom.

The approach and landing

It is difficult to give much advice on how to make foolproof approaches into small areas except to stress the need for planning. It is comparatively easy to arrive on the lee side of the field much too high and to fail to use up sufficient height before turning in to land, with a resultant risk of a serious overshoot.

The only practical difference between undershooting and overshooting is the speed at which the obstruction is hit. Undershooting, the glider hits at flying speed whereas, providing that it has touched down, the speed will be greatly reduced in an overshoot. In both cases the glider will probably be badly damaged and the pilot shaken.

Undershoot accidents are nearly always caused by underestimating the strength of the wind, or the turbulence if the field is in the lee of trees or hills. The wind strength can be assessed most accurately by making a comparatively long base leg instead of several short beats or S-turns to use up height. Undershooting used to be a common cause of field landing accidents, but with modern gliders having a very flat gliding angle, undershooting is almost unknown.

In general, bad approaches occur through getting too close to allow enough adjustment of height with the airbrakes to place the glider in the ideal position to turn in to land. S-turns are much more likely to result in poor positioning than a well-planned circuit type of approach. Naturally the pilot must be capable of making good landings with any setting of the airbrakes, across wind, and from short approaches. In fact he should be a complete master of his aircraft before attempting cross-country flights.

A particular warning is given against the temptation of trying to continue to soar at too low an altitude, waiting for what appears to be a certain source of lift to produce a thermal. It is very easy to sit just downwind of a steel works or similar thermal source waiting for the delayed sink to change to a gain of height, and to leave the actual choice of field and the method of approach to the last few hundred feet. This is much too late for safety.

Once the decision has been made to land, the wheel should be lowered and the airbrakes unlocked and any further lift should be ignored. It is particularly dangerous to attempt to soar in weak lift over the chosen field as it will upset the circuit planning and result in a poor approach.

It may also result in the glider drifting away from the field so that, if the lift fails, a new choice has to be made from a selection of poor fields.

The decision to land should be final and it is a good plan for the pilot to put the wheel down, trim the glider a little nose-heavy, unlock the airbrakes and to say to himself aloud: 'I am now going to land.'

In the case of inexperienced cross-country pilots, this should be done at about 800 feet.

It is easy to get into a bad position with too much height, downwind of the field, by circling and looking down at it. It is best to keep upwind and well to one side of the field, preferably several fields away. This makes it easier to look at the field and see any slope in the ground. Otherwise it is difficult to get a clear look at the field and to keep it in sight while getting into position for a good approach.

Once the choice of the approach path and circuit direction has been made, it is easiest to select certain features on the ground for the positions where it is planned to start the base leg and the final turn onto the approach. If the fields are of average size the base leg should be started at least two or three field lengths to one side of the landing area and the approach turn completed about one field length from the boundary of it. (Fig. 98.)

The tendency is always to get much too close to the field, particularly if the pilot is used to landing on an aerodrome or a large gliding site. Since the country surrounding the chosen landing area is usually unsuitable for a safe landing, the circuit and base leg must be made at a distance that will feel uncomfortably far away.

A similar position on the average gliding site might still be almost over the edge of the landing ground, and this may lead to the pilot keeping too close to the edge of the field instead of keeping well off to one side.

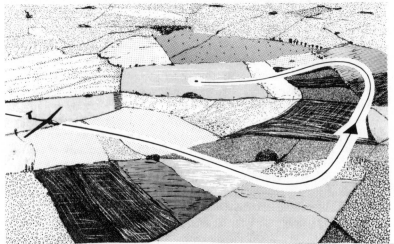

98. Making a field landing. Unless short of height, keep several fields away during the circuit and leave about one field length for the final approach.

Since the glider will glide about 600 yards for a loss of height of only 100 feet, a long cross-wind leg can be made quite safely, and more time is then available to adjust the height by using the airbrakes.

The altimeter must be ignored as it will not read accurate heights above any field which is a different height from that of the take-off. Heights below 500 feet are relatively easy to judge, and below about 200 feet a direct comparison can be made with the height of trees or buildings near the landing area. It is therefore best to use the airbrakes to descend to the position chosen for the base leg and to make sure that it is reached without too much height to spare.

Flying at the normal approach speed, the airbrakes should be used freely on the base leg so that the final turn can be completed without excess height and in a position to reach the landing area. It will be immediately apparent if too much height is being used up and therefore the most likely error to make is that of arriving too high. It is important to realise that any errors of judgement of height will be far greater above 300 feet than near the ground. (Fig. 99.)

The distance which the glider floats before touchdown is determined by the final approach speed. The approach should always be fast enough to allow a normal landing with full airbrake, or a heavy landing will occur if full airbrake has to be used unexpectedly at the last moment. However, in calm conditions the approach speed should not be faster than absolutely necessary or the glider may float a long way and overshoot the landing area.

After the final turn, the approach can be regulated with the airbrakes and, if the field is small, the boundary can be cleared by a small margin. Once it is certain that the boundary is going to be cleared safely, the pilot should concentrate on completing the landing well short of the far hedge.

The landing should be made with the tail well down so that the touchdown speed is as low as possible. Full airbrake should be applied immediately, if it is not already in use, to shorten the landing run and to prevent bouncing after touchdown. If there is any possibility of running into the far boundary, the wheel brake should be applied to get the maximum braking effect. The glider can be turned off to one side to lengthen the possible landing run and, if necessary, 'ground looped' by putting the wingtip onto the ground and applying full rudder to swing the glider round. This may damage the wingtip and skid but that is preferable to running into a fence or wall at speed. Remember, skids and wheel brakes are ineffective on wet grass.

In the event of the pilot misjudging the approach badly and overshooting the landing area, the glider can be flown onto the ground and held down with a forward movement on the stick. However, this nose-down type of landing is not recommended for normal landings as it often results in broken main skids and damaged bulkheads. The next field ahead, if any, may be less expensive.

Try to assess the situation during the final turn and if there is obviously

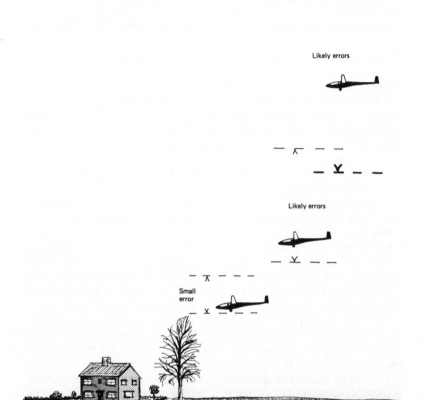

99. Height judgement errors. Whenever possible compare your height with trees or other tall obstructions.

plenty of height always open full airbrake and make quite sure that this would result in a slight undershoot. Then reduce it as necessary to make a normal approach. Remember that it is always far more difficult to recognise a slight overshoot situation than one where the glider is getting too low.

If full airbrake is required continuously, any misjudgement or area of rising air could result in an overshoot. Therefore, it is a sound policy to sideslip off any excess height at any time that full airbrake is being used for more than a few seconds on the final approach. Once the situation is back under control, stop the sideslip and continue a normal approach.

After landing, the pilot should first make sure that it is safe to get out of the glider. If the conditions are calm enough, he should get out and park the glider across wind, using the parachute as a temporary wingtip weight. In strong winds, it is wiser for the pilot to wait for help, trusting that someone in the vicinity has seen him land. When help arrives, the glider should be moved to the corner of the field nearest the gate. If it is parked near the gate or fence, it is much easier to keep people out of the field and this will reduce the possibility of crops or fences being damaged. It will also be easier to prevent any animals or small boys from damaging the glider. Some clubs equip their gliders with a set of pickets to hold the glider down securely after landing. However, it is nearly always possible to collect stones or earth and fill the parachute carrying bag or even a flying suit with them to use as a wingtip weight.

On *no* account should the glider be left alone in a field with animals. They can cause damage by chewing or licking the fabric, or by trampling on the wingtips or tail. A responsible-looking individual can be asked to keep both animals and onlookers out of the field or away from the glider while the pilot makes his way to the nearest telephone.

It is usually possible to recruit several bystanders to assist in derigging the glider and putting it into the trailer. They must be carefully briefed so that there is no risk of damage to the glider and, where possible, two persons should take the position usually held by one experienced club member.

If there is no prospect of a retrieve until the next day, if the weather looks stormy the glider can be derigged and the components can either be picketed down in the open, or, if possible, moved to some kind of shelter for the night.

If the flight is likely to be used as a qualification for Silver 'C' or a record claim, the barograph should not be unsealed. A landing certificate should be made out on any piece of paper and signed by two witnesses, giving the following information:

> Name of pilot.
> Aircraft type and number.
> Time and date of landing.
> The exact location of the landing area.
> The signatures and addresses of two reliable witnesses.

The police are always most helpful, and it is wise to telephone them if a landing is made in a place where a large crowd of spectators are likely to gather. One policeman is a match for a hundred small boys and may save a lot of costly damage to the glider and to neighbouring property.

Most farmers are very tolerant of any minor damage which may be caused by the glider. (In practice, the landing seldom makes more than a slight wheel mark across the field and this is usually undetectable after a few days.)

If any damage is caused to private property, the pilot should remember that the glider is covered by insurance for third party risks and that it may prejudice any claim if he makes an admission of liability. However, it should be clearly appreciated that a glider pilot has no right to trespass by landing on a farmer's field and that it is in the interest of the whole gliding movement to maintain the happy relationship which at present exists in most places.

23   Cross-country soaring

Training—Planning the flight—Preparing your maps—Picking good days—
Super days—Selecting the task—Turning-point photography—
Declarations—Cross-country briefing sheet for early cross-countries—
Reminders about field landings—Preparation—The flight—Map reading—
What to do when uncertain of your position—Food and drink in flight—
Retrieving arrangements—Preparations on the day—Advice for first
cross-country flights—Cross-country flying in motor gliders

Cross-country flying is not difficult, and in good conditions flights of over
100 miles can be made by comparatively inexperienced pilots on their
first attempts.

The art of cross-country flying combines many skills. Soaring ability,
practical meteorology and navigation all play a big part in enabling the
pilot to fly his glider where he wants to go.

Training

Not every glider pilot wants to fly cross-country and certainly no one
should unless he feels confident and really wants to go. Often there is a
certain amount of subtle pressure put on club pilots so that they feel that
they have to conform. This can be very dangerous.

Each pilot knows his own ability and should never do anything that
he is not happy about, least of all go off across country in a glider.

However, with modern facilities for dual instruction, a pilot who is
unsure of himself or his ability can usually have a chance of trying the
sport with an instructor or other competent cross-country pilot so that
he does not have the worry and responsibility for the safety of the aircraft.
It is also possible to practise selecting and making approaches into fields
in a two-seater motor glider so that the possibility of landing in a strange
field loses its worries.

After first solo, most glider pilots take about twenty to thirty flights
to settle down and establish confidence in their ability. From then on they
need to be given a programme of further training to develop their flying
abilities and judgement to the standard required for cross-country flying.
This will vary from place to place.

In England, where in many places there are plenty of reasonable fields,
it may be necessary to land in a very small field if the conditions suddenly
deteriorate while the pilot is flying over a bad area. Considerable experience
is needed to ensure that the pilot's flying will not go to pieces while under
this kind of pressure.

In many parts of Australia, the majority of the 'paddocks' are larger than many airfields and probably a lower standard of flying ability would be acceptable.

Each club will have developed its own standards based on their conditions and experiences.

At Lasham, for example, currently the normal minimum experience for a first cross-country is a hundred solo flights and thirty hours of solo flying. The pre-solo training includes two sets of spot landings (without the use of the altimeter), full airbrake sideslip approaches, solo spinning, and a minimum of three half-hour field landing sessions in a motor glider. There is also a dual cross-country in the Janus or motor glider to ensure the pilot has some experience of map reading.

The dual cross-country is mainly to coach the pilot in thermalling and cross-country techniques but also serves to check the pilot's airmanship and particularly his behaviour amongst other machines in busy thermals.

After a thorough training like this a pilot will be much more aware of his limitations and will know whether he really wants to go cross-country. The average club pilot should have no difficulties if he is well briefed and sent off on a suitable day at a time of year when there are plenty of landable fields.

However, there is no point in setting off unless your soaring ability is reasonably developed. Many pilots fancy their chances of a successful cross-country flight when their experience only consists of one or two thermal flights of an hour or so. Even a 5-hour duration flight in thermals is not much indication of ability if it is done in exceptional soaring conditions.

It is one thing to soar locally over the gliding site holding onto every scrap of weak lift and quite another to make progress from cloud to cloud in a predetermined direction. Unless a pilot has practised moving from cloud to cloud and being selective about which thermals he uses, he is unlikely to get very far on his first trip. It is also very important to gain experience in soaring and using very weak lift at only 1,000 feet or so, because in many cases this is going to be the height at which the decision to land will finally be made.

The great disadvantage of the 5-hour duration leg of the Silver 'C' is that it encourages the pilot to stay up using every bit of lift, rather than being selective and moving on when the lift is weak and there are better prospects elsewhere. The only good thing about it is that most people learn the need to get really comfortable and to relax more when they are flying.

However, it is an excellent opportunity to gain exerience at cross-country techniques if it is used to fly a small task round predetermined points within easy gliding reach of the home base.

For example, by choosing two or three turning-points about 8 – 10 miles away and upwind of the gliding site, there need never be any risk of landing out or getting lost.

In the course of the 5-hour duration flight such a course may be flown round several times, giving the pilot a good measure of his cross-country speed and ability. It is also an ideal opportunity to try taking proper photographs of the turning-points, which will be a necessary skill for the longer badge flights.

Once you become reasonably confident about your thermalling ability and the prospects of having to land in a strange field, you can seriously contemplate making a cross-country flight.

Planning the flight

Good flight planning is one of the secrets of successful cross-country flying. The beginner is generally fully occupied with the task of soaring efficiently and looking for promising conditions ahead and does not want to have to spend much time navigating.

On most glider flights the navigation consists of map reading from feature to feature along the required track. If part of the flight is in cloud it will be essential to know the compass course to steer between thermals. This should be estimated before the flight, when there is time to check it, and not in flight, when it is only too easy to make arithmetical mistakes.

A few minutes spent studying the map before the flight will reveal the most obvious features which will enable the glider's position to be checked quickly and without doubt.

Map reading is largely a matter of experience, logical thinking, and the refusal to become flustered. Great Britain is a difficult country for map reading because there are so many apparently similar features to confuse a beginner. It is always much more difficult to find out where you are than to confirm your position when it is known.

The pilot must be able to identify his position quickly by reference to a map and this necessitates a good knowledge of the symbols used on them, and the ability to recognise features on the ground. The glider pilot will find map reading easier if he knows the country below him either from previous flying experience or even by having travelled through it by road.

Seen from the air, only the most prominent features are of value and, in Great Britain, such features are often so close together that they can easily be confused with each other if taken individually. A reliable pinpoint is usually one in which two or three prominent features correspond exactly with those shown on the map. Air maps are specially produced to mark those features which can be easily identified from the air.

The most useful maps for gliding are the quarter- and the half-million series (1 : 500,000 is approximately eight miles to the inch). If anything the quarter-million shows too much detail and the half-million scale rather too little. The half-million has all the airways and other controlled air space, whereas the quarter-million only shows controlled airspace below 3,000 feet but is useful in poor visibility and for finding the turning-points and checking that you are in the correct sector for photographing them.

The quarter-million (1 : 250,000) is an over-printed version of the quarter inch to one mile road map.

Preparing your maps

Before you fold your maps in any way, draw in circles at 5 nautical mile (or some other convenient distance) spacings around your home base. This will enable you to know your distance from home without having to use a scale to measure it. Also shade in any permanent 'no go' restricted or danger areas or controlled airspace which are prohibited to gliders.

However you choose to fold your maps you will find the need to refold them quite often. Try to fold the map so that your home base is in a convenient position. Make sure that you have a good area of map in the direction you are most likely to go.

I use clips or even staples to hold my maps so that they cannot possibly become unfolded and be a nuisance in the cockpit. A transparent plastic envelope will do the same job and also provides good storage for the map between flights.

Most English maps are sold plain or with a shiny plastic finish which makes them more durable. Using these, the track lines that you draw in with a Chinagraph pencil or brush pen must be covered with Sellotape to stop them rubbing off when your hands get sweaty. Unfortunately, Chinagraph pencils break easily and for this reason I prefer just to use a soft 2B pencil on a plain map. This makes it easier to write notes on the map in flight and to put an 'X' and the time at each definite pin-point if the map reading gets difficult because of hazy weather. I usually buy a new half-million map each year.

Picking good days

Clearly an elementary knowledge of meteorology can be useful in choosing which day to go gliding. However, this is usually acquired during the course of learning to glide and a serious study of the subject is quite unnecessary.

It is well worth noting that in most countries the exceptional soaring conditions occur on the day after the passage of a cold front and when a ridge or other area of high pressure is approaching. At first this brings the cooler, clearer, unstable air which results in the stronger thermals.

The very gradual subsidence of the air in the high-pressure systems helps to prevent the over-development of the clouds and keeps the amount of cumulus small.

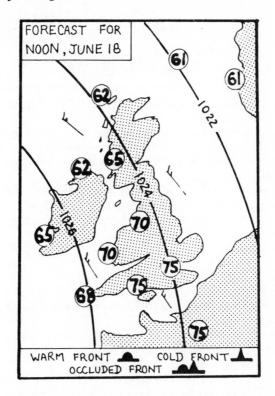

FORECAST FOR NOON, JUNE 18

WARM FRONT   COLD FRONT
OCCLUDED FRONT

100. The weather chart for an ideal day. Note the anticyclonic curvature of the isobars, giving light northerly winds.

If the air is unstable to a greater height, large cumulus and cumulo-nimbus clouds may form. With these there will be some very strong lift as the clouds develop but they will often kill the lift elsewhere for 30 or 40 miles around by causing a gradual subsidence of the air. If the upper cloud is ice crystals as is the case with a cumulo-nimbus, the cloud will persist for several hours until the ice slowly evaporates away and allows the sun to break through again.

Once the rain or hail begins from these clouds, a severe cold down-draught is produced at the upwind edge of the storm. Just ahead of this cold down-draught and on the edge of the rain it is normal to find a good area of rising air. The cold down-draught is acting like a small cold front and is shovelling up the air in front of it as it moves along at a greater speed than the normal surface wind.

Sometimes the cold air moves ahead of the storm as a layer of air only a few hundred feet deep travelling out at 20 to 30 knots. This results in a very big change in wind speed and direction at the top of that layer, which makes landing dangerous for any kind of aircraft. Since it cannot be seen, it presents an invisible hazard and has caused a number of airline accidents in the past. It could cause a complete loss of speed in a glider at a height where no recovery is possible.

With the approach of a low-pressure area, there is usually a tendency for the cumulus clouds to 'over-develop' and spread out as a layer of strato-cumulus. This cuts off the sun's heating and stops, or at least reduces, the thermal activity while it persists.

When the wind is blowing in directly from a coastline, the moist cool air will result in a low cloud base. Further inland the air will have warmed up and dried out so that the cloud base will be much higher and the thermals stronger.

Super days

For the best soaring conditions in England the statistics show that the following features are necessary:

Origin of the air: from the NW, N or NE. (NEVER from the S.)

Curvature of the isobars: anticyclonic (clockwise).

Mean sea level pressure: 1,023 mb ±7 mb.

5,000 feet wind: less than 16 knots from WNW to ENE sector.

Stability of the air: maximum surface temperature greater than 14°C higher than the temperature at 850 mb level (5,000 feet) with stable air above to limit the growth of the cumulus.

Surface dew point: 11 to 18°C below maximum temperature.

Sunshine: at least 8 hours of bright sun.

Rainfall: no overnight rain, ground dry at 06.00 G.M.T.

Visibility: more than 20 km.

Much of this information can be deduced from the shipping forecasts, and from VOLMET, which is a continuous broadcast for aircraft on the VHF aircraft waveband.

Selecting the task

The aim of most first cross-country flights is to fulfil the requirements for the Silver 'C' distance leg. The flight must be at least 50 km (32 miles) with a maximum difference of height between the release and the landing place of not more than 1 per cent of the distance covered. Fig. 101 shows the minimum distances required in different circumstances. It is usually easiest to fly downwind for such flights unless the wind is very light.

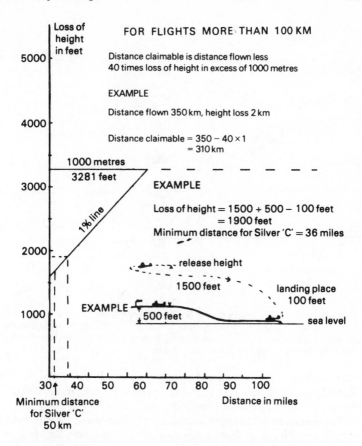

101. The 1 per cent rule for badge flights and records.

It may also be flown as an out-and-return, triangle or dog-leg flight as long as it is correctly declared and documented and the leg claimed is over the 50 km.

A remote 'start' point or remote 'finish' point may also be declared.

Our pilots seem to favour declaring their goal as a remote finish point so that if they get there they have made their distance leg for the Silver 'C'. After photographing their goal they are then free to try to fly home again and lose nothing if they cannot make it and have to land on the way back. If this is done it is important to make sure that the launch height is no more than would be allowed to make the flight and land at their goal. The 1 per cent rule still applies although the whole flight might be more than 100 km.

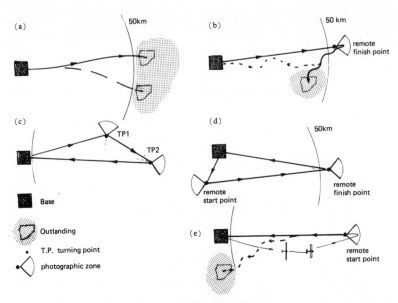

102. Tasks for Silver 'C' distance flights. (a) Distance over 50 km. (b) Distance to a declared finish point over 50 km. (Allows an attempt to return.) (c) Declared triangle with one leg over 50 km. (d) and (e) Distance from declared remote start point to declared finish point or anywhere over 50 km. (1 per cent rule applies to the leg claimed.)

A long flight round a declared course is obviously more creditable than a casual wander downwind. This is reflected in the requirements for Gold 'C' and Diamond awards. (See Figs. 103 and 104.)

The more experienced pilot should plan flights to suit various wind and weather conditions so that he has a number of possible flights in mind for each wind direction. After considering the weather forecast he can then select a suitable task, and test his judgement of the conditions and his skill as a soaring pilot.

Triangular courses and out-and-return flights are much more interesting than a straight dash downwind, and reduce the distance of any possible retrieve.

The selection of a task presents an interesting problem. The pilot must first consider the weather. How high is the cloud base and how high will it become during the day? Is it likely to over-develop or is there any high- or medium-level cloud to obscure the sun and limit the distance travelled? Will the thermals be strong enough to ensure a good average speed? Are there likely to be cloud streets which could help progress directly into or downwind?

On a really windy day an out-and-return flight directly upwind along good cloud streets is an interesting possibility. It will take hours to penetrate against the wind, but only a short time for the return journey.

If the wind is less than 15 knots at cruising height it should be possible to fly in any direction in a modern glider. But before declaring a task the pilot should always ask himself what average ground speed he can hope to make and how many hours of soaring he is likely to have.

Downwind flights for Gold 'C' and Diamond distance awards are only possible when the weather conditions are good over a large part of the country. This occurs on relatively few days in each year and it is not always possible to forecast them with certainty. Quite often after a seemingly perfect forecast a patch of upper cloud will form and cut off the sun's heating and the thermal activity.

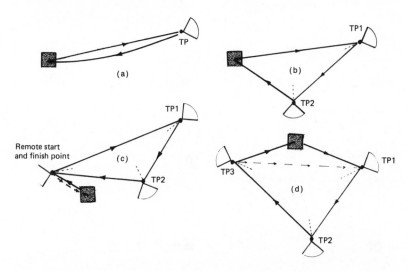

103. Options for 300 km Diamond goal flights. (a) Out-and-return flight. (b) Triangle. (c) Triangle with remote start and finish points. (d) Triangle declaring three turn points with take-off and landing at remote point (counting only the triangle for distance).

However, such distances can be flown on more frequent occasions if they are made in a number of legs. Careful planning may enable good soaring conditions in the vicinity of hills and mountains or the sea breeze front to be used to supplement the normal thermal soaring.

For example, if the wind strength is sufficient to ensure good wave or hill lift, it may be well worth while planning a flight across-wind in order to use this lift from a long ridge of hills at the beginning or end of the day when the thermal activity is likely to be poor.

Late in the day it may be possible to use the lift at the edge of the sea breeze to cruise at high speed parallel with the coastline. This sea breeze 'front' will vary in strength with the degree of heating of the land, and the direction and strength of the wind in relation to the coastline. The

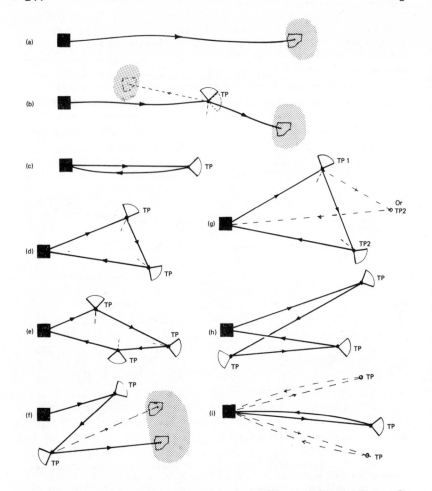

104. Options for 300, 500, 750 and 1,000 km distance flights. (a) Straight distance. (b) Distance with one declared turn point. (c) Out-and-return. (d) Triangle. (e) Quadrilateral. (f) Double zig-zag. (g) Triangle with alternative turn point. (h) Double out-and-return. (i) Out-and-return with alternative turn points. All turn points must be declared but need not all be used and may be flown in any order decided in flight.

lift will be strongest when the wind blows directly off shore, and will be poor and farther inland where the coastline bends parallel with the wind.

Areas which are poor thermal-producers must be avoided, and many of these are obvious from an examination of the map. Low-lying country such as an estuary is normally poor for soaring, but if the conditions are very unstable, the additional moisture from the damp ground may help to produce large cumulus clouds or even thunderstorms.

For a Silver 'C' flight, whenever possible, declare a recognised airfield as the goal, as there is then no risk of damage to the glider or of causing annoyance to farmers. A landing within the perimeter track of an airfield or within 1,000 metres of the declared place constitutes a goal flight.

For an out-and-return flight or a flight with multiple turning-points, the turning-points must be photographed or the glider must be identified by a reliable observer at the turning point. This is difficult unless it is a gliding site and you can call them on radio.

Turning-point photography

The detailed rules for records and International badge awards are laid down in the F.A.I. Sporting Code for gliders, obtainable from your National Gliding Association.

Briefly the rules require that the film is a single length of uncut film showing in the correct sequence:

The declaration taken in the presence of the Official Observer.

The 'Departure Point' taken from the correct location, if it is a 'Remote Start'.

The 'Turning-Points' and 'Remote Finish Point' (if used) from the correct location.

After landing, the declaration or the glider in the field showing the identification markings.

The film must be handed over to an Official Observer for developing.

The photographs of turning-points must be taken from a position within the Observation Zone which is a quadrant (90°) with its apex at the turning-point and orientated symmetrically to and remote from the two legs meeting at the Turning-Point.

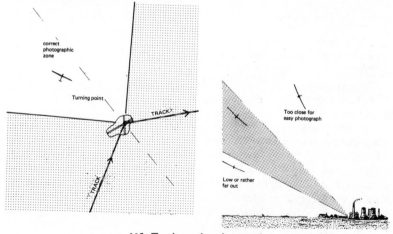

105. Turning point photography.

For a Remote Start or Finish the Observation Zone is symmetrical to the track line.

It is extremely difficult to take hand-held camera photographs from a glider in turning flight. Usually it costs several hundred feet and often the photos taken prove unsatisfactory.

It is best to fix the camera to the cockpit side viewing out towards the wingtip and it is ideal if it can be mounted on either side of the cockpit to allow for left- or right-hand turns. If it is sighted so that the wingtip is in the top of the frame in the viewfinder, it is an easy matter to bank over until the wingtip appears just above the feature to be taken. This will guarantee getting the turning-point in the picture.

At first it is best to go well beyond the turning-point so that your position is less critical.

Always double-check that you are well inside the Photographic Zone, which you should have clearly marked on your quarter-million map. Take several shots to make quite sure. No errors are accepted for badge flights; the photographs must show you were in the correct quadrant.

It is well worth while practising taking these turning-point photographs so that you waste the minimum of time and height on an actual cross-country.

In selecting a task it is important to choose a well defined feature for each turning-point. A particular town cannot be used whereas the market square or a particular church in the town will be acceptable. The declared feature should be in the photograph.

Declarations

```
                          Cross-Country
                         Declaration Form

Pilot's name:
Glider type and number:
Date:
Starting point:
1st turn point:
2nd turn point:
3rd turn point:
4th turn point:
Goal:
Distance:
Pilot's signature:
Official Observer's name:
Official Observer's number:
Time of declaration:
```

Cross-country briefing sheet for early cross-countries

To be filled in for every cross-country flight until cleared for unlimited flying and to be kept by the pilot.

Pilot's name:
Glider type:
Time:
Day:
Date:
Intended task:
Serviceable trailer available today?
Nominated crew chief for possible retrieve:
Max. launch height (for Silver 'C' attempts only):
Surface wind:
Visibility:
Cloud base now:
Expected:

CHECK THESE POINTS BEFORE FINAL BRIEFING

1 Correct maps with route clearly marked
2 Restricted or danger areas en route
3 Airways en route
4 State of fields
5 Warnings about slopes
6 Warnings about approach speeds for uphill slopes
7 Heights for selecting field and decision to land
8 Possibilities and hazards of sea breeze front
9 Permission to land at destination airfield?
10 Minimum height to leave airfield
11 Airfields to avoid landing at
12 Usable airfields en route
13 Royal flights and special restrictions in force today
14 Landing certificate for Silver 'C'
15 Briefing Instructor's Name (Block Caps)

Reminders about field landings (to be read before each early cross-country)

1. *By 2,500'* – Pick an area with two or three potentially suitable fields: consider the surrounding terrain.
2. *By 2,000'* – If landing appears probable—fly to suitable area—preferably flat and unobstructed—you will cover far more ground if you fly downwind.
   a. Are there hills to create turbulence or surface wind problems?
   b. Are there HT cables, TV masts or other large obstacles?
   c. Does the ground slope visibly? If it does, it is too steep!
   d. What is the general wind direction?
3. *By 1,000' – 1,200'* – Select your field considering the following:
   a. *Surface wind* – assess the wind by means of your drift or by smoke and cloud shadow movement. Always aim to land in a direction which will give you a headwind component. Do not land downwind.
   b. *Field length* – remember that the apparent size of any field is seen relative to the size of those surrounding it. An acceptable field for a modern glider would be 300 – 400 yards long with relatively unobstructed boundaries.
   c. *Obstructions* – choose a clear approach. Trees and buildings will create turbulence and seriously reduce the effective length of the field.
   d. *Slope* – any visible downslope in the field is unacceptable. A similar upslope is a good feature. Examine surrounding fields for slope indications. Choose uphill slopes if possible—what looks flat may be downhill.
   e. *Surface* – look for fields in the following order of priority:
      i. Stubble – look carefully for tram lines, do not land across them.
      ii. Grass – any areas or strips which are a slightly different colour indicate electric fences.
      iii. Short crop – the surface should appear more brown than green.
      iv. Other cropped fields may present a hazard on landing—remember half-ripe crops may look like stubble—consider the season!
   f. *Stock* – sheep panic, run and sometimes jump up. Cows are curious—horses bolt. A solitary cow is probably a bull! Try and avoid landing amongst animals. After landing never leave the glider alone with cattle.
4. *By 800' AGL* – Position the glider well upwind and well to one side of your field. Select an approximate position for the final turn, about one field length back from your field, and only move in closer if

you can see that you will be lower than you would want to be on the airfield. Be conscious of the tendency to cramp your circuit and plan to avoid doing so; you are far more likely to overshoot than undershoot. Use the airbrakes liberally to ensure you are not too high at the start of the base leg.

5. *Base leg position* – Plan to be abeam of your touchdown by 400 – 500'. Resist the common tendency to position the base leg too close. Select a safe approach speed, and monitor and maintain it. Allow an adequate margin of height over obstructions. Once you are certain you can safely clear them, use full airbrake to achieve early touchdown. Hold off fully for minimum touchdown speed on rough surfaces. Concentrate on keeping the wings level, especially in long grass or crop.

6. *Uphill landings* – Landing into wind uphill means a stronger wind gradient effect. Expect extra sink and use much more speed and maintain it until the roundout. It is *vital* to monitor the A.S.I. during the final approach to maintain this extra speed. Approaching into a field which has an appreciable upslope can give the visual illusion that the glide path and attitude are steeper than they actually are.

Preparation

First the intended track should be marked clearly on the maps and the direction of the track measured against a nearby north – south grid line. If the track passes near a control zone or airway, these should be marked clearly as a reminder to avoid cloud-flying in that vicinity. The maps should then be folded to enable the whole track to be read without the need for refolding them in flight more than is absolutely necessary. (There is nothing more awkward than trying to refold a map with one hand, or while attempting to fly the glider with the stick between your knees.)

Where the flight is a race or a record attempt, it may be a good idea to divide the track into intervals representing ten or fifteen minutes' flying at the estimated average cruising speed. This enables the pilot to judge how things are going without mental calculations.

In any case, if the flight is intended to be a long one, it is a sound scheme to make half-way and three-quarter way marks with the last time of arrival which will still allow the goal to be reached. If the conditions are poor, or time is wasted during the first two or three hours, it may be quite impossible to make up the time later in the flight and it may be better to turn back and reduce the retrieving distance.

Flying in mountainous areas and wild country with little or no habitation, it is prudent to mark every known safe landing area and airfield and to calculate the height required to fly from one to the next and mark it clearly on the map. The tactics are then to stay within easy reach of one place until sufficient height has been gained to be quite sure of reaching the next.

Where the track lies almost downwind there will be no drift off course, but care should be taken to allow for the variation to obtain the correct magnetic heading of the track. (See page 164.)

If the track is more than 20° across wind, an allowance for drift must be made during the glide between thermals. This has to take into account the effect of the wind during the climb and the glide, and is, therefore, quite a large angle for even moderate winds. An approximate course can be estimated by assuming a cruising speed of 30 – 40 knots and this will avoid serious errors if the glider is flown in cloud early on the flight.

Generally, it is better to keep slightly upwind of the desired track while the thermals are strong. It is then possible to cruise downwind when conditions deteriorate.

A well selected course allowing for drift may save many miles of fumbling, and this is one way in which an expert will score against an inexperienced pilot in competition flying.

A small knee pad strapped lightly to one leg and fitted with an attachment for a wrist-watch or stop-watch is most useful. A pencil should be attached to the pad so that it cannot be lost in the bottom of the cockpit. The information so far obtained can now be made up in a convenient form for use during the flight. The forecast winds, magnetic tracks, distances and times can be written at the top of the log for easy reference, and the rest of the sheet ruled off into columns.

The altimeter sub scale readings for the height of the airfield above sea level (known as the QNH) and the reading for a zero reading (known as the QFE) should be noted before take-off. This will allow for re-setting it to determine the base of an airway (1,013 mb or 29.92 inches) and you then have both settings if you subsequently need them.

The flight

The time and height of the launch should be noted on the log and, if necessary, the launch point must be emphasised by descending to register a low point on the barograph. (See page 169.)

If the first town or pin-point near the track has been spotted during the climb, it is a simple matter to stop circling as the lift peters out and turn towards this point straight away so that height is not wasted trying to get on the right course by direct reference to the compass. However, if there is a crosswind remember that you will need to select a cloud well upwind of that place so that by the time you have reached it *and* climbed back up you have drifted to a position above it. If you do not allow for this you will be miles off track after your next climb.

Map reading

The map should be orientated so that features shown on it can be easily compared with the actual features on the ground. It is easiest to note distinctive features on the map and then look for them on the ground; this is the correct method to use provided that the position of the glider is known to within a few miles. Combinations of railways, rivers, main roads and towns are generally satisfactory for pin-pointing, particularly if the feature is across the track and is unlikely to be missed. For example, if the map shows a main railway line running across the track with a distinctive shaped side-line joining it by a small town and a canal running alongside, the pilot need only look out for the railway and canal. When these are spotted, a further glance at the map will show the relative positions of all the features and so determine the exact position of the glider. Care must be taken not to jump to a conclusion based on the appearance of one feature. It is comparatively simple to get miles off track by a combination of course errors and a change in wind, so that it is quite likely that there may be two or three features inside the possible area which taken singly would satisfy that shown on the map.

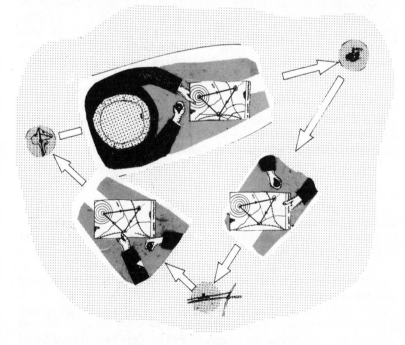

106. Orientating the map. For easy map reading, turn the map so that ground features can be compared with those on the map.

It is vital, therefore, to check any pin-point to make sure that all the features confirm the position. No map is completely up to date, and it is always possible to miss a feature which is marked clearly on the map.

Most beginners attempt to find every detail instead of relying on main features spaced at reasonable intervals. This leads to a feeling of uncertainty if something is not marked on the map or if some feature slips by unnoticed on the ground in the shadow of the clouds. There is also a tendency to forget the scale of the map and the relative distances between features on the ground so that they may be wrongly identified. This is often the case using the quarter-inch to the mile map, when small villages and roads are easily confused and seldom constitute a sound pin-point by themselves.

Airfields are not good landmarks unless they can be definitely identified by the letters near the signals area or other confirming features. A very large number of disused airfields will not be found marked, and many marked ones will only have almost un-recognisable signs of old runways or taxiways. However, they are good thermal-producing areas since they are well drained and may have large areas of concrete runways and perimeters which warm up quickly in the sun. A slight diversion to identify the airfield is, therefore, worth while but remember that you must be over 2,000 feet to keep clear of the traffic area.

Roads do not in themselves constitute good pin-points since only the major roads are shown on the half-million map, and it is difficult to distinguish between main roads and other wide roads from several thousand feet high. Also, many of the main roads are, in fact, mere lanes.

Rivers and canals are useful features because in most parts of the country they are sufficiently rare to be unmistakable. However, from 4,000 feet or so it is sometimes difficult to distinguish between roads, railways and canals because of the shadows thrown across them by trees. Small rivers and lakes may become dried up in summer or may flood over the surrounding countryside, making them difficult to identify. Often the distinctive shape of the river may provide an accurate pin-point and road or rail bridges over them may provide an easy way of identifying the exact position.

Small towns often have a collection of minor features which provide definite identification, but larger towns and industrial areas may be very difficult to identify because of the mass of conflicting evidence which can be seen. The town may have increased in size and may even have railway junctions running to the factories which are not marked on the map.

Large areas of woodland may be identified by their shape on the map, but may have changed since the survey.

Physical features such as hills and mountains form good aids to pin-pointing but are not easily seen from high up.

A useful tip is to check your position and heading by looking back at the last two places which you have flown over. This is often easier than trying to spot a place ahead, since you have already identified these places as you flew over them and can recognise them quickly. For example, if our required track passes over an airfield and a few miles further on over a town, we can then check if we are still on track or to which side we have wandered by looking back to those landmarks and seeing if we are still in line with them. Using this method, we can check the direction in which we need to head, so that we can straighten up accurately as we prepare to leave a thermal.

If you are doubtful about your ability to navigate over strange country it is worth while making a route plan listing all the obvious landmarks and their position relative to your track line. A table like the one shown will make this easier.

DIST. n. mls	LEFT OF TRACK	ON TRACK	RIGHT OF TRACK
5			Basingstoke town 2 n. mls
11		Kingsclere Mast	
15			Greenham Common airfield 2–3 n. mls
23	Hungerford Town railway/canal 2 n. mls		Welford bomb dump 3 n. mls
26		Membury M4	
35	Swindon Town 2 n. mls	South Marston airfield	

What to do when uncertain of your position

Although it is comparatively easy to map-read from place to place along a track, it is much more difficult to find where you are once you have become lost. The chances of putting things right are greatly reduced when the pilot is perturbed by the situation and starts making wild guesses, at the same time flying inefficiently and losing height. In a glider, provided that there are no prohibited areas or controlled airspace nearby, there is no additional risk in carrying on. It is better to accept the fact that you are temporarily lost and settle down to find where you have gone wrong.

The flight should be continued using the course as planned and no change should be made, except to keep in good soaring conditions, until a definite pin-point has been found.

Unless the ground is known from previous experience, it is almost always a waste of time trying to find out your position until a straight course is resumed.

The first thing is to check back on the map to the last reliable pin-point. This may mean considering whether the last pin-points were correct or might have been wrong. A wrong pin-point might be based on one or more rather unreliable feature. If a note of the time and place was made on the map or in the log, it is easy to find out how long it is since leaving that position and the approximate distance flown can then be estimated. In general, it is unlikely that the error in position will ever exceed one-third of the distance travelled from the last pin-point, except in very poor soaring conditions when virtually no progress may be made. If a rough circle is drawn round the estimated position with a radius of about one-third of the distance from the last definite pin-point, the search can then be concentrated on that part of the map. A good lookout must now be kept for features on the ground which may be identified on the map. Where the feature is a railway or similar straight-line object, the direction should be carefully noted so that it can be distinguished on the map from other similar features running in different directions.

The position of several main features relative to each other along the direction of flight will normally narrow down the search to one or two possible positions on the map. It is then easy to confirm the position by the next feature.

Unless the glider has been in cloud for some time, it is unlikely that it is far off track and, in practice, the most common reason for being uncertain of position is impatience in waiting for the expected features to appear on the ground. This gives rise to the assumption that they must have been overlooked and soon the pilot may be attempting to map-read many miles ahead of his actual position, naturally without success.

The identification letters on service aerodromes and the aerodrome name sometimes marked on the hangars or field of civil aerodromes may provide a positive pin-point when all else fails. The identification letters are usually the first and last letters of the place-name, so that, even if the airfield is not marked, it may be recognised by the letters corresponding to a town within the area of uncertainty. Sometimes, the types of aircraft on the airfield provide the final clue when there are several aerodromes close together and the pilot has some idea of the types of aircraft used at the aerodromes.

In England, do not land on a strange airfield unless you see gliders on it. Most airfields regard gliders as a nuisance and hazard to other traffic and you will usually be wiser to keep clear of them and land in a field, especially if you are lost.

When it is required to fly back onto track, it is useful to note that an error of 1 mile off track in 60 miles' distance is the same as a 1° track error. This is known as the one-in-sixty rule for estimating angles, and it can be used very easily for measuring angles on maps.

For example, 5 miles off track in 30 miles is an angle of 10°; 2 miles in 10 miles is an angle of 12°.

$$\text{Track error} = \frac{60}{\text{distance in miles}} \times \text{error in miles}$$

It is not suggested that track errors should be calculated accurately in flight, but some knowledge of the alteration of course needed for getting back onto track will prevent wild estimates which waste valuable height.

In conclusion, finding your way in the air will be easier if you:

1. Plan the flight thoroughly and prepare a flight plan and maps. Note the course required, allowing for the wind velocity and variation.
2. Study the map and try to memorise the main pin-points.
3. Keep the map correctly orientated.
4. Read the map first and then look on the ground for the features shown, unless lost.
5. Note each pin-point and the time on the map or log.
6. Never rely on a single feature unless it can be confirmed by others in the area or is an indisputable natural feature such as coastline, large lake, river or range of hills.
7. Never try to account for every minor feature seen on the ground or keep an exact pin-point all the time.
8. Look back and check your line of flight by reference to any clearly identifiable features that you have passed over.
9. If uncertain of the position, work from the last reliable pin-point, check the time elapsed and search the circle of uncertainty round the estimated position on the map. Keep on the same course.
10. When uncertain of your position note the features on the ground and then look for similar ones on the map. Never guess or jump to conclusions.
11. If you become really lost, unless you are certain that you are well clear of restricted airspace, select a good field and land without delay.
12. Never let the map reading interfere with the soaring; it is more important to keep up. Any passer-by will delight in telling you where you are after you have landed.

Food and drink in flight

It used to be thought that chocolate and glucose sweets should be taken to ward off hunger and provide instant energy. However, it is now recognised that on a long flight sandwiches and proper food are far better and that sweets leave the body worse off after the initial benefit has gone.

Although there are obvious problems if the glider pilot drinks too much liquid before and during the flight, it is now becoming universally accepted that the consequences of becoming even slightly dehydrated can be very serious indeed.

Even in relatively cool climates the human body is constantly evaporating off moisture without obvious sweating, and after a few hours is becoming significantly short of liquid. This needs to be replaced or eventually there will be trouble.

In some ways dehydration has rather a similar affect to lack of oxygen. Without realising it the pilot may lapse into a state of well-being and indecision which makes him less efficient and much more liable to make serious errors without being conscious of them.

On a hot day the only solution is to keep drinking and not to risk dehydration. Obviously, strenuous exercise such as rigging and pushing gliders should be avoided in the heat of the day just before flying. It is wise to try to get these things done early in the morning and to keep out of the sun as much as possible. A white cloth hat will help to reduce the loss from your head and this is vital in the summer.

In hot climates it becomes necessary to carry extra water for drinking in case you have to walk miles to the telephone after landing and have to wait many hours for the retrieve team to arrive.

Retrieving arrangements

If possible, arrangements for the retrieve should be made before take-off, in order to reduce the time taken to collect the glider after landing. In marginal conditions, particularly for competition flights, it is worth using radio between the glider and the retrieving crew and for the trailer to attempt to keep up with the glider during the flight.

The retrieving team can keep in contact with their glider and share the excitement throughout the flight. When conditions are poor they can even help by pointing out promising-looking clouds, other gliders, or even suitable fields for landing.

In most clubs, the trailer-towing vehicle is often unable to leave the gliding site until the evening. In this case, it is easier to report the position of the landing to the club by telephone and settle down for a long wait. 35 miles per hour is a good average speed for a car towing a trailer, and unless careful map reference and directions for finding the glider are given, it may take some time to locate it, particularly in the dark.

The requirements for the Silver, Gold and Diamond awards allow for out-and-return flights, triangles and zig-zag flights provided that they are properly declared before take-off and conform to the regulations laid down by the international body, the F.A.I. These save the pilot a considerable expense by eliminating the long road or air retrieves inevitable with a flight downwind, in some cases of several hundred miles.

It is useful to know that with British roads, the road mileage for the retrieve can be estimated by multiplying the direct distance by 1.3.

For example: the road mileage for a flight of 52 air miles is 52 × 1.3 = 70 miles (approx.).

The cost of retrieving by air will usually be more expensive but it is enjoyable and saves time and trouble.

The glider should carry the necessary tools for derigging so that the pilot can have all the controls disconnected and ready for when the trailer arrives.

The tools should include a hammer, pin punch and a pair of pliers, or any special tools needed for that type of glider.

Preparations on the day

It is a good idea to plan possible flights in various directions from the gliding site. Then, when a suitable day for cross-country flying occurs, it is much easier to choose a goal and very little last-minute planning need be done. This is particularly necessary for attempts at 300 km and 500 km distance flights which generally need to be started earlier in the morning than shorter flights.

It is worth making a list of the things which need to be done before take-off so that there is no possibility of overlooking some vital item and spoiling a flight.

The following list will provide a basis for readers to add their individual 'wants'.

1. Obtain the best possible meteorological forecast and check the sky for signs indicating that the weather is moving faster or slower than expected from the forecast.
2. Refold maps. Check that they are clearly marked with your task, with control zones and airways and with the minimum distance required for Silver or Gold 'C' distance flights.
3. Consider possible tasks and make out a flight plan taking into account the position of the airways, cities and bad areas for landings. For reference, note the magnetic course, magnetic track, wind

direction and strength at various heights and the distance for each leg.

4. If the proposed flight is in a club glider or away from your home site, ask permission or give warning that you hope to make a cross-country flight.

5. Organise a retrieving crew and arrange communications, check that they have similar maps for pin-pointing the landing point.

6. Prepare sandwiches and a thermos of hot drink if required.

7. Dress sensibly for the type of glider being flown: cold weather—all the clothes available including gloves and extra socks; hot weather—adequate clothes to keep warm and dry after landing but a long-sleeved shirt and a white hat for protection against the sun.

8. Check the instruments for serviceability and log the altimeter settings when the altimeter is reading both zero and the airfield height above sea level for reference in flight.

9. Check that the tools required for derigging are in the glider.

10. Check the parachute, and adjust the harness until it is tight.

11. Reload, wind, check, and have the barograph sealed. Start it and stow it in the glider.

12. Move the glider to take-off point and stow the maps, etc, in the cockpit as early as possible to avoid a last-minute rush.

13. Go to the lavatory.

14. Write out a declaration of the proposed task and give it to an official observer and photograph him holding it.

15. Give any special instructions to the tug pilot if the launch is to be by aerotow.

Advice for first cross-country flights

Never wait until the conditions are perfect before taking off. On a suitable day they improve rapidly.

For record attempts or flights for F.A.I. Certificates, the barograph record should show the point of launch clearly. Descend with the airbrakes open for a few moments if the glider is launched into lift.

Climb as high as possible before setting course (at least 3,000 feet above the site). Make sure the conditions ahead look reasonably good and, if possible, aim for the next promising-looking cloud more or less on track.

Note the times of release, setting course and each positive pin-point.

Divert to keep in the areas of the best soaring conditions. If necessary, wait rather than fly across an area in the shadow of complete cloud cover.

If you get lost and there is a risk that you might inadvertently fly into an airway or controlled airspace, select a good field and land at once.

Check the surface wind whenever possible by noticing any indications from smoke, etc., *en route*.

Start looking for a suitable field for landing at any time you get below 2,000 feet.

Select a definite field at about 1,500 feet and look for lift within easy reach of it.

Pick the largest suitable field available. Check the surface, the slope and the approaches. NEVER attempt a landing downhill.

Make a firm decision to go in and land at about 1,000 feet. Open the airbrakes and make a definite descent to a position from which a long base leg and a straightforward approach can be made.

After landing, park the glider and, if possible, leave it in the care of a responsible person while telephoning the retrieving crew.

Give adequate information to make the retrieve easy. Whenever possible give the telephone number of the farm or place of landing for the retrieving team to contact in the event of a breakdown.

Obtain a landing certificate giving time and place of landing, signed by two witnesses; and thank the farmer.

Cross-country flying in motor gliders

The chances of having to make an inadvertent field landing are not eliminated by having an engine, as it is easier to get out of reach of the gliding site and always possible that the engine will not restart. Inexperienced pilots must, therefore, keep within easy gliding reach of the site and should never depend upon restarting to get home.

As a precaution against the day when the engine refuses to restart, a suitable field should *always* be chosen in plenty of time. Unless the engine starts immediately, a normal circuit pattern should be begun so that, if unsuccessful, the aircraft is in an ideal position for a normal base leg and approach for landing. By then all attempts to restart should be abandoned in order to concentrate on a safe landing.

Student pilots must on no account attempt a take-off from a field without obtaining their instructor's permission by telephone. Many factors can adversely affect the take-off, and these need to be assessed by an experienced pilot or instructor. The height and temperature at the field, slope and surface and the effects of turbulence in the lee of obstructions all have to be considered. It is wise to pace out and mark the mid-point of the field with a handkerchief or similar marker. Then if the aircraft is not off the ground by that point, cut the power and abandon the attempt to take-off. It is always better to derig and have a road retrieve than to crash into the hedge or wires attempting to take off.

With self-launching sailplanes which have 'tuck away' engines and propellers, it is essential to practise approaches and landings with the engine up. When the engine is folded away these aircraft handle and perform identically to the glider versions.

However, if the engine fails to start when required, there will seldom be time to retract it again before a landing has to be made. Therefore, it is prudent to practise landings with the engine up since any actual field landing will almost certainly be in this configuration.

It is just as vital to select a good field for a possible landing as with a glider and to keep close to it until the engine is running normally. Then if it does fail to start it is a simple matter to complete the circuit and land.

Remember in selecting your field that, although an uphill slope is ideal for the landing, it will probably make the take-off impossible. Even a slight uphill slope increases the take-off run dramatically.

24 Cloud flying

The limitations of the senses—The sense of balance—Muscle sense—
Learning to fly by instruments—Sensations—Turbulence and icing—
Lightning

Most countries do not permit cloud flying at all. However, it is allowed in England, except, of course, in airways and in controlled airspace.

The ability to fly a powered aircraft in cloud or at night enables it to be used as a reliable means of transport in all conditions and at all times. The power pilot who cannot fly in all weathers would find himself seriously restricted and might, on occasion, be grounded altogether for long periods of bad weather.

The glider pilot, however, is not under any compulsion to learn to fly on instruments since it is always possible to postpone flying until another day. He will seldom want to fly when the conditions are bad, with low cloud or poor visibility; but the time will come when he climbs in a thermal up to the base of a large cumulus cloud and then has to leave the strong, smooth lift because he cannot fly by his instruments.

The ability to fly gliders in cloud enables great heights to be obtained which, in turn, enables longer and easier cross-country flights to be made. The cloud base in summer in England is generally between 3,000 – 5,000 feet, which makes a cross-country flight below cloud a series of short climbs and rather worrying searches for the next area of lift. If a cloud can be successfully exploited, each climb will be much higher, and this immediately increases the probability of finding the next thermal. The rate of climb in the cloud is often up to two or three times the strength of the thermals feeding it from below so that, if some of the flight can be made above cloud base, less time will be spent climbing and more on cruising flight.

The disadvantages often outweigh these factors: map reading becomes difficult or impossible; above cloud base it is difficult to select the next usable area of lift and, worst of all, wet or iced-up wings have a disastrous affect on the performance of any glider.

Unless there is a large gain of height possible without risk of icing, it is usually more efficient to stay below cloud base and use dolphin techniques. (See page 287.)

The limitations of the senses

It is not difficult to fly by instruments. A pilot must understand the instruments and build up his confidence by constant practice. He must also have an elementary knowledge of the physiological requirements and limitations of his own body.

The main difficulty when learning to fly by instruments is the need to ignore all bodily sensations of balance, and concentrate on the readings of the instruments. This requires practice, to build up the confidence to accept the readings of the instruments rather than the sensations of the brain, when the two contradict each other.

Confidence is based on a knowledge of all possible difficulties which may arise, together with the experience of having successfully dealt with such situations before. Over-confidence can be dangerous, particularly in cloud flying, and pilots must never be tempted to conclude that it is easy because their first attempts seem successful. Instrument flying always seems easy until something goes wrong, and a pilot who has never lost control in cloud can have no conception of the real problems.

The instruments would be almost unnecessary if only the senses of balance were reliable. These notes would then only consist of a few comments on the use of the compass. In order to appreciate the need for ignoring the senses, it is worth knowing a little more about the mechanism responsible for our sense of balance.

There are three sources of information which enable the brain to assess balance and position; the eyes, the semi-circular canals of the inner ear, and muscle sense.

The eyes are by far the most reliable sense organ. But when flying in poor visibility or cloud, it is usually impossible to see anything to act as a datum from which to deduce the attitude of the aircraft. It is generally impossible to see beyond the wingtips to see either the angle of bank or the position of the nose in relation to the horizon.

The sense of balance

The semi-circular canals form a part of the vestibular apparatus, which is a tiny organ of the inner ear. It consists of three semi-circular tubes mounted in three planes at right angles to each other and filled with a liquid. Each tube records movements in a different direction, one in the tilting plane, one in the pitching and the third in the horizontal plane. Each tube is connected to a common reservoir which forms a fourth instrument, the otolith organ, which can detect the direction of the force of gravity or any acceleration acting on the body.

The system has severe limitations, particularly when flying. Normally the information from the semi-circular canals is monitored by the eyesight and misleading sensations are disregarded without conscious effort.

However, false sensations of tipping or turning become so vivid when no correction is available from the eyesight that at first it is impossible to believe that the instruments are reading correctly.

After a few moments of steady turning there is no sensation of turning and a vivid impression of turning in the opposite direction occurs as the turn is stopped.

Small changes are not detected by the semi-circular canals, with the result that the glider may get into a very steep turn without the knowledge of the pilot, provided that the entry into the turn is gradual and smooth.

The most disturbing sensations caused in this way occur when recovering from a tight turn or spin. Here the impression of turning or spinning in the opposite direction is most marked as soon as the corrective action begins to take effect, with the result that the pilot may easily stop the correction and continue the spin or turn again. It is unwise to move the position of the head suddenly during instrument flying, as this changes the planes of the semi-circular canals and may give violent sensations of turning or pitching which can be most disturbing.

The reservoir to which the canals are connected forms a further instrument consisting of minute hairs with small crystals of lime at the ends submerged in the liquid. If the head is tilted, the weight of the crystals bends the hairs, giving an indication of tilt. However, when a glider is turning, the loading of the turn will keep the hairs upright provided that the turn is accurate and there will be no sensation of bank. If the turn is not accurate, the load created by the slip or skid will bend the hairs, giving an impression of bank which may be false.

Clearly the vestibular organs of the inner ear, although essential for the normal sense of balance, can give misleading and confusing information, which must be disregarded by a pilot flying by instruments.

Muscle sense

Muscle sense is the impression of attitude deduced by the brain from the sensations of load on the muscles of the body. When these impressions can be used in conjunction with those of vision, they can be most useful. The glider pilot is able to centre accurately in a thermal by the feel of the lift and he can also detect inaccuracies in turns by the sensation of slip and skid. For example, a skidding turn can be detected by the feeling of being thrown towards the outside of the turn.

Since the load on the body varies considerably during normal man-oeuvres, the small loads resulting from leaning the body are undetectable and completely swamped by changes in attitude of the aircraft, so that muscle sense is of no assistance in keeping the glider upright in cloud. Furthermore, this sense is unable to distinguish between pitching nose-up and flying into rising air, with the result that the pilot will have the impression that the nose of the glider is rising and that a forward movement of the stick will be needed, when, in fact, the glider is in the same attitude but is accelerating upwards. A few seconds later, if sinking air is encountered, the false impression of the nose dropping will be felt and the pilot may over-control and stall the glider. This is nearly always the cause of difficulty when flying in turbulent conditions in cloud and it can only be completely overcome by ignoring the sensations or, with experience, by distinguishing between pitching movements and changes in the rate of climb by the readings of the instruments.

So far, it has been shown how and why the senses of balance cannot be relied upon without the help of a visual horizon or reference point. However, there are other factors which help to confuse the pilot.

Hearing plays a very important part in gliding because the sound of the glider in flight gives the pilot a fair idea of speed and, in particular, changes in speed. If the airspeed indicator becomes inoperative because the pressure head is iced over, the pilot must use his judgement of the noise to keep the glider flying at the right speed. This may seem simple at first, but in turbulent conditions the pilot soon forgets what the ideal speed sounds like, and as the speed increases it may soon sound like a terminal velocity dive and be very frightening.

The sound of hail or thunder and of the cracking ice on the wings as it melts and breaks away, nearly always affects the ability of the pilot to fly on instruments accurately by disturbing his state of mind and morale. It is, therefore, necessary to fly armed with the knowledge of what can happen and what action should be taken, so that nothing is unexpected and, for that reason, disturbing.

Even the most experienced instrument fliers will show a loss of ability towards the end of a long spell of instrument flying. This loss of ability will be accelerated in a less experienced pilot because he is unable to relax and is over-anxious.

Flying fatigue is greatly increased by discomfort, cold and lack of oxygen. It produces an inability to co-ordinate the controls in steady and accurate flight, and a lack of critical sense. By making a conscious effort to relax physically and mentally for a few seconds, it is usually possible to improve the standard of flying.

Learning to fly by instruments

The art of instrument flying in a glider can either be self-taught by trial and error flying solo, or learnt by receiving dual instruction. In practice, many self-taught pilots never reach a proficient standard because of the rather alarming experiences which occur all too frequently, unless the pilot has a good fundamental knowledge of the problems involved. Very useful experience can be gained by observing the instruments closely when not in cloud so that the readings of the instruments can be interpreted very quickly. It is also possible to wear a visor or fit a small cloth hood over one pilot in a two-seater glider, so that instrument flying can be practised without any possible unconscious cheating.

It must always be remembered that an adequate lookout must be kept when practising instrument flying in clear conditions and that cloud flying may only be carried out away from control zones and civil airways.

There is always the possibility of a failure of one or more instruments in cloud, with the result that control may be lost and the glider may be damaged by the excessive speeds and loads encountered during the descent through turbulent areas. For this reason, parachutes should always be worn whenever it is intended to enter cloud. Furthermore, unless the pilot is a skilled instrument flier, the glider should be one fitted with limiting airbrakes, so that, in the event of loss of control, he can open the airbrakes and prevent high speeds and consequent damage to the glider.

No attempt should be made to fly in cloud unless the glider has adequate serviceable blind flying instruments, i.e. a turn and slip, A.S.I., altimeter and compass. It is impossible to fly without at least turn and slip indicator for more than a few moments without getting into difficulties.

The ideal way of learning to use the instruments in a glider is by flying for short periods in small cumulus clouds. Any difficulties can then be overcome by opening the airbrakes and descending into the clear air below. Unfortunately, attempts to get into cloud are often unsuccessful and the surest method of getting instrument flying practice is to have dual instruction using a hood or visor so that only the instruments can be seen. The Link trainer or flight simulator can also provide valuable experience although it can never completely take the place of actual flying.

The first essential is to adopt a philosophical frame of mind and to settle comfortably in the cockpit long before entering cloud. The pilot should always transfer his full attention to the instruments 200 – 300 feet below the cloud in order to be absolutely calm and settled down by the time that he enters cloud. If the glider is fitted with an elevator trimmer, it should be adjusted to enable the glider to be flown 'hands off' at the correct speed so that it will need the minimum of effort to fly. The position of the turn needle should be noted so that the approximate relationship between the rate of turn indicated and the angle of bank is known.

Normally, the glider will be circling in a thermal when it enters cloud and, in order to continue to use the lift efficiently, a steady turn must be made. In most cases, the pilot is eager to gain as much height as possible and should continue to circle until the lift begins to fail or is lost. Even a short period of straight flight may result in flying out of the cloud or into a down-current and for this reason, as long as the glider is gaining height, the turn should be continued.

The would-be instrument flier should, therefore, concentrate on learning to circle smoothly and accurately by reference to the instruments and should not worry too much about straight flying in the early stages. If the glider has been carefully trimmed in the turn before reaching the cloud, it should not be difficult to maintain the turn. When flying by instruments, attention must be paid to all the significant instruments, i.e. the turn and slip indicator and the airspeed indicator, with occasional glances at the variometer and altimeter to check whether the glider is still climbing. Over-concentration on one instrument will result in erratic flying, since it is only by interpreting both the turn and slip and the A.S.I. that the attitude of the aircraft can be pictured. It is probably easiest to consider the handling of the glider in exactly the same way as in visual flying—the ailerons controlling the angle of bank and consequently the rate of turn, and the elevator controlling the speed. If the rudder is used in co-ordination with the ailerons as it is in normal visual flying, no excessive slip or skid should occur. Errors in slip and skid are the least important and only small corrections will be required on the rudder provided that the pilot remains relaxed and allows his normal instinctive rudder movements to occur.

The rate of turn must be kept under complete control, and prevented from increasing by the use of small, but positive movements of the ailerons. Any increase in the rate of turn must be checked immediately by taking off the bank until the correct rate of turn is obtained again.

At first it will be difficult to believe that the turn has steepened because of the lack of any sensation of turning, but action must be taken without delay if a smooth turn is to be resumed without difficulty.

The rate of turn depends on both the angle of bank and the amount of backward movement on the stick. When the nose is raised by moving back on the stick while the glider is being brought out of a diving turn, the turn indicator will register the increase in the rate of turn caused by the pitching movement.

Any increase in speed must be corrected by first ensuring that the rate of turn is not excessive and then by making a small backward movement on the stick followed by a movement back to its normal position. The rate of turn and airspeed can then be checked again after allowing time for the speed to settle down.

It is important to reduce a large rate of turn before attempting to correct for flying too fast, since if the bank is steep, pulling back on the stick will only tighten the turn and cause the nose to drop instead of rise. In this way, a turn can easily develop into a steep diving turn or spiral dive in which speed is gained very rapidly.

The movement of any control should consist of the following stages (merged smoothly into one action):

a. A movement of the control to change the glider's attitude.
b. A small check movement to prevent the change going too far.
c. Adjustments to maintain the new attitude.

For example, the turn needle is showing too great a rate of turn to the left. Correction: move the stick to the right to reduce the bank; make a small check movement to the left to prevent over-correction; and then make adjustments to keep the correct position of the turn needle. (The rudder would also be used to assist the aileron, and a correction on the elevator might be needed to readjust the airspeed.)

If the turn has become erratic, only calm and patience will enable a smooth turn to be resumed. The use of the airbrakes will prevent excessive speeds and help normal flight to be resumed, but once things have got out of hand, the pilot must *expect* to stall and dive several times before sorting it out again. The sensations during this period of oscillation are rather disturbing, but the pilot will be far less worried if he understands the worst that is likely to happen, and knows how to deal with it.

The most usual way in which control is lost is by allowing the glider to become semi-stalled during the turn. Since both the nose and wing will drop, a steep spiral is imminent and will be detected by the high rate of turn and the ever increasing speed together with a rapid loss of height. The correction is to reduce the rate of turn and then ease back to normal flight, guarding against any tendency to over-correct and stall again. (Always open the airbrakes if the speed has already increased by more than 20 knots.)

If the speed has already increased by even 20 knots a very definite pressure will be required to operate the ailerons in order to reduce the bank, and the pilot may make what he considers to be a normal correction without obtaining the desired effect. In recovering from the dive, the tendency is to over-correct and pull the nose up too far, resulting in a stall and then another dive.

In exceptional cases the glider may even begin to spin. Present-day gliders, however, will only continue to spin if the pilot keeps the stick back and rudder applied in the direction of the spin. Therefore, unless the stick is held back, the glider will become unstalled during the first half-turn of the incipient spin. The speed will then increase very rapidly as the glider spirals down in a steep diving turn. The recovery action is once again: airbrakes out, reduce the rate of turn and then ease the glider out of the dive.

Should the speed remain low and almost constant with a maximum rate of turn and a rapid loss of height, the glider is spinning.

If the glider is fitted with a nose pitot and static vents, the needle of the A.S.I. may move back beyond the zero so that it appears to read a high airspeed in the spin. The airbrakes should be opened and the normal spin recovery action should be taken. The direction of the spin is indicated by the turn indicator which will be showing a maximum rate of turn in that direction. Apply full opposite rudder to the direction of the spin and then move steadily forward on the stick until the turn needle flicks across to the other direction. This indicates that the spin has stopped and the rudder should be centralised. The glider is then usually in a steep diving turn, and the rate of turn must therefore be reduced before attempting to raise the nose of the glider to recover to a normal gliding speed. The sensations during a spin or spiral dive recovery are very vivid, and care must be taken to centralise the turn needle before attempting to recover from the dive, or the spiral will only become steeper and faster. The slip indicator usually shows a full deflection in the opposite direction to the turn needle in the spin, but this depends on the spinning characteristics of the glider. Provided that there is at least 2,000 feet of clear air below the cloud, the pilot can feel quite secure in the knowledge that, with the airbrakes open, he can, if need be, wait until the glider falls out of the cloud. In many hours of cloud flying in gliders I have never known a glider to spin fully except when deliberately put into a spin for practice. The airbrakes should be used as soon as things get out of hand, as they make it much easier to regain steady flight and to prevent excessive speed.

In turbulent conditions, it is impossible to maintain exact readings on the instruments but the aim should be to make the needles average the correct position. It is much easier to maintain a steady gentle turn than a steep one, and accurate and completely controlled flight should be the aim. Losing control almost inevitably means losing both height and the best area of the lift.

Centring into the best lift in cloud is not easy. A Bohli or Cook compass or directional indicator may enable the pilot to orientate himself in the lift and centre accurately. If the turn is partly in lift and partly in sinking air, the turn can be opened out into a gentle turn just after the worst indication of sink. Then as the lift is felt to improve, the turn can be tightened up in order to put the complete circle into the stronger lift. With practice steady steep turns are quite practicable and enable the method recommended on page 106 to be used in cloud.

Difficulty in keeping an accurate turn is often caused by the failure to use the elevator correctly when changing the angle of bank. If the angle of bank is allowed to increase (intentionally or otherwise) the backward movement on the stick *must* be increased to maintain an accurate turn. Otherwise the nose will drop and the speed will increase. Similarly, when reducing the bank, the backward pressure *must* be reduced or the glider will become stalled.

Sensations

The sensations of flying into rising or sinking air are at first indistinguishable from those of the nose rising or dropping. The natural reaction to the impression that the nose has risen is to move forward on the stick, with the result that the glider is actually put into a dive. This usually results in the glider flying out of the area of lift into a downdraught. Then the pilot raises the nose acting under the impression that it has dropped. These effects, combined with the increase in airspeed occurring as the glider enters rising air, and the decrease as it enters sinking air, result in over-controlling with the risk of diving or stalling. The beginner should ignore everything except the actual readings of the instruments. These, subject to their individual inherent errors, are the only reliable guide to the pilot flying in cloud.

A most disconcerting sensation of flying upside-down occurs whenever the nose of the glider is lowered too rapidly—generally if the pilot overdoes the stall recovery action. On instruments, it is usually easier to allow the nose to drop naturally when a stall occurs, checking any change in rate of turn with the rudder and keeping the stick more or less in the normal position so that no extreme attitude is reached. It is almost impossible to get into an inverted position unintentionally and, in any case, the glider would fall into a normal dive after a few seconds so that no special recovery need be considered.

The delay in changing speed after a change of attitude becomes very large when the glider gets into steep climbing or diving attitudes. A useful guide to recovery to level flight is to apply the correction until the change in speed is arrested and then to make a check movement to hold that position while the speed settles down. This will enable extreme attitudes to be damped out quickly without over-controlling and a series of violent stalls and dives will be avoided.

For example, if the speed is increasing rapidly, a backward movement is made until the increase in speed is checked and is about to decrease. A small forward movement on the stick then prevents the nose rising farther and, after a few seconds, the speed will fall to approximately cruising speed so that final adjustments can easily be made. This idea can be tested in clear conditions and it will be found that the nose of the glider is at approximately the correct position as the speed is momentarily constant.

As the turn is stopped by levelling the wings until the turn needle is central, care must be taken to maintain the correct speed by easing forward on the stick. There is a tendency to stall the glider when coming out of a turn, because during the turn a constant backward pressure or trim is used to prevent the nose from dropping and this has to be taken off in contradiction to the sensations felt at the time, which produces a feeling of diving when in fact the nose may be too high.

This will be avoided by ignoring the sensations and trusting implicitly in the readings of all the instruments. A few seconds' over-concentration on the turn indicator will almost certainly result in a very low airspeed and a possible stall before any correction can be made.

When the glider is circling, the readings on the compass are confusing, and in some cases, the compass may spin freely so that no indication of direction can be obtained. In this case a gradual reduction in angle of bank and rate of turn may allow it to settle down so that some idea of the heading can be deduced in spite of the turning and acceleration errors at the time.

The pilot should try to picture the attitude of the glider from the indications of the instruments, and anticipate the possible movements of it so that no change comes as a surprise. This is considerably simplified by the use of the artificial horizon, which has no time lag and suffers only minor errors. However, even when an artificial horizon is fitted, it is essential that the pilot is able to manage on the turn and slip indicator and airspeed indicator, since unless the batteries are fully charged and in good condition there is always a chance of it failing.

The artificial horizon is best interpreted by imagining the view from the tailplane looking forward. The wings and body of the glider are represented by the miniature aeroplane and the horizon by the horizon bar of the instrument. In the normal gliding attitude, the little aeroplane will take up a position on or just below the horizon bar with the wings level. In a nose-up position, the aeroplane will appear higher in relation to the horizon bar in exactly the same way as the pilot would see the real horizon if he was sitting on the tail. The miniature aeroplane in the instrument is fixed and the horizon tilts and moves up and down to register the changes in attitude of the aircraft.

After a little practice turning in clear air and referring to this instrument, the use of the artificial horizon becomes more or less instinctive and a very high standard of accuracy can be maintained. However, it is vital to observe all the instruments and not just concentrate on one, or a difficult situation will arise if the artificial horizon fails.

Perhaps the most essential thing with an artificial horizon is to keep the batteries fully charged and in good condition. An unreliable horizon is much worse than no horizon at all. Avoid testing the instrument unless it is absolutely essential because the starting load on the accumulators is very large. It is best to allow the instrument to run for several minutes, before uncaging it while the wings are held level for a moment. If it does topple in flight it will re-erect itself gradually. It should always be caged for take-off or landing and for aerobatics.

Turbulence and icing

Turbulence in clouds is rather unpredictable and varies considerably from cloud to cloud. If the cloud is developing from a large cumulus into a cumulo-nimbus or storm cloud, the conditions may at times be very violent, with rates of climb of 1,000 – 2,000 feet per minute and similar down-draughts in places. These powerful air currents can be smooth and cover a large area, making a climb on instruments a comparatively simple matter. However, it is usual to find very turbulent conditions near the top of the cloud—generally above freezing level, making it difficult to continue climbing and sometimes even desirable to steer out of the cloud. If the pilot concentrates on maintaining just a gentle turn, most of the bumps can be ignored; indeed any attempt to correct for them will only result in over-concentration and subsequent over-controlling. Most of the bumps will be vertical currents lifting the whole glider up or down, or banking it over, and few will cause much nose-up or nose-down change in attitude, in spite of the misleading sensations to the contrary which are felt by the pilot.

The decision whether to enter a particular cloud should be taken while there is still time to fly away from it without being sucked into the bottom. If the day is one with only small cumulus, there is little risk for the most inexperienced instrument pilot, providing that the aircraft has adequate airbrakes. But if the cloud is massive and tending to develop into thunderheads, it is not the right day for starting to learn to fly by instruments.

In a modern glass fibre glider thunderstorms are things to be avoided at any price.

There is always some risk of structural failure flying in them, although if the glider is kept down to normal flying speeds, this is almost negligible. However, when the turbulence is violent, it is easy to lose control of the situation and overstress the glider in regaining control or in failing to do so.

It is vital to keep the speed from becoming too high, since if the glider flies from a violent up-draught into a down-draught or vice versa at high speed, the loads on the wings may exceed the design strength with consequent risk of failure.

Damage may also be caused by large hailstones penetrating the leading edges, etc. Because of the very narrow gaps between the control surfaces there is serious risk of having them jammed by even slight icing. In addition the stability and control may be seriously affected by ice.

As the glider reaches the freezing level, ice will begin to form on the nose, leading edges and the front of the canopy or windscreen. This will increase steadily until either the glider is too high for ice to form, or the weight and drag of the ice forces it down. Unless some form of nose vent or pitot heating is fitted, the ice will gradually obstruct the pressure head for the airspeed indicator until it ceases to read changes in speed. It is then necessary to judge the airspeed by the sound of the airflow.

Exercising the controls from time to time will free them or give warning of serious icing. The airbrakes are probably best left alone unless required in emergency to check the speed, as they will easily jam open if only a slight film of ice forms on the front. This will prevent them being closed again until the ice has melted off lower down, and in an extreme case it might mean a forced landing with the brakes jammed out. However, if control is lost and the speeds become rather high, open the airbrakes immediately.

Most modern machines are specifically prohibited from flying in icing conditions and it would probably infringe the insurance rules if control was lost because of icing.

Icing generally occurs at temperatures between 0°C and −25°C (32°F and −15°F) which represents a layer of cloud about 5,000 feet in depth. Above this level the water droplets have normally frozen into ice crystals or snow. It is interesting to note that water droplets can exist unfrozen as water at temperatures far below freezing point provided that they are comparatively undisturbed. These super-cooled water droplets, as they are called, freeze immediately on impact with the surfaces of the aircraft, forming ice. The glider pilot should avoid staying in the icing region unless the glider is climbing rapidly, and should straighten up and look for stronger lift, or leave the cloud if the lift is poor, to avoid collecting more ice than is absolutely necessary. A thin layer of ice will start to melt once the glider is below the freezing level. When the pieces of ice are swept away by the airstream, the noise of the ice breaking and striking other parts of the glider can be quite alarming, and the pilot should be prepared for this or he may think that the aircraft is breaking up.

Sometimes hail or melting ice does considerable damage to the glider which cannot be seen from the cockpit and it is therefore unwise to carry out any aerobatics or fly at very high speeds after flying in severe conditions.

At very low temperatures the controls may become excessively stiff because of the contraction of the control rods and cables. Also the wood, perspex, and other materials in the glider may be temporarily below their normal strength because of shrinkage or frozen moisture.

A further considerable difficulty is the moisture from the pilot's breath condensing and freezing on the inside of the canopy, so that it is difficult to see out except through the clear vision windows. This can be prevented by wiping it with a rag soaked with an anti-icing fluid such as glycol which can be carried in a tin.

Flying in any shower cloud there is also the risk of having to descend in heavy rain or snow. The visibility can be reduced to a few yards and with no way either of telling the wind direction or of selecting a good field, only luck can prevent a serious accident. The cloud base may be reduced from several thousand to only a few feet in a matter of minutes, making it folly to attempt cloud flying unless the showers are isolated and the general cloud base is high. When driving a car in heavy rain it is not uncommon to have to slow right down or stop, in spite of windscreen wipers. Imagine trying to see to land a glider in such conditions!

Lightning

The greatest danger from lightning in a glider is probably the risk that the pilot may be panicked into losing control.

However, experience in the past has shown that there is a considerable risk of gliders being struck and that severe damage is often caused. Even on occasions when no external damage has been found and the pilot was unaware of a strike, control cables have been found burnt through to the last few strands. For this reason it has become the recommended practice to remove and inspect all control cables after any flight in an active thunderstorm.

When the glider does become heavily charged with static electricity the pilot may feel 'pin prick' shocks from the control column or other metal parts of the aircraft. This is quite common when the glider is being launched in very dry or thundery weather even when there are no actual storms near by. In this case sparks several inches long can be drawn from the cable release knob by putting a hand anywhere near it.

Severe shocks may be felt if the glider is actually struck and these are particularly unnerving because there is no way of knowing when they will occur or when they are likely to stop. The strikes cause burn marks and slight damage to the glider.

I was once struck by lightning in flight in a glider and it was very alarming. It is a sobering thought that the strikes were probably only minor 'feeler' sparks or this would never have been written.

It is worth mentioning that in a moment of mental stress the pilot may start to breathe heavily, which can result in a condition known as hyperventilation of the lungs. This upsets the critical balance of carbon dioxide in the lungs, which stimulates the respiratory system and may cause unconsciousness in a few minutes. Care should be taken to avoid deep breathing as this will increase the pilot's susceptibility to lack of oxygen. Even at sea level it is fairly simple to produce fainting by over-breathing, so that at $10,000 - 15,000$ feet the effects of lack of oxygen may be pronounced if the pilot gets a nasty fright and begins to breathe heavily. Rapid shallow breathing does not have this effect and is quite safe at any time.

Cloud flying has opened a whole new range of experiences for the glider pilot. Some of them are pleasant and peaceful, others overawing and spectacular. Few pilots will deny that there is a tremendous thrill to be gained from surging upwards at thousands of feet per minute to come out of cloud on top of the world with a view of, for example, the whole of the south coast from Portland Bill to the Thames Estuary.

To be really successful at cloud flying the pilot must be able to interpret the instruments and fly the glider accurately while censoring any sensations of pitching and turning which might cause him to doubt or disbelieve the instruments. At the same time, he must maintain a mental picture of the strength and position of the best lift by the combination of his sense of feel and the readings of the variometer.

As Philip Wills said, 'instrument flying is a state of mind'. Try it first, before deciding whether you consider it is a sane one or not!

25 Flying high

Anoxia—Symptoms—Points to watch when using oxygen equipment

Glider flights to over 20,000 feet in large-scale standing wave conditions are now becoming sufficiently common for many of the dangers to be overlooked in a rush of enthusiasm to take advantage of the conditions when they exist.

The ambitious glider pilot must face many of the same problems of survival at high altitudes as the jet pilot, and must understand the need and use of oxygen equipment if such flights are to be made safely. Without this equipment, high flying is dangerous, since the glider may be carried up several thousands of feet while the pilot is attempting to fly out of the lift. This might well result in the pilot losing consciousness at the controls.

Anoxia

The seriousness of the effects of lack of oxygen cannot be overstressed. The tolerance of each individual varies considerably and is affected by day-to-day health, so that it is difficult to give a safe height not to exceed without oxygen. It is certainly dangerous to assume that because glider pilots have reached over 20,000 feet without oxygen and lived to tell the tale that others can safely do so. Such heights without oxygen involve a considerable risk even when the pilot is well aware of his personal capacity from experience at those heights or by tests in a decompression chamber.

The exhilaration of an exciting height climb, together with the effects of slight anoxia may lead to over-confidence and cause the pilot to make serious blunders in airmanship and judgement. Special care should be taken when making field landings after any climb which may have been high enough to cause even slight anoxia.

Symptoms

It is the nature of the symptoms of lack of oxygen which makes it particularly dangerous. The brain is affected in much the same way as with alcoholic intoxication. At first, there is usually a feeling of well-being and over-confidence, and inaccuracies in flying go unchecked. This is followed by a progressive lack of concentration so that, even if the aircraft is not completely under control, the victim is neither really interested nor able to do anything about the situation. Finally, loss of consciousness and even death occurs unless the supply of oxygen is restored.

Oxygen is absolutely essential for life and a continuous and adequate supply must be available all the time, since, for all practical purposes the body is unable to store it up. The oxygen is absorbed into the blood which is pumped to the brain and all the parts of the body. Moreover, a shortage of oxygen has an almost immediate effect on the brain, causing a loss of mental acuity, although this is normally undetected by the person concerned.

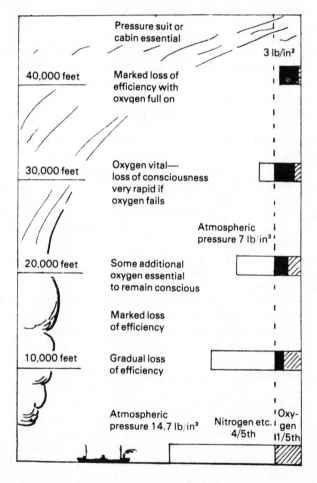

Pressure suit or cabin essential

3 lb/in²

40,000 feet — Marked loss of efficiency with oxygen full on

30,000 feet — Oxygen vital— loss of consciousness very rapid if oxygen fails

Atmospheric pressure 7 lb/in²

20,000 feet — Some additional oxygen essential to remain conscious

Marked loss of efficiency

10,000 feet — Gradual loss of efficiency

Atmospheric pressure 14.7 lb/in²   Nitrogen etc. 4/5th   Oxygen 1/5th

107. The need for oxygen at high altitudes. Cross-hatched areas show the pressure of oxygen in normal air. Shaded areas show the additional oxygen needed to maintain sea level conditions.
Note. At 40,000 feet even using 100 per cent oxygen the pressure of oxygen is less than at sea level and the pilot will suffer.

The atmosphere consists of a mixture of about one part of oxygen and four parts of nitrogen and very small amounts of other gases. The pressure decreases with height but the proportions of oxygen and nitrogen remain the same, so that oxygen is still available in the air at height, but only in greatly reduced quantities. When the air is breathed, the atmospheric pressure forces the oxygen into the blood. However, if the pressure of the air is reduced, less oxygen can be absorbed by the blood, and oxygen starvation occurs. This can be averted by providing additional oxygen to take the place of some or all of the nitrogen in the air so that the required pressure of oxygen is maintained all the time. Above about 38,000 feet the pressure is so low that, even breathing pure oxygen, there is insufficient pressure to force an adequate supply into the blood and the only satisfactory solution to the problem is to provide the pilot with a pressure mask, pressure suit or cabin. In effect the situation in this case is similar to that above 15,000 feet without any oxygen equipment.

The human body is most suited to the atmospheric conditions found at sea level. There, the air pressure is about 14.7 pounds per square inch, providing the equivalent pressure of 3 pounds per square inch of oxygen. Although we are able to acclimatise ourselves to heights of 10,000 or even 20,000 feet over a period of days or weeks, a slight but definite loss of efficiency occurs when flying as low as 10,000 feet if that height is maintained for more than an hour.

At about 15,000 feet, a marked deterioration begins in the average individual which would be noticed by an observer although quite unobserved by the individual himself. It is unwise to attempt flights above this height without oxygen equipment. Even the slightest anoxia is enough to prevent most glider pilots from flying accurately on the turn and slip indicator, particularly in turbulent conditions.

Decompression chamber tests show that most pilots pass out after a short time between 15,000 and 20,000 feet.

In a well-sealed cockpit there is not much ventilation so that, after a time, the oxygen available in the air becomes depleted. In this way the effects of lack of oxygen may well occur below the normal height, and symptoms should be watched for when flying above 10,000 feet. Most gliders have one or more clear vision panels in the canopy which should be opened periodically at height to introduce fresh air into the cockpit.

Fatigue and exposure increase the effect of oxygen starvation and the pilot must keep warm and comfortable if he is to soar efficiently.

The effects of lack of oxygen at height are summarised in Fig. 107 but it cannot be too strongly emphasised that every individual varies in tolerance.

It has been shown that smoking lowers the pilot's resistance to lack of oxygen. Smokers should use supplementary oxygen about 3,000 feet lower than non-smokers.

If the pilot keeps a constant check on his reactions a descent can be made immediately any symptoms of trouble are noticed. These may include light-headedness, over-confidence and any kind of visual aberration, such as difficulty in reading the instruments or even the figures appearing upside-down.

Airsickness, or a fit of coughing, can be dangerous at great heights since they make it difficult to use an oxygen mask. In a tandem two-seater, a careful check should be kept on the second pilot, who is far more prone to sickness than the pilot handling the controls. If he does have to remove his oxygen mask or suffers from lack of oxygen through some other cause, he may be unable to attract attention to the fact, even if he realises it in time.

The reduction in atmospheric pressure at great heights causes other uncomfortable effects on the body which may, in extreme cases, necessitate the curtailment of a flight. Starchy and gassy foods should be avoided, as they can give rise to great discomfort at height when the gases formed in the stomach expand under the reduced pressure. It is also possible to suffer from 'bends', a very painful kind of cramp caused by bubbles of nitrogen forming in the bloodstream and obstructing the flow of blood. In some cases this can result in sudden unconsciousness without warning. The nitrogen bubbles redissolve in the blood when height is lost, putting right the cause of the trouble.

It is unwise to attempt a height climb with a cold, when the sinuses may be blocked. The change of pressure gives rise to acute pains across the eyes, and the ear-drums may be damaged if the descent is very rapid and the pressure in the inner ear cannot be relieved. This can usually be done by swallowing or chewing, or by pinching the nose and blowing. In any case, flying with a cold should be avoided as it can give rise to inner ear infections and deafness.

Height climbs to over 10,000 feet in open gliders are mainly a matter of physical endurance, as the temperature is usually well below freezing, and ice and hoar frost form on the pilot's head and shoulders. Exposure reduces the pilot's efficiency to such a degree that keeping warm is probably the most important single factor governing how high it is possible to go without special equipment.

There can be no doubt that safe and successful high flying can only be the result of careful preparation and the use of efficient oxygen equipment.

The normal glider oxygen systems consist of a steel cylinder of compressed oxygen at about 1,800 pounds per square inch pressure supplying a steady flow of oxygen into a reservoir (known as the economiser) from which it is drawn breath by breath.

It is usual to have a main ON – OFF supply valve, a contents gauge showing the amount of oxygen left, and a flow indicator and adjustment valve so that the quantity of oxygen delivered can be accurately adjusted. Oxygen is supplied at low pressure to the economiser, from which it can be breathed through a simple type of face mask. In most installations, the economiser takes the form of a small plastic bag attached to the mask.

A supply gauge may be calibrated for height so that the supply can be adjusted according to the height at the time, or there may be only a flow indicator and a regulator which may be switched to NORMAL—HIGH—EMERGENCY. (NORMAL: 10,000–25,000 feet; HIGH: 25,000–40,000 feet; EMERGENCY: 40,000 feet or at any time lack of oxygen is suspected and immediately before baling out at high altitudes.)

The fitting and condition of the oxygen mask are most important as the oxygen will be seriously diluted by air leaking into a badly fitting mask. Above 25,000 feet, a leakage of this sort might be disastrous, as pure oxygen is needed to maintain consciousness.

It is also vital that the main ON–OFF valve is turned on as far as it will go and not just until the contents gauge indicates the contents. Unless this is done, the flow of oxygen will be restricted and may be inadequate at height in spite of the indicator reading correctly.

Moisture from the breath may freeze in the mask and block the inlet valve. In most cases this can be easily broken up by flexing the mask or the inlet tube, but a constant check for this and all other possible causes of failure must be *kept all the time* above 20,000 feet.

For any attempt to climb above 20,000 feet, a small emergency 'bail out' bottle of oxygen should be carried. This could be a life-saver in event of a failure of the main supply or if it became necessary to bail out at height.

Above 25,000 feet you only have about thirty seconds of consciousness if your oxygen supply is cut off.

Points to watch when using oxygen equipment

1. No oil or grease may be used on or near oxygen equipment as this may cause an explosion on contact with the oxygen.
2. Check the complete system regularly, including mask, for leakage.
3. Before take-off, check the contents indicator and turn on the main valve as far as it will go.
4. Ensure that oxygen flows freely into the mask.

Remember that oxygen is no use if the pilot is insufficiently skilled to make use of the conditions, or if the aircraft or instruments are unserviceable. Only systematic care will ensure that all the vital things are serviceable on the day they are needed.

26 Going faster and farther

Factors governing cross-country performances—Cruising technique—Wind effects—The polar curve—Speeds to fly—Pull-ups—Gliding to a goal—Determining the speed to fly for maximum distance in various conditions—General rules and advice

The average glider pilot will find his time fully occupied with the problems of staying up and map reading during his first few cross-country flights. However, as he becomes more experienced and sets himself more difficult tasks, he will want to travel faster.

Factors governing cross-country performances

It is difficult to make a long-distance flight in this country because Great Britain is so small. Also, even in the summer-time it is unusual for the weather to be soarable before 10.30 a.m. or after 6.30 p.m. and it is even more unusual for these conditions to exist for 200 or 300 miles. The aim of the glider pilot must be to travel as fast as possible to make the most of the good thermals while they are available.

The pilot attempting a long-distance flight must normally set off as soon as he can be fairly sure of staying up. However, if a short flight is planned, the pilot can choose his time. An early start will waste time because the thermals will be weaker and it may be difficult to stay up: whereas by waiting until conditions appear ideal there is always the risk that the weather will deteriorate later in the day, making the task impossible.

The most important factor affecting cross-country performance is the ability of the pilot to find and make the best use of the strongest lift for climbing. This is largely a matter of practice.

Unless there are other gliders climbing in the same thermals or attempting the same task it is difficult to judge the efficiency of the individual pilot. The expert is constantly striving to improve the rate of climb by exploring the extremities of his thermal for even stronger areas of lift. Frequently a small change in position of the circle will double the rate of climb and since nearly half the flight is spent climbing, this improvement will mean a much greater distance covered.

It is just as important to avoid flying through strong down-draughts as it is to climb well in the thermals. This is largely a matter of experience in judging whether a particular cloud is still growing, and it is useful to watch the clouds and also gliders soaring to learn to distinguish between good and bad clouds.

The strength of the thermals may vary considerably and the pilot must select the strongest ones if he is aiming to fly a long distance. Unless the glider is desperately low, the search for stronger lift should be continued if a thermal does not come up to expectations after several circles. Similarly, if the thermal becomes weaker with height it should be left, provided that there is good prospect of finding another stronger one.

Whereas the beginner is advised to try to stay as high as possible in order to avoid a premature landing, the would-be expert must be more critical of the thermals he uses, and be prepared if necessary to descend much lower in search of the stronger lift. If he is careless or too critical, or if he fails to realise that the conditions ahead have deteriorated, his urge for better lift and more speed will result in a landing. In this case he would have flown farther by cruising more carefully and conserving height.

The performance achieved on a particular day depends to a great extent upon the efficiency of the glider. A good pilot in a low-performance glider may well be easily beaten by a high-performance machine even flown by an inexperienced pilot. In competition flying, the gliders are divided into Open or unrestricted, 15 metre restricted and 15 metre standard classes so that the results depend more on the skill of the pilot than the design of the glider.

Cruising technique

Thermal soaring can be considered in its simplest form as a series of units of a glide and a climb. In this case, the average speed across country (ignoring the effect of the wind) depends mainly upon the average rate of climb in the thermals. However, particularly when the thermals are strong a significant improvement in average speed is possible by cruising between thermals faster than the speed for the best gliding angle.

Fig. 108 shows a practical example. Flying at the speed for best gliding angle, less time is spent in gaining height but this is offset by the slower speed in straight flight. At the optimum cruising speed a greater number of thermals have to be used but the average speed over the ground is raised. On a poor soaring day, there is little to be gained by this technique, which assumes that the next thermal will be found. The moment that assumption cannot be made it will pay to reduce speed and conserve height.

The cruising speed between thermals should be based on an estimate of the strength of the *next* thermal. Otherwise, following a rapid climb, the pilot might jeopardise his chances of staying up by cruising at high speed into an obviously poor thermal area. In good conditions it is usual to assume that the next thermal will be as strong as the previous one. The speed to fly between thermals can then be based on the rate of climb obtained in the last thermal. However, the pilot must be prepared to slow

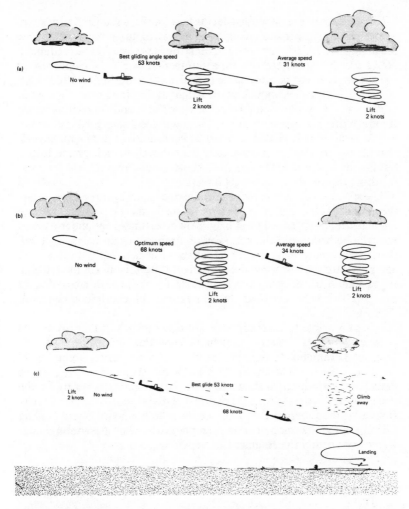

108. Cross-country cruising speeds. (a) Flying at less than the optimum cruising speed keeps the glider much higher but gives a lower average cross-country speed. (b) Flying the optimum cruising speed gives a better average but increases the risk of a landing. (c) The 'optimum' cruising speed may result in getting too low unless the next thermal is within easy gliding range.

up and change his technique the moment that there is any doubt about the conditions ahead.

Cruising at too high a speed between the thermals will reduce the average speed across country by making it necessary to climb more often. The 'best' cruising speed can be calculated from the performance curve of the particular glider.

During a flight the pilot must decide how low he is prepared to descend before slowing down and changing to a 'staying up at any cost' policy. He must also decide what strength of lift he is prepared to discard in the search for the best thermals. On a summer day with the cloud base at 5,000 feet, it would be reasonable to cruise at the optimum speed down to 2,000 feet or so, i.e. about half the height of the cloud base. From then on the pilot would be well advised to slow down and concentrate upon finding a thermal to keep him up. The lower the glider gets, the weaker the thermal strength which is acceptable. For example, the pilot may decide that on a particular day he will only use thermals which give at least 4 knots if he is above 4,000 feet, 2 – 3 knots if he is above 3,000 feet, and anything he can find below 2,000 feet.

The speed to be flown between thermals will also have to be varied when the glider flies through rising or sinking air. It may be possible to cruise for many miles without losing height by diverting to fly under a cloud street. This will avoid the necessity of circling to gain height and will therefore increase the average ground speed considerably. In this case, and at any time when the glider is flying through rising air, the cruising speed should be reduced. Similarly when flying through areas of sink, the speed should be increased until more favourable conditions are found. (See Fig. 113.)

It is impossible to determine the average strength of down-draughts between thermals, because in unstable conditions the air is alive with varying movements. Since the speed should be varied according to conditions the usual arrangement is to have a 'speed to fly' ring on the dial of the variometer to show the pilot the correct speed to fly for the rate of sink which is indicated at the time. This is known as a 'MacCready ring' after the inventor, Paul MacCready, who was twice World Gliding Champion and the designer of the man-powered and solar-powered aircraft which flew across the English Channel.

Wind effects

Once the glider is in the air it can be considered as being in free flight in the air mass. The aim is to achieve the best progress through the air mass since that will give the best ground speed regardless of the wind strength and direction.

It is important to realise that, except for a final glide when there is no need for or no hope of another climb, the strength of the wind should not be taken into account in deciding what speeds to fly.

In cruising flight the speed should not be increased against a headwind. This will simply use up more height so that a longer time will be spent climbing. The average speed through the air mass will be worse and not better.

For example, with 2 knot thermals and cruising at the 'optimum' cruising speed the average speed through the air mass might be 34 knots. When flying against a strong, 30 knot wind, it would just be possible to make a few knots' headway.

Flying faster than the optimum, the average speed would drop. Because of the extra height lost, more time would be wasted climbing and no progress would be made forward against the wind.

Notice that if the pilot has to use a weaker thermal, he will be losing ground and drifting slowly back downwind.

To make progress against such a strong wind, he must use dolphin techniques and avoid any circling unless the lift is above 2 knots.

Owing to the variations in the rate of climb in a thermal, it is difficult to assess the average rate of climb exactly by reading the variometer. The rate of climb indicated by the variometer is usually much greater than the average measured by the gain of height timed with a watch. Often considerable time is wasted in getting into the best part of the lift and this reduces the average rate of climb.

A rate of climb of over 6 knots is unusual in England except when cloud flying, even though the readings on the variometer may seem to be between 6 – 8 knots most of the time.

It is useful to time the height gained in thermals with a stop-watch to obtain a better idea of the real rates of climb and how they compare with the readings of the variometer. This will also make the pilot painfully aware of the time wasted by poor centring and using weak thermals.

Most skilled pilots achieve rates of climb of a half to three-quarters of the average variometer reading.

Electronic variometer systems usually show a running average of the achieved rate of climb for the last half-minute. Immediately the rate of climb drops significantly the pilot is made aware and can decide whether

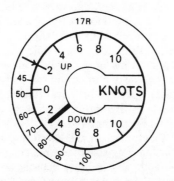

109. The MacCready 'speed to fly' ring. In this case the ring is set for a 2 knot climb and the variometer needle indicates that the speed should be 70 knots.

to move on to another area or re-centre in the lift. These systems are also able to give an average for the complete climb and this is very useful in deciding on the best setting for the 'speed to fly' director or MacCready ring.

When the lift is rather broken, it often takes time to realise that although the variometer is flickering to very high rates of climb, the actual achieved rate is quite low. A better assessment can be made by watching the altimeter. The hand will be moving steadily if the lift is really worth while.

With a dial type variometer, a MacCready ring can be mounted round the face of the instrument and calibrated in speeds to fly. This sub-scale can then be turned to point to the average rate of climb expected and the position of the needle will then indicate the best speed to fly at any given moment.

This simple system is ideal for teaching the principles of speeds to fly, but for the competitive pilot there are more sophisticated instruments available. By using transducers to measure the changes in speed and height and feeding them into a micro-computer, at the touch of a key the instrument will give this and even more useful information. Many can be switched from a normal variometer reading to give 'air mass' or a 'director' mode to tell the pilot to go faster or slower as the lift and sink changes. All of these are usually indicated by both a visual and audio presentation. They will also do the necessary calculations for a final glide and tell the pilot if he is falling below the glide path needed to reach his destination, how many miles he has flown and how many more miles he has to go to a turning point or his base.

At high altitudes most types of variometer over-read because of the reduced density of the air. This can be allowed for when compiling the tables or by flying a little slower than they indicate. The error is about 10 per cent per 5,000 feet but is eliminated in most of the electronic systems.

In the case of two-seater gliders, the effect of reducing the all-up weight when flying solo can be allowed for by flying a few miles an hour slower than the calculated best speeds for full load.

Near the top of each climb, the pilot should try to assess the strength of the next thermal and set his 'speed to fly' scale to the appropriate rate of climb. As soon as the rate of climb drops off seriously, he should leave the thermal, increasing speed to his best cruising speed and varying it according to whether he is flying through sinking or rising air until the next area of strong lift is encountered.

If the glider flies slowly into an area of strong sink, several hundred feet may be lost while gaining speed and reaching better conditions. It may often conserve height and improve the average cross-country speed to increase flying speed in anticipation of the down-draughts usually encountered just after leaving the thermal, or before passing through or near to clouds which are obviously decaying.

The polar curve

The performance of a glider can be measured in flight tests by checking
the rates of descent at a series of speeds and plotting them to produce
a polar curve as in Fig. 110. It is extremely difficult to do this at all reliably
because of the inevitable up-and-down movements of the air which occur
even on a seemingly smooth, early morning flight starting at 10,000 feet.
However, tests are done and the results published by the manufacturers
and various research groups.

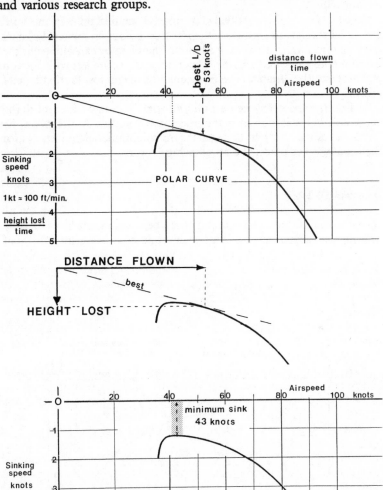

110. Using the polar curve to determine the speed for the best gliding angle (53 knots)
and the speed for the minimum rate of sink (43 knots).

Theoretical estimates are also liable to error because of the impossibility of calculating the total drag of a glider accurately.

Fig. 110 shows a polar curve for a typical 15 metre glider of average performance. The rate of sink for any speed can be found from this curve. The lowest rate of sink (minimum sink) is at 43 knots.

The actual gliding angle may also be found by dividing the speed by the rate of sink. For example, if at 60 knots the rate of sink is about 1½ knots the gliding angle, sometimes referred to as the L/D or lift to drag ratio, is 40 : 1.

Speed is simply distance divided by time (60 nautical miles in one hour, etc.), and the rate of sink is the height lost divided by time (1½ knots is 1½ nautical miles down in one hour). Therefore by cancelling out the time on both the speed and the rate of descent, we are left with a graph which shows the distance covered against the height lost for that type of glider.

To find the speed for the best gliding angle we draw a tangent to the curve and where it touches is the best speed possible. At this point, 53 knots, we get the furthest distance for the minimum height lost. Notice that at any other point, the relationship is worse.

Speeds to fly

It can be proved that the optimum speed between thermals is found by drawing the tangent from a point corresponding to the achieved rate of

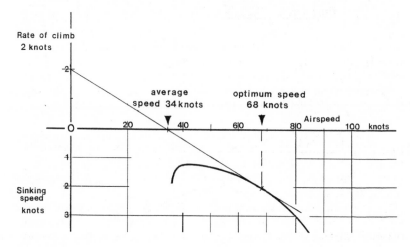

111. Using the polar curve to find the optimum cruising speed. Here for a 2 knot rate of climb the optimum speed in normal air is 68 knots, giving an average cross-country speed of 34 knots.

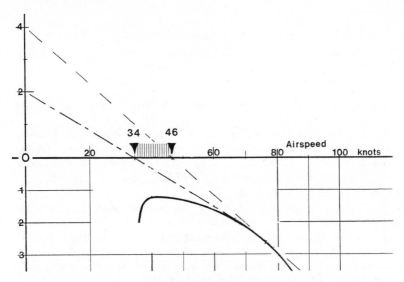

112. Increasing the achieved rate of climb from 2 to 4 knots can give an increase in average speed of over 10 knots.

climb anticipated in the next thermal, assuming that it can be reached. In the example shown, for a rate of climb of 2 knots, the best speed to fly is 68 knots. (Fig. 111.)

It can also be shown that the average speed for each glide and subsequent climb is given by the point at which this tangent cuts the speed axis of the graph. In this case the speed will be seen to be only 34 knots. One obvious way to increase this average speed is by using only the stronger areas of lift. Fig. 112 shows that in this case the average speed can be increased by over 12 knots if 4 knot thermals can be found.

However, it can be seen that if the glider flies slowly through even weak lift so that level flight is possible, it will be cruising considerably faster than this average speed.

This is the basis of 'dolphin' flying where the glider is cruised slowly through any lift which is not worth circling in, and speeds up while flying through sinking air. By selecting the course so that the glider flies through more lift than sink, long glides are possible without circling, and also very much higher average speeds are possible.

Having decided on the minimum strength of lift which is worth using for a climb, the glider is flown from cloud to cloud using the lift to extend the glide. When it flies into some lift which is stronger than the minimum selected it is efficient to use it for climbing until the strength of the lift drops below the minimum, when it is abandoned in favour of another straight cruise.

113. Dolphin flight. Pull up and fly more slowly through rising air, speed up through sink.

Improvements in glider performance at higher speeds has made dolphin flying easier and more effective. At high speeds, the effects of flying through sinking air are reduced and the excess speed is quickly changed back into a height gain of several hundred feet as the glider is pulled up to fly slowly through the lift.

Using cloud streets, glides of 50 miles or so are possible without circling and the average speed is sometimes as much as 80 to 90 m.p.h.

In practice, the cruise is far from straight and it pays to divert at quite large angles to use a cloud street rather than cross a blue area. Each pilot will select his own route and the one who makes the best decision will travel fastest. This is the real skill in cross-country flying.

In considering what speeds to fly between thermals it should be noted that the improvement in average cross-country speeds made by flying the 'optimum' speed instead of the speed for best angle of glide is only 3–4 knots unless the lift is very strong.

This advantage can easily be cancelled out by even one scrape when

114. Follow the energy! By diverting to stay under the most promising-looking clouds, long distances are possible without circling to climb.

perhaps 10 or 20 minutes are spent grovelling at low altitude in weak lift. In view of this fact it is important for the inexperienced pilot to be very conservative about his choice of ring setting and cruising speeds. Probably if the achieved rate of climb is 4 knots it would be wise to set at about half that value. This will improve the chances of recognising lift because of the lower speed, and the next thermal will be reached higher up, reducing the worry of getting too low.

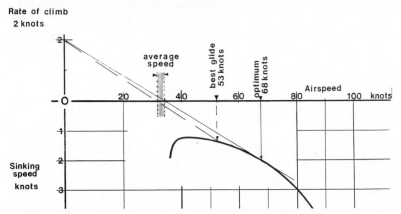

115. Exact cruising speeds are not critical. The advantage to be gained by flying at the optimum speed compared with the best gliding angle speed is only 2 – 3 knots unless the lift is strong.

But the strength of the next thermal is not the only factor involved in choosing the ring setting. If the thermals are a long way apart it clearly makes no sense to fly at speed and then to have to land because the next area of lift is still out of range. Even if the lift in the last thermal was very strong and the conditions still look very good ahead, if the next cloud looks a long way away, a ring setting should be selected which will get the glider to that thermal at a safe height. This will always be a matter of inspired guesswork.

Having determined the basic cruising speed for the next glide, the 'speed to fly' ring or speed director will indicate the need to slow down in lift and speed up in sink. The instrument will then indicate a suitable speed from moment to moment. Notice that it will reduce the average speed to slow right down to the speed for minimum sink in weak lift unless the conditions ahead look poor. However, if more height is needed, the moment the variometer shows a rate of climb much above the one set, a climb should be made.

When the glider is close to the cloud base or an inversion it will not be worth while making a climb unless the conditions ahead look tricky. A climb of 200 – 300 feet will almost always waste time unless the pilot is lucky enough to get straight into very strong lift.

It will almost always take one or two circles to centre on the lift and this will wreck the average rate of climb for such a short climb. If you are high and conditions ahead look good, glide on until you are well below cloud base so that you can take a reasonably long climb. This will result in a much better average rate of climb.

Below a cloud street, if you need more height, the speed setting should be low enough to result in a gradual climb to reach the cloud base or very near it by the end of the street. If possible the glider should always be cruising more slowly in lift and faster in sink.

Pull-ups

In a modern glider on a good day, the optimum cruising speeds will be about 75 knots for 5 knot climbs. This means that the correct speed in strong sink will be as high as 80 to 90 knots. The question arises how best to slow down to a lower air speed as the sink changes to rising air.

Certainly the pilot must be very quick to respond to the change, or at that speed he may well be back into more sink before he has even slowed down.

It is particularly important not to get caught flying into strong sink at a low speed. Once in the sink it can cost several hundred feet while the speed is being increased. On days when the sink is very strong, it is often worth while speeding up in the lift during the last turn before leaving to ensure the glider is already flying faster when it hits the sinking air.

Theoretical studies show that the pull-up should be surprisingly violent, pulling 2g or more and bringing the glider up into a steep climb to slow down in order to spend more time in the lift.

If it were possible to predict exactly where and how wide an area of lift was ahead, the optimum pull-up could be prescribed. It might be a + 2g pull-up followed by a 0g push-over.

However, the penalty for getting the timing of these changes wrong would probably cancel out the advantages and it seems unlikely that we would get it right very often. Moreover, for most pilots + 2g and 0g every few minutes is too hard and too tiring on the stomach.

Totally disagreeing with these theories, one of the German universities has shown by computer studies that it is much more efficient to hold a steady cruising speed and ignore the changes in lift and sink. Of course if the flight consists of a violent porpoising up and down the glider has to fly much further than at a steady speed.

There is still much to learn about problems of this kind, and for the time being each pilot has his own way of doing things.

One thing is certain: it is dangerous to fly directly above or below another glider in straight flight. Without warning it may dive down steeply to gain speed or pull up violently as it hits lift and you may be in the pilot's blind spot and unable to prevent a collision.

Gliding to a goal

In competition flying, the problem of knowing how high to climb for the final glide to a goal can be crucial, since time spent climbing further than is necessary can never be made up by flying at a higher speed. On other occasions it can also be important, since it is easy to waste time and height searching for further lift, perhaps unsuccessfully, when in fact the goal has been within gliding range. The incredibly flat gliding angles of modern gliders make the judgement of these long straight glides almost impossible without a calculator. Even then the glide can be completely upset by a change in wind strength or an unexpected area of sinking air.

Simple calculators can be bought or made to suit the performance of the particular glider. (See Fig. 116.)

At many times the cost, more accurate results can be obtained with an electronic navigation system. These compare the actual height lost with the distance flown and give the pilot a continuous read-out of his position relative to the required glide path. If he runs through a bad area the computer shows immediately whether he needs to slow down or take another climb to reach his destination.

Theoretically, the last climb should be just high enough to allow a straight glide at the best cruising speed based on the strength of the lift *at the top* of the last thermal. Depending on the conditions, some spare height must be allowed, but this can be whittled down during the last few miles by flying a little faster. As the glide progresses, the height and distance to go must be checked by getting accurate pin-points, and an early decision must be made to find more lift if there is any doubt about reaching the goal. Normally the final glide speed will be well above the speed for best range, and even if there is a strong headwind it is possible to extend the glide slightly by slowing down to the best speed for penetration against that strength of wind.

If during the final climb the strength of the lift increases as height is gained, the calculator should be reset to the higher rate of climb and enough height taken to fly faster to the goal.

Even a small layer of ice on the leading edges of the wings will ruin the gliding performance. The cruising speed should be cut down and an allowance should be made for the gliding angle being reduced by at least a third. Since the ice takes considerable time to melt, it does not pay to risk icing even though the rate of climb in the clouds is very good and a large gain of height is possible.

Similarly it is vital to allow for a reduction in performance if the leading edges of the wings are badly contaminated with squashed insects. The

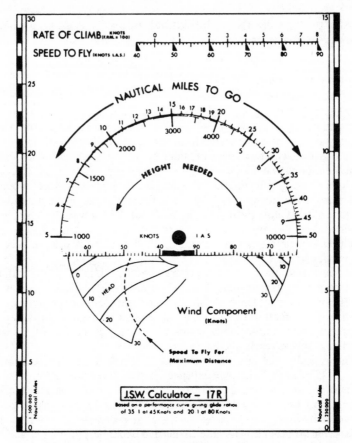

116. Gliding to a goal using the John Williamson final glide calculator.
(1) Measure or estimate the rate of climb at the top of the last thermal and read off the 'speed to fly' on the top scale.
(2) Set this speed against the wind speed curve by turning the centre piece.
(3) Measure the distance to fly and read off the height needed against the 'miles to go' scale.
(4) Add allowances for the height of the goal and for down-draughts.
(5) Check the distance to go and height required at each pin-point.
  Example: Rate of climb 2 knots, distance to goal 28 nautical miles, height of goal 600 feet, weak thermals and down-draughts. Rest speed is 60 knots. Height needed 5,500 feet. Safety margin, say 500 feet. Indicated height required 6,600 feet minimum.

loss may be as much as 20 per cent on some types of glider.
  It is not difficult to determine the best speeds for final glides in various circumstances and the following diagrams explain the principal cases and the rules to be applied. The exact speeds are not very important, because the wind strength and the strength of any down-draught are seldom accurately known. Performance curves for most gliders are obtainable from

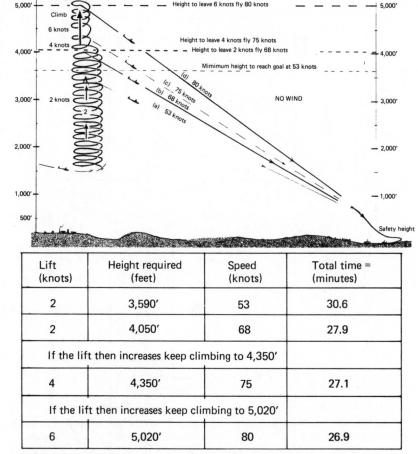

Lift (knots)	Height required (feet)	Speed (knots)	Total time = (minutes)
2	3,590'	53	30.6
2	4,050'	68	27.9
If the lift then increases keep climbing to 4,350'			
4	4,350'	75	27.1
If the lift then increases keep climbing to 5,020'			
6	5,020'	80	26.9

117. The final glide. In this case the wind *must* be taken into consideration. If the lift becomes stronger during the last climb it pays to climb higher and to fly the optimum speed for the new rate of climb.

their manufacturers but it must be remembered that dead flies and other imperfections on the leading edges will prevent them from achieving the claimed performance.

Determining the speed to fly for maximum distance in various conditions (See Fig. 118)

a. In still air. Fly the speed for best L/D to cover the greatest distance for a given loss of height. (Usually about 15 knots above the stalling speed.)

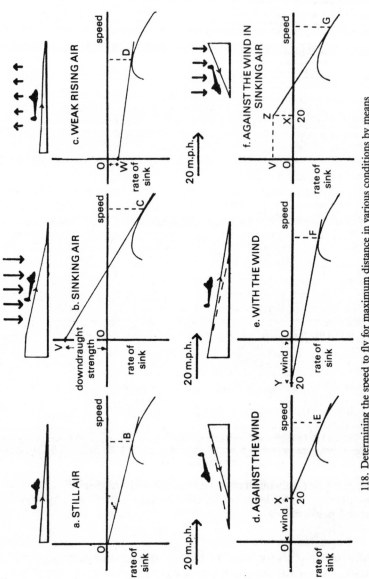

118. Determining the speed to fly for maximum distance in various conditions by means of the performance curve.

Draw the tangent from the origin *O* to touch the curve at *B*. The speed for best gliding angle in still air corresponds to the point *B* on the curve.

b. In sinking air. Increase speed to fly through the sink with the minimum loss of height.

Measure off the down-draught strength *OV* above the airspeed axis. Draw the tangent *VC* to the curve. The best speed corresponds to the point *C* on the curve.

c. In weak rising air. Reduce speed to just above the speed for minimum sink and circle if the lift becomes strong enough and more height is required.

Measure off the up-draught strength *OW* below the airspeed axis. Draw the tangent *WD* to the curve. The best speed corresponds to the point *D* on the curve.

d. Against the wind. Increase speed to best gliding angle plus one-third of the wind speed.

Measure off the wind strength *OX* along the airspeed axis. Draw the tangent *XE* to the curve. The best speed corresponds to the point *E* on the curve.

e. With the wind. Reduce speed to just above the speed for minimum sink.

Measure off the wind strength *OY* in the negative sense along the airspeed axis. Draw the tangent *YF* to the curve. The best speed corresponds to the point *F* on the curve.

f. Against the wind in sinking air. Increase speed to well above the speed for the strength of the head wind.

Measure off the wind strength *OX* (as in *d*) and the down-draught strength *OV* (as in *b*). From *Z* corresponding to points *X* and *V*, draw the tangent *ZG* to the curve. The best speed corresponds to the point *G* on the curve.

General rules and advice

Although there are still many new ideas and theoretical studies going on about cross-country cruising speeds, there are several generally agreed principles.

At all times the pilot must be thinking ahead to what is likely to happen and must not be influenced by the previous situations and thermal strengths. What has happened has happened and nothing can improve what has gone before!

While the thermals are consistently spaced and within easy gliding distance of each other, the 'speed to fly' setting should be to the rate of climb expected in the next thermal. The speeds flown in lift and sink during the cruise should be as shown by the speed ring or speed director. Only thermals strong enough to result in a climb of more than the ring setting should be used for circling climbs, and then only if there can be a worthwhile gain of height before reaching the cloud base or height restriction. (Note that the indicated rate of climb in straight flight will be more than the rate of climb circling because of the increased rate of sink of the glider in a turn.)

If it is necessary to climb in weak lift, only climb to the minimum height from which a stronger area of lift can be reached and then leave for it.

If the thermal is strong, always climb to the maximum altitude.

If it is a long distance to the next thermal, fly at a speed that will ensure that you reach it at a safe height.

If possible, for the last thermal, climb to the height required to reach the destination safely at the optimum speed for the rate of climb at the top of the lift. If that is not feasible, climb as high as possible and glide using the speed which will still take you to your goal. If during the final glide the normal rate of sink is not experienced, adjust the speed to that which will enable the goal to be reached safely, e.g. slow down if dropping below the proper glide path or speed up as necessary to use up any excess height *en route*.

During cruising flight, every effort must be made to avoid areas of sinking air and divert to fly through areas of lift.

Carrying water ballast in order to increase the wing loading is of particular benefit where conditions allow long glides using dolphin techniques with a minimum of circling climbs. It is a particular disadvantage for circling in small or weak thermals because of the increased radius of turn and rate of sink.

With all the aids and theoretical knowledge about gliding, cross-country flying is still a very inexact science.

The pilot must try to assess the situation at the time, and judge what conditions he will be meeting ahead.

After a flight it is often obvious where mistakes were made, but without a 'crystal ball' it will remain a matter of skills, judgements and decisions, which can never be automated.

27 Motor gliders and self-launching sailplanes

Motor trainers or high-performance two-seater light aircraft—Motor gliders for training glider pilots

Since a glider is a motorless aircraft it may seem strange that we have aircraft known as motor gliders. However, this kind of aircraft was called a motor glider during the early years and somehow the name has stuck. An alternative and much more legitimate name for them is 'motor soarer'. They are aircraft designed for soaring but having an engine to get them off the ground or to keep them up once they have been launched. Those which are not capable of taking themselves off the ground are usually referred to as 'self-sustaining sailplanes'.

There is nothing new about the idea of putting an engine into a glider to make it independent of launching equipment. However, it is only since the 1960s that really satisfactory machines have been produced in numbers.

The initial idea was to produce a glider to soar well but capable of launching itself and flying across country to better conditions when necessary. This required a reasonable power performance but also an ability to soar well.

The early attempts were a rather poor compromise. Most of them turned out to be under-powered aeroplanes with a poor rate of climb and not a very good gliding performance. However, they were capable of flying on very low power because of the efficient glider type of wing.

In the same way that yachtsmen have adopted the idea of an auxiliary engine, it seems likely that eventually most new sailplanes will have the option of a tuck-away engine. There already are several single- and two-seaters available and they perform well.

There are various advantages for the self-launcher. On the gliding site, of course, it is totally independent of any form of launching, which means that the pilot can launch when he likes and also to what height he likes. On a busy gliding site this is a great advantage for any ambitious cross-country pilot who is liable to experience a great deal of frustration at the launch point, particularly when the winch breaks down or there is a long queue of other gliders waiting to go.

It also enables the pilot to climb much higher than normal to explore signs of wave or to cruise out in unsoarable conditions to a hill or wave site some distance away.

Without the constant worry of the time wasted and frustration caused by a field landing miles from home, the pilot can make bolder declarations and go across country in conditions which are more marginal but which might turn out to be the start of a record-breaking day. Once the engine is folded away, the fun of soaring is just the same as with a normal glider.

With a two-seater, dual cross-country soaring becomes more practicable because there is no need for an out landing, which would normally be the end of the day's flying. So the utilisation can be much higher and it is possible to go much further afield, knowing that it will only be a relatively short cruise home if the soaring finishes unexpectedly.

Although these machines are far more expensive than a normal glider, or for that matter, than a normal light aircraft, they can be more highly utilised and, therefore, it becomes practicable to form a much larger syndicate, with the members able to get more flying than with a normal glider. They are particularly suited to people who have very little spare time and don't really want to get involved with normal gliding operations. Some may live near to an airport but have to drive a long way to their soaring site. What could be easier than to rig, taxi out to the runway and take off from the airport rather than waste half the day travelling. With radio, almost any airport or airstrip could be used without causing any special problems.

At present many club pilots worry that these aircraft will just be used as powered aircraft for flying noisily round the gliding site or from place to place under power. However, with the present breed of self-launchers there is very little chance of this happening. In the cockpit the noise level is extremely high, with the fuselage shell acting as a sound box. Ear defenders are absolutely essential and it is a blessed relief to shut off the engine after climbing to height. Also with most of the two-stroke engines there is a certain amount of rough running when they are throttled back for cruising. This makes cruising from place to place a matter of climbing normally to height and then gliding the next fifteen or twenty miles before repeating the process.

The self-sustaining sailplanes are in effect a rather less powerful and simplified version of the self-launchers. Fitting little engines to many of the best-performing gliders allows them to fly home if they are away from base when the soaring conditions fade.

In producing the Turbo Ventus, Turbo Nimbus 3 and Turbo Janus two-seater, the German manufacturer Schemp Hirth has led the field with this interesting development.

The engine is a lightweight two-stroke, driving a five-bladed propeller which folds and tucks back into the fuselage just behind the wing root, leaving no trace once the doors are closed over it. One switch raises the engine electrically, the ignition is switched on and a valve lifter is operated during a gentle dive to about 70 knots. The airflow revolves the propeller and starts the engine. There is no throttle and the power is sufficient to give a climb of about 200 – 300 feet per minute or a cruise of about 70 knots.

These machines are very quiet and because they do not have the power to make a normal take-off, they do not require a pilot's licence like a self-launching machine. They can be launched by car, winch or aerotow. Because like a normal glider they require rigging, ground handling and launching, the pilots have to be sociable and take a launch like any other glider pilot. In this way they are more likely to remain firmly in the club atmosphere rather than as outsiders using the gliding club as a base for take-offs and contributing very little to the club.

The question has been asked whether having such a low rate of climb is safe, because of the risks of running into strong down-draughts and gradients. However, since they are all being flown by glider pilots who understand the likelihood of meeting bad sink and are used to dealing with such situations in a glider, perhaps the risks involved are not too serious. Of course, it is sensible to do the restart at a fair height and not a few hundred feet up over bad country, where a failure would be disastrous. At worst they can make a normal field landing like any other glider.

Machines like these offer immense possibilities for an enterprising pilot. Provided that it is landed at another gliding site, it would be perfectly practical to fly across the channel and soar south down into Spain or the French Alps on one day and get a launch and fly home the next.

Possibly on an open airfield all that would be needed is a tow with a car to 50 feet for a start and then to climb away slowly using any thermals or other lift to gain height for the return flight.

With all these types, whether they are self-launching or self-sustaining, it is vital to select a field at about 1,000 feet as in a normal glider and to start a normal circuit procedure. If the engine does fail to start it is important to abandon trying to start it in plenty of time to be able to make a normal field landing. Note that in most cases the landing would have to be made with the engine up because of the time taken to realign the propeller before retracting it. So an essential exercise is to practise engine-up landings to get used to the much steeper gliding angle caused by the extra drag.

It must not be forgotten that with any form of electric starting and electric drive to raise and lower the engine, the system is entirely dependent on the state of the battery.

To be safe against a power failure, all these machines could do with a totally independent emergency power supply.

Doubtless there will be many improvements over the next few years which will make these machines even more dependable and easier to operate.

Motor trainers or high-performance two-seater light aircraft

Although it is difficult to define a difference between some of these machines and other self-launching sailplanes, at present the two-seater motor glider with the engine in the nose is considered by most glider pilots to be more of a light aircraft in spite of the gliding performance being even better than many of the older two-seater training gliders.

The Scheibe SF25 Falke series of designs showed the way to a practical motor glider and many hundreds are still flying today. This is a two-seater with wood wings, steel tube fuselage, fabric-covered, with side-by-side seating; it uses a Volkswagen engine mounted in the nose like a normal light aircraft.

The undercarriage is usually a single wheel with outrigger wheels to keep the wings level during taxiing and it has a very positive steering tail wheel.

The Falkes have proved the value of a motor glider for all phases of glider pilot training but in addition have been used in many countries for cheap pleasure flying. Later versions use an 80 h.p. engine with a feathering propeller and have a rate of climb of about 600 feet per minute and a gliding angle of about 26 : 1 at quite a low speed.

More recently several glass fibre designs have gone into production. All are basically along similar lines to the Falkes but use modern aerofoils and take advantage of the possibilities of the new materials. They have conventional aircraft-type undercarriages and foldable wings to reduce the hangarage costs. This makes them very attractive and efficient machines with gliding angles of about 28 : 1 and capable of cruising at over 100 knots using only 3 gallons of fuel an hour. Moreover, they are capable of using thermals, hill lift or wave conditions just like other gliders.

They are not ideal for thermal soaring, however, because their minimum circling speeds and rather high rates of sink make them difficult in weak conditions and in small thermals. All of these types are magnificent for exploring wave systems. With the fast cruising speeds, a day trip of 100 miles or so to the mountains for wave or mountain soaring is practical.

Often wave lift is illusive and the ability to fly over to the next range of hills or climb an extra 1,000 feet makes a wave climb possible. A typical day's flying in Scotland gave five students climbs to over 10,000 feet for only a few minutes' engine run each, and the possibilities are almost unlimited.

Motor gliders for training glider pilots

Why is learning to glide such a long-winded and time-consuming business? The answer in most cases is the time spent between flights manhandling the glider and waiting for the next launch to be available.

Often the problems are compounded by the restricted landing grounds or by the number of gliders on the site.

Launching is usually limited by congestion so that an extra winch, car or tow plane does not make much improvement on the launch rate. Moreover, as the potential launch rate increases, so does the number of gliders making landings and these hold up the launches and block the landing areas. Each site seems to have a certain capacity for launches and even strenuous efforts do little to improve it.

However, using a motor glider for the basic training can offer a vast increase in training facilities without increasing the congestion.

'Touch and go' landings can be made, leaving a clear area for the gliders after only a few seconds. Also the motor glider can always taxi away without delay and it does not involve the manhandling of a glider.

But perhaps the main advantage of the motor glider flying on a normal gliding site is that if it is used for the initial training, it releases a large number of launches for gliders. Launching facilities are always limited and if a large proportion of the launches are used for training, there are not many left for launching solo machines.

In most British gliding clubs each member under training will have either an aerotow flight or two or three car or winch launches as their turn of the flying. Perhaps, if they are lucky, they may get a second turn of flying late in the day, but at busy times like the weekends this would be unusual. All day long they will be helping with the launching and retrieving of the other students while waiting for their turn to fly. Often, of course, the weather intervenes and they go home disappointed.

But the awful truth is that by far the majority of the people being flown on any one day will never reach solo, let alone become soaring pilots. Without them the flying list would be surprisingly short and there would be plenty of launches for both dual and solo flying.

When a motor glider is used for the basic training, all of these people get their trial flights and discover whether they really want to glide or have the time to do it while they are on the motor glider. Only the instructor is involved and the training goes on more rapidly than with any glider. This saves large numbers of launches for those members who have persisted through the basic stages. Their progress is bound to be more rapid and less frustrating during their glider flying.

During the initial handling stages, the flights will be similar to an aerotow with a climb to height followed by a glide down practising turns, etc. However, if the cloud base is too low, the instructor can still give good value by making several shorter climbs and glides.

With all the advantages of an aerotow, the student gets more of the flying by being able to practise his turns during the climbs; the launch to 2,000 – 3,000 feet uses only a fraction of the fuel burned by the tow plane; only the student and instructor are involved and a launch is released for a glider.

Gliding

At a later stage the student will need to learn to land his aircraft. In a glider this is more of a problem because you cannot possibly learn much from one individual landing.

In the motor glider it is possible to make at least six landings per half-hour session. True, most of the motor gliders are a little more difficult to land than gliders: but this just raises the standard of skill required and makes the conversion onto the glider that much easier.

At the circuit planning stage the student can practise at least five glider-type circuits and approaches in half an hour. The very vital exercises like running short of height and having to choose an alternative landing area, and cable break procedures, can be practised many times with no physical effort or wasted time at all. While they all have to be repeated again on the glider before solo, practising them in the motor glider can save a lot of glider flights and unnecessary manhandling of the glider at the later stages.

Surprisingly, a few experienced instructors still profess to doubt the value in this kind of training. Few will dispute that it is easier to teach a student who has already done even a few hours of normal power flying. Motor glider students have the advantage of being able to learn to co-ordinate correctly with the stick and rudder. They can also learn the fundamentals of circuit planning and the use of the airbrakes. And of course the stalling and spinning characteristics are similar to a normal glider. So, at worst, the student is getting some power experience in an aircraft which handles like a glider, glides like a glider and simulates it very closely in most respects.

Other instructors fear that students will rely on the engine to get them out of trouble. This could happen, but is avoided by treating it as a glider once the engine has either been stopped altogether, or is throttled back and left idling.

It is vital that it is *never* used for convenience or to avoid difficult situations which the glider pilot would have to deal with. For example, there can be situations where because of flying through strong sink the glider must be turned in to land early, perhaps even cutting in ahead of another glider. If this situation arises on a flight in the motor glider the engine must not be used. The engine should be stopped altogether for every flight at the later stages when the student is learning about planning and decision making.

For advanced training the motor glider is the only practical way to teach field selection and approaches without time-wasting retrieves. It is also ideal for map reading and even for advanced cross-country soaring.

Speed flying can be simulated by improving the gliding performance with a small amount of power and using more power to artificially increase the rates of climb. In this way poor soaring conditions can be improved and the experienced pilots can be put under extra pressure so that their work load is similar to racing on a good day. The motor gliders are also excellent for practising final glides, as these can be made in stable conditions or on any day when the cloud base is high enough.

Of course our present motor gliders are not ideal for this work. They are not designed specifically for training and are compromises between having a passable glide performance and a reasonable speed in level flight to satisfy the pilot who wants to tour as well as glide.

In most of the present breed the rudder loads are far higher than on most gliders and since learning to use the rudder is one of the major problems for the student, this is not a good thing. The circling speeds are also unrealistically high and the larger radius of turn changes the situation for the final turn and also of course for thermal soaring.

The other problem area is on the landing, not because of the difficulty of making good landings, although this may worry a number of the less experienced instructors. It is the combination of the rather high weight and the touchdown speed which make it undesirable to make bumpy landings on the relatively rough ground of a gliding site. Everything is fine if the landings are good but the impact of these machines when the landing is bouncy can too easily result in expensive damage. It seems unlikely that the weight of these machines can be reduced, so they need more wing area or a higher-lift aerofoil to reduce the touchdown speed to make them better as a basic trainer.

One future possibility would be to design a machine specifically for glider pilot training. The most important features required are glider handling, airbrakes and stalling speeds, together with the best rate of climb obtainable.

The glide performance is not so important, because the glide can be simulated by leaving a small amount of power on during the descents. Above all it must be rugged in order to reduce the risk of damage during landings. Since the gliding angle is not critical, the whole machine would not be such a difficult compromise as a normal motor glider.

With a machine of this type, the time spent climbing would be minimal and the task of teaching circuits and landing would be made quicker and easier. It might not be quite so economical for touring but it might well double as a tow plane as it would probably climb as well as many tow planes.

Another practical alternative is the idea of attaching a power 'egg' to a standard two-seater glider for training purposes. In this case the engine is not retractable but is mounted above the fuselage when required. The drag of this kind of installation usually ruins the gliding performance, but of course this can be overcome with a little power during the descents. The beauty of the system is that the handling is almost identical to the glider and apart from the noise, the student might be flying the glider version.

It remains to be seen whether the noise level inside the cockpits can be made low enough to be acceptable for normal instruction without the need for headsets and an intercom system.

Operationally, it is obvious that the motor glider is ideal for a large proportion of glider training. However, it does have some problems. For youth training schemes it has the disadvantage that apart from the actual flying there is nothing for the student to do, unlike glider training where team work and co-operation are essential. In a normal gliding club the motor glider training also tends to encourage people to sit and wait for their turn to fly without helping with the necessary work on the airfield. A few drop out when they find at the glider stage that they are expected to play their part at the launch point.

To be economical a motor glider must be fully utilised and this makes it unsuitable for a small club.

The other major problem is that the instructors have to reach a high standard both as pilots and as instructors. It is easy to do many hours of flying and to waste the student's time and money. Utilising the flying time efficiently, the work load on the instructor is higher than on a glider or a normal powered aircraft. For example, teaching a group of five pilots on a week's course, I have frequently made 70 or 80 landings in a day at the stage when they were all learning to land. This kind of work load is tiring and not everyone's idea of how to spend a pleasant summer's afternoon. Obviously, it is much more difficult to find instructors who want to spend their time doing this kind of work rather than making a few glider launches an hour. However, the instructor certainly has his reward in seeing the rapid progress of his students on the motor glider, particularly when compared with their progress on a glider.

The amount of training required to reach a safe standard seems to be very little different with any type of training. With the motor glider the student has much more training in landings and circuit planning than would be normal with all aerotow training. This must be considered a good thing, as many students going solo on all aerotow training have less than 30 landings. In terms of cost to the student again there is very little to choose between the various types of training. However, the motor glider will usually reduce the number of days spent at the gliding site and this can be a considerable saving to the student.

It is probably better not to calculate the cost of glider training too carefully. Unless a fair proportion of soaring flights are made, the cost per flying hour is much the same as for powered flying.

The cost of motor glider flying is similar to car or winch launching for short flights. On longer flights much depends on the particular system of charging in use at the time. The motor glider offers the greatest advance in glider training since the introduction of two-seater trainers but it remains to be seen if it will be developed and adopted universally.

APPENDICES

1 Gliding awards and records

National badge awards—F.A.I. badge awards—World records

National badge awards

Nothing encourages an enthusiastic sportsman so much as keen competition and a sense of pride in personal achievement. This is particularly true of gliding, in which the award of certificates and badges, which are recognised all over the world, has played a great part in the encouragement of a healthy competitive spirit amongst both beginners and expert pilots.

Unlike most club or society badges, a gliding badge is an award for actual ability and achievement. It cannot be bought by money or prestige alone but must be earned by skill, adventure and, in some cases, endurance.

Gliding is an international sport, and the regulations for world records and the tests for the Silver, Gold and Diamond 'C' badges are laid down by the Fédération Aéronautique Internationale, which also controls record flights for powered aircraft.

The requirements for the 'A', 'B' and 'C' certificates vary from country to country and are determined by the National Aero Club or Gliding Association of the country concerned.

In some countries, the 'C' certificate test includes examinations in Principles of Flight, Meteorology, Navigation and Flying Regulations, and is a glider pilot's licence.

British gliding suffers far fewer restrictions and regulations than most of the Continental countries and no licence is required by law. Pilots who have a Bronze or Silver 'C' are granted certain concessions if they wish to become private (powered aircraft) pilots and can count some of their gliding exierience towards the hours needed for their licence.

The requirements for the British certificates are now as follows:

'A' Certificate. One solo circuit in a glider (or a motor glider in unpowered flight after launch) together with a knowledge of the basic rules of the air.

'B' Certificate. A soaring flight of at least five minutes at or above the previous lowest point after launch.

Bronze 'C'. A minimum of 50 solo flights in a glider. (A 2,000 feet aerotow counts as 3 flights and a PPL or similar service or foreign equivalent counts as 25 flights.)

Two soaring flights each of 30 minutes' duration, if launched by car, winch or bungee, or each of 60 minutes after an aerotow release not exceeding 2,000 feet.

Two or more flights with a rated instructor, demonstrating good general flying, understanding of stalls and incipient spins, and ability to land accurately.

A pass in a written Air Law and General Paper.

The Bronze 'C' is the minimum qualification for a glider pilot to fly out of gliding range of his base and the test usually incorporates simulated or actual field landings.

F.A.I. Silver 'C'

Duration. A flight of not less than five hours.

Height. A flight in which the gain of height registered by the barograph is not less than 1,000 metres (3,281 feet). Gain of height being the difference between the maximum height recorded and the lowest previous point registered after release.

Distance. A flight of not less than 50 kilometres (31.07 miles) carried out in a straight line or as one leg of a declared task.

The loss of height between the release and the place of landing or destination must not exceed 1 per cent of the distance covered. (Also see Figs. 101 and 102.)

F.A.I. Gold 'C'

Duration. A flight of not less than five hours (usually already completed for Silver 'C').

Height. A flight in which the gain of height registered by the barograph is not less than 3,000 metres (9,843 feet).

Distance. A flight of not less than 300 kilometres (186.42 miles) carried out in a straight line, a broken line with up to four turn points, a triangle or an out-and-return flight.

A written declaration must be made before all except straight-line distance flights. (See Fig. 104.)

Photographic evidence is accepted as proof of having reached the declared turning points and this method has totally superseded the old system of ground observers.

Diamonds

The holder of a Gold 'C' badge is entitled to wear a diamond on the badge for each of the following performances:

Height. A gain of height of 5,000 metres (16,405 feet).

Goal flight. A triangular or out-and-return flight of at least 300 kilometres (186.42 miles). (See Fig. 103.)

Distance. A flight of at least 500 kilometres (310.7 miles).

Distance flights may be made in a straight line, or a broken line with up to four turning points, all or some or which may be used in any order decided in flight. (See Fig. 104.)

With the F.A.I. badges any flight may count for Silver, Gold and Diamond awards; a sealed barograph must be carried on all flights except for the duration flight which may be visually observed from the ground.

The exact requirements for these F.A.I. awards are changed from time to time and the reader is advised to check them carefully at the start of each gliding season.

National and International gliding records are divided into two main classes: solo flights, and flights made by two or more persons flying together. There is also a separate category of records for women.

In each class there are records for distance, out-and-return flights, distance to a pre-determined goal, speed over triangular courses and set distances, and absolute and gain of height. Until 1955 there were also duration records but these had become feats of endurance and because of the danger of the pilots falling asleep at the controls they have been discontinued. In the early days of gliding, long-duration flights had great publicity value and served some purpose in investigating soaring conditions at night. But flights of over 40 hours prove nothing except the will-power of the pilot.

World records (as at January 1986)

Absolute height: 46,268 feet (14,102 metres) P. Bikle, U.S.A.
Straight distance: 908.61 miles (1,460.8 km) H. W. Grosse, W. Germany.
Out-and-return: 1,024.5 miles (1,646.68 km) T. L. Knauf, U.S.A.
1,000 km triangle speed: 90.38 m.p.h. (145.32 k.p.h.) H. W. Grosse, W. Germany.

2 The gliding movement in Great Britain

The British Gliding Association is the central body representing the gliding clubs and associations in Great Britain. The Headquarters of the B.G.A. are at Kimberley House, Vaughan Way, Leicester, telephone Leicester 531051; it is able to answer any inquiries about the gliding clubs and courses of instruction.

There are gliding clubs in most parts of the country and these are expanding and increasing in number each year. Most of the larger clubs have full-time instructors and ground engineers, and operate throughout the week. The smaller clubs are usually run on an entirely voluntary basis and fly mainly at weekends and holiday periods.

The three services have their own gliding clubs, and gliding is a recognised sport. Their aim is to provide gliding facilities for all ranks at a low cost.

There is also the Air Training Corps scheme, which trains cadets to glide. Approximately twenty gliding schools operate at aerodromes throughout the country and train many thousands of boys up to solo standard. These schools are run mainly by unpaid volunteer instructors and R.A.F.V.R. (T) officers. They have just been re-equipped with modern glass fibre two-seater gliders and most of their launching is by winch. It is of very real value to the country in spreading airmindedness and in developing the character and spirit of adventure of the boys. There is no doubt that far greater value could be derived from this gliding if the training were to be continued to include more solo and more soaring flights.

Training throughout the clubs and associations affiliated to the B.G.A. is carried out on dual control, two-seater gliders with approved instructors.

Most of the larger clubs run training courses for beginners lasting one or two weeks and these are an excellent way of spending a holiday and finding out whether you enjoy the sport.

Most gliding clubs have an entrance fee of about £60 and then a yearly membership fee of about £80. However, most clubs have reduced rates for students and for members who live a long way from the club.

*Flying fees are £2.50 to £3.50 a launch by winch or motor car, and an additional £10 to £15 an hour is charged for soaring flights. Launching by aerotow costs £9.50 to £10.50 for a launch to 2,000 feet.

---

*All fees and costs in this chapter refer to 1986 and, of course, include all instruction and the use of the club glider.

Training in a motor glider costs £30 to £35 per hour depending upon how much of the flying is done with the engine running. However, all these charges include instruction.

Most clubs have their own catering and sleeping facilities and encourage their members to stay at the club at weekends. Flying often takes place from dawn to dusk and the keen pupil can get extra flying by making an early start.

The cost of gliding is kept relatively low by the voluntary work of the club members themselves. In the smaller clubs almost all the glider and vehicle maintenance is carried out by members and everyone is expected to lend a hand with some aspect of club life.

Gliding is by no means only a rich man's sport. There are people from every walk of life and every income group at a gliding club. This is one of the attractions of joining a club which can be enjoyed even by an associate member.

What of the future? It now seems clear that special light aircraft designed to simulate the characteristics of modern gliders will be introduced to provide quicker and perhaps more economical training. In addition there will be many more self-launching, powered gliders capable of good soaring performances for those enthusiasts who live too far from a gliding club or who cannot spare the time for normal gliding. The performance of new designs continues to improve, with the best having gliding angles of almost 60 : 1 or nearly 12 miles' glide from only 1,000 feet.

3   Owning your own glider

Members of a gliding club place their names on a flying list and take turns to fly club gliders so that, if they arrive late in the day, they may be unable to fly until the evening, when there is no hope of thermal soaring. The advantages of owning your own glider are, therefore, obvious.

There is nothing, legally, to prevent any enthusiast from building and flying a glider of his own design if it is insured against third party risks and is not flown at a recognised gliding site. However, if it is to be flown at a club site, it must have a Certificate of Airworthiness.

The Technical Committee of the British Gliding Association is responsible for the testing of new types of British glider to ensure that they have safe flying characteristics and are structurally sound. It also issues Certificates of Airworthiness which are valid for twelve months.

Very few gliders have been constructed by amateurs in this country since 1980, whereas on the Continent it is common for people to build their own gliders or to asssemble gliders from kits of parts. This is a lengthy business requiring considerable skill in carpentry and a full understanding of the principles of wooden aircraft construction.

Most enthusiasts who want to have their own glider prefer to buy a proven design.

The choice of design will depend mainly upon how much the prospective owner can afford. A new Standard Class competition outfit will cost over £20,000. This is clearly beyond the means of the average enthusiast. However, pre-war gliders such as the Kite, Gull and Tutor occasionally change hands for under £1,000 and are capable of good soaring flights. A glider such as a K6 or Skylark makes a good first cross-country machine and may cost only £3,000 to £4,000. Shared between four pilots, this would be a good investment for anyone who wants to fly regularly.

Although the initial cost of a new glider is high, it is a reasonable investment if it is well cared for and flown regularly. The capital depreciation is small and the market for modern second-hand gliders is growing rapidly as gliding becomes more popular.

A trailer is essential, but it may be either the open frame type or a completely weatherproof closed one. An open trailer is quite satisfactory for retrieving, provided that a dry garage or hangar is available to store the glider.

Almost any car can be fitted with a ball hitch for towing trailers, as they are fairly light and easy to tow. The average driver will have no problems except with backing, which takes some practice.

The names and addresses of glider manufacturers and details of second-hand machines for sale are to be found in the national gliding magazines (*Sailplane and Gliding in U.K.*).

In general, the higher the performance of the glider, the easier it is to fly and the less likely it is to be damaged by an error of judgement on the part of the pilot. Even if the pilot does not aspire to cross-country flying, it is worth buying the machine with the best possible performance.

Modern production gliders are structurally sound and have good handling qualities in the air. The choice is largely one of price and performance.

However, expert advice should be sought to avoid buying a machine which looks nice. Some have a relatively poor climbing performance or poor airbrakes. Although there are a few high-performance gliders which are quite suited to an inexperienced pilot, there are some which cannot be recommended for beginners.

Most of the modern designs are now built entirely of glass fibre and this gives them a superb finish and almost unbeatable performance. However, repairs are more expensive than for a wooden machine and, as yet, it is difficult to know whether there will be problems as they get older. Carbon fibre promises even lighter gliders for the future.

The choice between a single-seater and two-seater is a personal one. A two-seater can, of course, be flown solo but in practice some people do not feel inclined to do this. It is a great pleasure to be able to take friends for flights, but many pilots find that both they and their passengers are prone to airsickness when they are not actually handling the controls. Also it is surprisingly difficult to agree amicably about sharing the flying. Most pilots, like yachtsmen, have their own ideas on how things should be done and are not content to sit and watch for very long. In my experience, there is nothing more agonising than watching another pilot 'fumbling' and wasting opportunities on a really good day. (However, I get paid to do it!) The B.G.A. requires a minimum of 50 hours' solo gliding before a pilot may carry passengers.

There are many advantages in sharing a glider and most privately owned machines are shared by a syndicate of from two to six people. This makes operating and ground handling easier, and reduces the initial outlay and running costs. The success of any syndicate depends upon the personalities of the members, and the greatest care is required when selecting possible members.

If any members of the syndicate are abnormally tall or large, the size of the cockpit has to be considered when choosing the glider. Long flights are only possible when the pilot is comfortable and able to relax in the cockpit.

Running costs

The major annual expenses for the private owner are:
Third party insurance for at least £250,000 (premium about £80).
Comprehensive insurance against accident (optional).
Certificate of Airworthiness inspection (known as the C. of A.).

The third party insurance is compulsory for all gliders, but most owners also insure comprehensively against accident. The premium for a comprehensive insurance depends almost entirely upon the record and experience of the pilot or pilots who will be flying the glider. Insurance for a few, named, pilots, is much lower than for a club machine which will be flown by any club member.

The cost of comprehensive insurance for a glider and trailer valued at £2,000 (such as a second-hand Olympia) shared by four pilots of Silver 'C' standard would be about 8 per cent of its value per annum. However, the costs of repair in event of damage could be several times the purchase price.

Usually the insurance companies are very fair with owners who have no accidents and will reduce their premiums considerably. It is normal for the pilot to pay the first £100 to £200 of any claim.

The cost of the C. of A. inspection depends entirely upon the amount of work required to make the glider fully serviceable for another year. The cost can be reduced if the owner does most of the work himself under the supervision of a B.G.A. approved inspector. This is possible at most gliding clubs, which usually have workshop space available for private gliders.

Briefly, a C. of A. inspection involves cleaning and inspecting the whole glider, replacing any damaged or worn parts, and making good any temporary repairs and patches.

Assuming that the glider is only a few years old and that there are few outstanding repairs or replacements to be made, the cost of the C. of A. carried out professionally might be between £200 and £400. However, with older machines, every seven years or so the wings and tail surfaces may require re-covering with fabric and the whole glider re-finishing. This is expensive because of the large amount of work involved, and may raise the cost of a C. of A. to several thousand pounds.

Apart from the annual C. of A. inspection it is usual for the pilot to carry out a thorough inspection of his glider after rigging it and before the first flight of the day. Most private owners will also carry out minor repairs and fabric patches themselves, but send the machine away for repair if they are unfortunate enough to damage it seriously.

The life of a wooden glider seems to be at least thirty years and depends mainly upon the state of the glue joints. Gliders built before 1945 were usually glued with casein glue, whereas all modern ones use Aerolite, a synthetic resin.

Casein glue has a rather unreliable life. There are many casein-glued gliders over 40 years old in which the glue is perfectly sound. However, if it remains very damp for a long period it develops a bloom and eventually goes bad. This can be detected by the bad smell of rot. Extensive inspection and rebuilding is necessary where the glue is suspect and often the glider proves beyond economic repair.

Gliders built with Aerolite or other synthetic glues should last almost for ever, since the glue is oil- and water-proof and does not deteriorate with age. However, particularly in warm climates, the wood gradually dries out and becomes more brittle. This reduces the strength of the glider until eventually it is no longer airworthy. Wood shrinkage in hot climates will also reduce the strength of the glued joints.

Glass fibre machines usually require less maintenance and this offsets the higher initial cost to some degree.

Index

Figures in italics refer to illustrations when separated from text

adverse yaw, 36, 103-6
aerobatics, 149-50
aerotowing, 41-3, *45,* 63
aileron controls, 14-15
aileron drag, 103-5, 126
ailerons
  differential, 104
  Frise, *104,* 105
  use of, 122, 129-30
aiming point technique, 76-7
air mass variometer, 159-60
Air Training Corps, 308
airbrakes, 39, 73, *74,* 75-6,
  78-80, 135
airspeed, 216-17, 266, 267
airspeed indicator (A.S.I.), 152-4
airspeed log, 154
'all-out' signal, 24
altimeter, 154-5, 228
  see also barograph
angle of attack, 120
angle of bank, 103, 106, 107
anoxia, *see* oxygen, lack of
approach angle control, 76
approach landing, 229-32
  speeds, 74-5
artificial horizon, 167-8, 270
attitude, flying, *17,* 31, *32,* 37
autorotation, *68,* 123-4
awards, 305-8

balance indicator, 162-3
balance sense, 262-3
ballast requirements, 10, 30
ballooning, 38-9
bank, angle of, 103, 106, 107
banking movements, 14-15, 98-9
barograph, 168-70, 233
base leg, 82

bat signals, *24*
belly hook, 22
bends, 277
blue days, 200
BOHLI compass, 167
boxing the wake, 49-50
briefing sheet, cross-country, 247
British Gliding Association, 9,
  308
  glider testing, 310
Bronze awards, 305, 306
bucking, 114
bumps, 27-8

'C' certificates, 305-6
cables, *see* tow ropes
'can't release' signal, 52
car launching, 41, 59-60, 163
  in high winds, 134-5
  speed, 111-12
CB SIFT CB (cockpit check), 30
centring, 189-92
  in clouds, 68
  quicker, *200*
certificates of airworthiness, 310,
  312
c.g. hook, 22, 54
chandelle, 149, *150*
checklists
  aerotowing, 63
  cockpit, 30
  cross country, 247-9, 258-9
  field landing, 248-9
  flying, 40, 71-2
  landing, 79-80, 93-4, 248-9
  launching, 63
  navigation, 255-6
  oxygen equipment, 278
  pre-landing, 85-6

soaring, 202
tug pilots, 55
windy conditions, 139-40
circling, *89,* 90, 115
circuit planning, 81-4
climbing in, 29-30
clothing, 10-11
cloud flying, 194, 261, 264-8
cloud 'streets', 200, 288
clubs, gliding, 308-9
for training, 8-9
coast line, effect on thermals, 178
cockpit checks, 30
cockpit loading, 126
cockpit size, 10
collision avoidance, *144,* 201-2, 205
compass, 164-6
errors, 165-6
special types, 166-7
compass steering, 145
control column, 13, 30
controls, 13-15
layout, 30
use of, 31-2
Cook compass, 166
costs, flying, 308-9
crabbing, 116, *117*
cross-country flying, 92, 144, 216, 218, 235
briefing sheet, 247
check list, 247
declarations, 246
first flights, 258-9
improving performance, 279-80
planning, 237-45
preparation for, 249-50, 257-8
principles, 294-5
selecting task, 240-5
training, 235-7
crosswind effects, 115-19
cable break procedure, *61*
cruising, 147-9
speeds, 280-1, 286-90
technique, 280-2
cumulus clouds, 171-2, 239-40
'curl over' effect, *206,* 210
'cycling', cloud, 173

declaration form, cross-country, 246
design, choice of, 309-10
deviation, 164-5
Diamond 'C' award, 168, 170, 242, 243, 306
directional indicators, 167
distance flights, 240-4
see also under cross-country flying
dolphin flying, 160, 287, *288*
drag
creation of, 73
effects of, *89,* 90
drag forces, 100-3
drifting, 115
drinking restrictions, 26-7
dual controls, 27
'dust devils', 177

economiser, oxygen, 277-8
electronic systems, 146-7
elevator control, 14-15
emergency signals, towing, 51-2

F.A.I. awards, 305-7
fatigue, 264
field landings, 230
check list, 248-9
final glide, 291-5
calculator, 291, *292*
final turn, landing, 87-90
fishtailing, 142
flick roll, 123
flight, theory of, 16
flight director, 161
flying attitude, *17,* 31, *32,* 37
flying log, 19
Frise ailerons, *104,* 105
full spins, 69-71
FUST (landing checks), 85

glider parts, 12-13
controls, 13-15
Glider Pilot Rating (USA), 49
gliding angle, 147, 286, 309
gliding clubs, 9, 26, 308-9
gliding schools, 26

glue joints, 311-12
Gold 'C' awards, 49, 168, 170, 242, 243, 306
ground contours, effect on thermals, 175-7
ground handling, 19, *20, 21*
in high winds, 131-2
ground run, 43, *118*

'hands off' flying, 33
hearing sense, 264
height
losing excess, 75-6
landing judgement, 231, *232*
measurement, 154-5
high flying, 274, 276-7
hill lift, 203-4
hill soaring, 210-12
rules, 206
techniques, 206-7
hold off, *38*
hyperventilation condition, 273

icing conditions, 271-2, 291
'in spin' aileron, 129
incipient spins, 121-4
recovery from, 128-9
indicated airspeed (IAS), 216
instrument flying, 262, 264-8
insurance requirements, 311
inverted spins, 130

jet streams, 220
John Williamson final glide calculator, *292*
joining other gliders, 201

lamp signals, 24
landing, 37-40
approach, 229-32
downwind, 212-13
emergency, 52-3
failures, 86-7
on hill sides, 208-13
preparations for, 84-5
procedure summary, 93-4
wind checks, 229
landing field selection, 221-9

lateral damping, *68, 124*
lateral instability, *68*
launching, 17, 43-4
methods, 23, 41-2
signals, 23-5
speeds, 111-12, 114
lee waves, 214
lenticular clouds, 214
licences, flying, 12
lift/drag ratio (L/D), 147, 148-9, 286
lift forces, 100-3
lift 'streets', 180, *181*
lightning conditions, 272-3
load factor, 103
log, flying, 19
log book, pilot's, 11
loop turn, 149, *150*
low 'g' sensations, 71
low tow position, 48

MacCready leak, 160
MacCready ring, 282, *283,* 284
magnetic heading, 164
map reading, 145, 237-8
cross-country, 251-6
preparatory, 249
materials, construction, 13, 230, 312-13
medical requirements, 12
motor gliders, 9, 27, 297-9
cross-country, 259-60
launching, 41
Scheibe SF25 Falke series, 9, 299
training, 9, 299-303
muscle sense, 263-4

navigation system, electronic, 291
Netto variometer, *see* air mass variometer
north, magnetic and true, 164
nose hook, 22

one-in-sixty rule, 255
one per cent rule, 240-1
Ottfur hook system, 22

'out spin' aileron, 129
overdevelopment, cloud, 173
overshooting, 229
ownership, glider, 309
oxygen, lack of, 273, 274-7
    symptoms, 274
oxygen systems, 277-8

parachutes, 29
parking, *21*
penetration, in high winds, 137-9
performance figures, 18
periodical magazines, 11
photography, turning-point,
    245-6
pilot-induced oscillation (PIO),
    53-4
pilot's log book, 11
pitching, 14-15, 99, 113-14
pitot tube, 152
placard speed, 153, 154
polar curves, 285-7
post-landing actions, 233-4
'pot' pitot, 152
power 'egg', 303
pre-landing checks, 85-6
pull-up, 290

QFE, 250
QNH, 250

radio communication, 25
rate of climb and speed, 52-3,
    287
rate of climb/descent indicator,
    155-7
rate of descent, 147-8
rate of turn, 266
rate of turn indicator, 161-2
refreshments, 256
Reichmann centring method,
    196, 197
release hooks, 22-3
release knob, 30
releasing in lift, 50-1
residential courses, 8
retrieving arrangements, 256-7
reverse pully launching, 59

ridge lift, 205-6
rolling, *see* banking
rotor cloud, 219
rotor flow, *215,* 218-19
round out, *38*
route plan table, 253
rudder
    control of, 13-15
    effect of, 98-9
    movements, 33-6
    spin recovery, 128-9
rudder waggling signal, 51, *52*
running costs, owner's, 311

safety harness, 29-30
Scheibe Falkes gliders, 9, 299
sea breeze front, 178, *179*
self-launchers, 297-9
self-sustaining sailplanes, 297-9
sensations
    flying, 27-8, 183
    Low 'g', 71
    use of in flying, 262-4, 268-70
side slipping, 141-3
signals
    'all out', 24
    emergency towing, 51-2
    launching, 23-5
    stop, 24-5
    'too fast', 114
    'too slow', 130
    wave off, 51
Silver 'C' award, 49, 168, 306
    distance leg, 240, *242,* 245
    duration leg, 206, 236
sink, moving from, 197-8
sinking speed, 108
site locations, 204-5
skidding turn, *107,* 108
slip indicator, 109, 162-3
slipping turn, *107,* 108, 142
small landing areas approach,
    229
snap roll, 123
soaring
    hill, 206-7, 210-11
    local, 145-6
    selecting conditions, 240
soil surface, effect on thermals,

176-7
solo flying, beginning, 95-6
speed control
    landing, 78
    turning, 106
speed determination rules, 285-7,
    293-4
'speed to fly' ring, 156, 282, *283*
speeds
    approach, 74-5
    optimum, 16, 18, 286-90,
    293-5
    sinking, 108
spin, 123-4, *125, 127,* 267
    incipient, 67-9, 121-4, 128-9
    inverted, 130
    recovery action, 124-6
spiral dives, 127
spoilers, 73, *74*
spoiling lift, 73
'square circuit', 82
stalling, 64-7, 71-2, 120-1
    symptoms, 65
    turning, 122, 149
stalling speeds, 66, 121
    variation with banking angle,
    103
static vents, 152
steep diving turns, 267
'stick lift', 157, 189
'stop signal', 24-5
'streets', cloud, 200, 288
stubble fires, use of, 181-2
S-turns, 61-2, 90-2
SUFB (landing checks), 85
surge
    straightening up, 198-9
    tightening on, 192-3
swinging, *see* yawing
swinging the compass, 164-5

'Take up slack' signal, 23
taking-off, *see* launching
thermal bubbles, isolated, 182-4
thermal lift, 108
thermal soaring, 108-9, 144, 280
thermals, 171
    centring, 189-97
    development of, 173-8

locating, 172-3, 185-9
safety in, 201-2
using on hill sites, 207-8
visible indications, 178-81
'wind shadows', 175-6
thermic days, 207-8
total energy compensation, 157-8
total energy variometer, 157-9
towing
    accidents, 53-4
    emergency signals, 51-2
    positions, 44-5
    speeds, 50
tow ropes
    attaching, 22-3
    bowing, *46,* 47
    breaks, 52-3, 60-3, 93, 135
    checking, 22
    releasing, 49, 57-8
track errors, 255
training courses, 8, 9, 26
triangular flight, 146
trimming, 33
    resetting, 149
true airspeed (TAS), 217
true heading, 164
tugging, 54-5
tug pilots, 54-5
turbulence, 135-6, 270-1
turn and slip indicator, 161-3
turning, 16-17, 33-7, 106, 149
    aerotowing, 48-9
    co-ordination need, 105-7
    efficient, 107-9
turning forces, 100-3
turning point photography, 245-6

UFSTAL (landing checks), 85
undershooting, 229, 137, 139

variometer, 155-7
    air mass, 159-60
    dial type, 284
    electronic, 283
    total energy, 157-9
vehicle driving, 20

washout, 122

wave lift, 216
'wave off' signal, 51
wave systems, 219-20
  lee waves, 214
  rotor systems, *215*, 218
weak links, launching, 59-60
weather conditions, 9, 26
  crosswinds, 115-19
  selecting, 238-40
  windy, 92-3, 131
weathercocking, 115, 119
weight limitations, 10
wheel brake, 227
wheels, 12
winch launching, 41, 56-9, 63
  high winds, 134-5
  speeds, 111-12
wind gradient effects, 93, 132-6

wind shadow thermals, 175-7
winds
  high, 131-40
  precautions, 137
  use of, 92-3, 177, 282-3, 284
  see also crosswind effects
wing-down landing method, 117
wingover, *see* chandelle
wingtip, running, 19
wire launching, *see* car
  launching; winch launching
world records, 307

yaw string, 109-110, 163
yawing movement, 15, 98-9, 101
  adverse, 36
  spinning, 126